Serving Teen Parents

Recent Titles in
Libraries Unlimited Professional Guides for Young Adult Librarians
C. Allen Nichols and Mary Anne Nichols, Series Editors

Teen Programs with Punch: A Month-by-Month Guide
Valerie A. Ott

Serving Young Teens and 'Tweens
Sheila B. Anderson, editor

The Guy-Friendly Teen Library: Serving Male Teens
Rollie Welch

Serving Urban Teens
Paula Brehm-Heeger

The Teen-Centered Writing Club: Bringing Teens and Words Together
Constance Hardesty

More Than MySpace: Teens, Librarians, and Social Networking
Robyn Lupa, Editor

Visual Media for Teens: Creating and Using a Teen-Centered Film Collection
Jane Halsall and R. William Edminster

Teen-Centered Library Service: Putting Youth Participation into Practice
Diane P. Tuccillo

Booktalking with Teens
Kristine Mahood

Make Room for Teens!: Reflections on Developing Teen Spaces in Libraries
Michael G. Farrelly

Teens, Libraries, and Social Networking: What Librarians Need to Know
Denise E. Agosto and June Abbas, Editors

Starting from Scratch: Building a Teen Library Program
Sarah Ludwig

Serving Teen Parents

From Literacy to Life Skills

Ellin Klor and Sarah Lapin

Foreword by Maryann Mori

Libraries Unlimited Professional Guides for Young Adult Librarians
C. Allen Nichols and Mary Anne Nichols, Series Editors

LIBRARIES UNLIMITED

AN IMPRINT OF ABC-CLIO, LLC
Santa Barbara, California • Denver, Colorado • Oxford, England

Library of Congress Cataloging-in-Publication Data

Klor, Ellin.
 Serving teen parents : from literacy to life skills / Ellin Klor and Sarah Lapin ; foreword by Maryann Mori.
     p. cm. — (Libraries Unlimited professional guides for young adult librarians)
  Includes bibliographical references and index.
  ISBN 978-1-59884-693-5 (acid-free paper) — ISBN 978-1-59884-694-2 (ebook) 1. Libraries and teenage parents—United States. 2. Libraries and families—United States. 3. Family literacy programs—United States. 4. Teenage parents—Services for—United States. I. Lapin, Sarah. II. Title.
  Z711.92.T44K56 2011
  027.6—dc22   2011010670

ISBN: 978-1-59884-693-5
EISBN: 978-1-59884-694-2

15 14 13 12 11   1 2 3 4 5

This book is also available on the World Wide Web as an eBook.
Visit www.abc-clio.com for details.

Libraries Unlimited
An Imprint of ABC-CLIO, LLC

ABC-CLIO, LLC
130 Cremona Drive, P.O. Box 1911
Santa Barbara, California 93116-1911

This book is printed on acid-free paper ∞

Manufactured in the United States of America

The publisher has done its best to make sure the instructions and/or recipes in this book are correct. However, users should apply judgment and experience when preparing recipes, especially parents and teachers working with young people. The publisher accepts no responsibility for the outcome of any recipe included in this volume.

To the teen parents who have taught us so much.

CONTENTS

SERIES FOREWORD

We firmly believe that all teens deserve distinct and diverse library services. They also should be provided equal access to library services, and those services should be equal to those offered to other library customers. The wide array of titles in this series supports these beliefs. We are very excited about *Serving Teen Parents* as the newest addition to our series. Teens who are parents have a wide variety of needs as they juggle, and often struggle, with being teens and taking care of their child. For this reason, library services to them must take into consideration their multiple roles. Authors Klor and Lapin's collaboration has done a fine job in offering ideas to reach this often overlooked group of teens.

We are proud of our association with Libraries Unlimited/ABC-CLIO, which continues to prove itself as the premier publisher of books to help library staff serve teens. This series has succeeded because our authors know the needs of those library employees who work with young adults. Without exception, they have written useful and practical handbooks for library staff.

We hope you find this book, as well as our entire series, to be informative, providing you with valuable ideas as you serve teens and that this work will further inspire you to do great things to make teens welcome in your library. If you have an idea for a title that could be added to our series, or would like to submit a book proposal, please email us at lu-books@lu.com. We'd love to hear from you.

Mary Anne Nichols
C. Allen Nichols

FOREWORD

When I was a newly appointed Teen Specialist Librarian (back in 2006), I was given the task to build a teen program. I took my appointment seriously and was constantly on the lookout for opportunities to create programs, develop professional partnerships, and make the library an important part of teens' lives. One such opportunity came when I least expected it. Having seen a notice on my library's community bulletin board about a local teen group with which I was unfamiliar, I contacted the coordinator of that group and arranged to meet over coffee in my library's café. (Surely this is one of the benefits of having an in-house library café—the chance to schedule meetings with cappuccino and a muffin!) When I met the director of the group, she told me exactly the kind of audience she worked with (teen parents), and I thought, "Oh. End of conversation." But as we continued to chat, I rethought and suddenly said to myself, "Oh! Beginning of an opportunity!" It was definitely a light-bulb moment. I had just started a baby lapsit program in the library's children's department shortly before moving to the teen department. It only made good sense to combine those infant storytime programs with the teen parent audience. I was on to something! The group's coordinator and I began to develop a wonderful collaborative effort that allowed me to present early childhood literacy programs to the teen parents in her group.

I had thought—upon leaving the children's department—that I would have no future use for those storytime ideas as the Teen Specialist Librarian. But was I ever wrong in those original assumptions because the storytime ideas were exactly what these teen parents needed. Since that time, I have successfully started and led countless early childhood literacy programs for pregnant/parenting teen audiences. It is work that I have personally found extremely satisfying, although admittedly not always easy. One of the most exciting outcomes of these programs was one I did not anticipate; for some of these teens, it is the first time they realize books are enjoyable.

When Sarah and Ellin contacted me at the end of 2009 with questions about my activities with teen parent audiences, I was thrilled to learn that they were developing a book about library services for these young parents. Having "been there, done that," I could assure Sarah and Ellin that few resources on the topic existed. In fact, I had searched for help and guidelines in developing my own programs, but I found either very old and limited resources or (more often) no resources at all. I was even more thrilled—and extremely honored—when Sarah and Ellin asked me to contribute to the book you now hold in your hands.

Serving teen parents and pregnant teens is a natural extension of what you likely already do in your library. It is a service that can incorporate the best of library services from the children's and teens' staff, and it is an ideal opportunity to collaborate with other library staff from neighboring departments and/or partner with countless youth services organizations in the community. And don't think you have to work in a library to incorporate these ideas; anyone working with teens will benefit from the practical, easy-to-use ideas Sarah and Ellin present in this book. What a tremendous benefit this book will be to those of us already working with teen parents and those of you just getting started with this audience. The impact of this book will undoubtedly touch the lives of many teens and babies—and the lives of many library staff—as a multitude of literacies are shared.

Maryann Mori, MSLIS

ACKNOWLEDGMENTS

I would like to thank my coauthor, Sarah Lapin, for her enthusiasm, great intellect, and powerful editing skills. Our work together far surpassed my personal expectations. I could not have done this alone. I would also like to express my appreciation to my former supervisor and dear friend, Julia Passalacqua, who jumpstarted my personal reinvention as an outreach librarian and continues to support my efforts. The teachers at the Young Parents Center, Liz Adrian and Vickie Shelton, who for over twenty-five years have helped teen parents in Santa Clara make better lives for themselves and their children, are an ongoing inspiration to me. Shanti Bhaskaran and Priya Macarenhas, colleagues at Read Santa Clara, have helped me hone my family literacy skills and listened endlessly as I worked my way through the writing of this book. I thank Barbara Ittner and Libraries Unlimited for giving me the opportunity to fulfill my lifelong dream to write a book for publication. Last, but hardly least, I owe a huge debt to my husband, Hal Jerman, and my daughter, Callista Jerman, for their patience during the many months I was distracted while writing.

Ellin Klor
Palo Alto, California

I would like to thank my coauthor, Ellin Klor, for believing that we could accomplish this endeavor, and for sharing her vast knowledge and expertise, allowing me to grow both personally and professionally. I would also like to thank our contributing author, Maryann Mori, for adding great value and insight into this book, and Jacquie Brinkley at the California State Library for connecting Ellin and me. The READS team members at San Mateo County Library, Jeanine Asche, Pamela Bilz, Darwin Eustaquio, Nathalie Jackson, and Linda Roderick, have each helped me continue to build my literacy knowledge base. I express great appreciation to Janice Clark, from New Creations Home Ministries, and Samantha Johnston, from Coastside Mental Health, for sharing their passion and dedication to the teen parents in their communities. I would also like to thank the women at Mothers' Club Family Learning Center, where my journey in family literacy began. It is impossible to express the gratitude I feel for the support and guidance from my friends and family. Special thanks to my mother, Karen Lapin, for her invaluable editing expertise and input; my father, Richard Lapin, for the comic relief; and Becca and Martin Brinkhuis, for the motivation from afar. Finally, I am forever grateful for my fiancé, Michael Nordhausen, for his unwavering encouragement, patience, and belief in me.

Sarah Lapin
San Francisco, California

The authors would like to express their appreciation to Aimee Strittmatter of the Association for Library Service to Children who assisted them in previewing the revised version of the Every Child Ready to Read® program.

INTRODUCTION

A CRITICAL NEED: LIBRARIES SERVING TEEN PARENTS

Maria, a seventeen-year-old mother of one, sits at a small table in the community room of her local library, listening to the librarian's directions on how to create her own children's book for her baby. Surrounded by other young mothers, today is Maria's first time attending the Teen Parent Program; she watches the other participants drawing pictures and writing stories about their children. She is unsure of what to include in her own book. Noticing Maria's hesitancy and wanting to help her generate ideas, the librarian asks what the title was of the last book she read to her one-year-old child. Slightly confused, Maria looks at the librarian and answers, "Oh, I've never read a book to my baby." Nodding, the librarian gently explores a little further and asks, "What was your favorite story that was read to you when you were a child?" Without wavering, Maria answers, "I was never read to when I was young." Realizing the need to begin with the basics, the librarian shows Maria examples of various children's books appropriate for a one-year-old. Over the next month, the librarian works patiently with this young mother to convey the critical importance of reading to her son and integrating literacy-rich activities into their daily routines.

Maria's situation is similar to that of many of the 750,000 girls in the United States ranging in age from 15 to 19 years who are likely to become pregnant this year (Guttmacher Institute 2010). These very young parents face challenges, often well beyond the scope of their limited experience, that significantly impact their lives. While navigating the ups and downs of their own transition to adulthood, these teens are also faced with trying to find their place in society and are striving to understand the basic principles of effective parenting. They are often unprepared to face the realities of teen parenthood and are forced to grow up very quickly. How they respond to the challenges inevitably affects the lives of their children, families, and communities. The support they receive on this difficult path will help to promote a more successful journey for teen parents and their children.

Libraries are in a unique position to offer assistance, information, and encouragement to these young patrons. While it may be beyond the scope of what many people consider the traditional role of library staff, by providing free access to critical information and services, library staff can play a pivotal part in supporting these teens and their children. Such involvement can significantly help to reduce many of the negative outcomes associated with teen parenting and greatly impact two generations at one time. Incorporating programs for teen mothers and fathers and their children into the library's core services helps to meet a critical and growing need in the community.

THE SCOPE OF THE ISSUE

After almost 14 years of a steady decline, the most recent data indicates that the teen birthrate has increased, resulting in 435,436 births in the United States in 2006 (Martin et al. 2009). This reversal has spurred renewed concerns about the short-term and long-term negative outcomes associated with teen pregnancy and parenting. Teen pregnancy is more common among adolescents with existing socioeconomic disadvantages, often compounding the obstacles faced on the way to creating a life for themselves and their children. Additionally, approximately 82 percent of teen pregnancies were unintended at the time of conception (Finer and Henshaw 2006), leaving the young mother unprepared physically, emotionally, and financially. The inadvertent nature of these pregnancies is linked to unhealthy behaviors and consequences before, during, and after the birth of the baby for both the mother and the child. Compared to women with intended pregnancies, mothers with unintentional pregnancies are more likely to consume less of the recommended amounts of nutrients, smoke prenatally, smoke postpartum, and report postpartum depression (Cheng et al. 2009). In addition, the vast majority, approximately 84 percent, of these births occur outside of marriage, often placing the single parent and child in multiple living arrangements with less support, increased instability, and more family disruption (Lichter and Graefe 2001).

The United States, a country often revered for its strength and international leadership, has the highest rates of teen pregnancy and birth among comparable countries (World Bank 2010). According to the most recent data, the teen birthrate in the United States is 35 births for every 1,000 teens (World Bank 2010). This is one and a half times as high as the teen birthrate in the United Kingdom (which has the highest teen birthrate in Europe), almost *three times* as high as the rate in Canada, and more than *seven times* as high as the teen birthrate in Japan (World Bank 2010). While the rates vary from state to state, it is overwhelmingly evident that the high birthrate, and its associated adverse consequences and human and economic costs, holds significant bearing on the young family and society at large.

The Human Cost on the Parent

It is difficult to measure the human costs of a teen pregnancy in terms of individual challenges, lost potential, and displaced opportunities. Further, considering the fact that teen parents tend to experience preexisting socioeconomic and familial disadvantages prior to getting pregnant, it is often a complicated task to decipher the causality of the consequences. Regardless, most experts agree that ample research exists demonstrating the negative outcomes for the young mothers as a result of a teen pregnancy (Constantine, Nevarez, and Jerman 2008). Pregnancy in adolescence creates a strong potential for disruption of the young parent's own social and emotional development, potentially impacting relationships, capabilities, and the teen's self-concept and sense of self-worth (Coley and Chase-Lansdale 1998).

Compared to their nonparenting counterparts, teen mothers are more likely to drop out of school and to never graduate (Hoffman 2008), affecting future employment opportunities and earning power. Accordingly, teen mothers experience a higher risk of living in poverty, having to rely on public assistance, and having a less stable employment (Meade, Kershaw, and Ickovics 2008). Adolescents who become mothers also experience poorer psychological functioning (Coley and Chase-Lansdale 1998), which can directly impact their capacity to take care of themselves and their children. Physically, these young mothers are more likely to experience pregnancy-related problems and give birth to less healthy infants (Constantine, Nevarez, and Jerman 2008). These adverse outcomes for teen parents can be damaging and are likely to perpetuate an intergenerational cycle, creating high risks for their children.

The Human Cost on the Child

As a product of teen pregnancy, children of these young parents contend with a diverse array of challenges, often even before they are born. Compared to children born to older mothers, babies born to teen moms are more likely to have a low birth weight and to be born prematurely (Martin et al. 2009). This can increase the newborn's risk for serious health problems, long-term disabilities, and even death. These children are also at higher risk for academic and behavioral problems in school. They are more likely to begin kindergarten with lower levels of school readiness, including lower math and reading scores, language and communication skills, social skills, and physical and social well-being (Terry-Humen, Manlove, and Moore 2005). Further on in their academic career, children of teen parents are 50 percent more likely to repeat a grade and have lower performance on standardized tests (Hoffman 2008). The nature of these academic disadvantages could partly be attributed to the teen parents' lack of knowledge of effective parenting practices. Young mothers are less likely to be verbal with their babies, provide stimulating environments, and have realistic expectations of what is developmentally appropriate (Coley and Chase-Lansdale 1998).

The child's overall welfare and well-being is also impacted by the young age of his or her mother. According to the National Campaign to Prevent Teen Pregnancy (2010), not only are adolescent mothers in foster care more likely to become pregnant, children born to the young mothers are more likely to end up in foster care and be victims of abuse and neglect early on. Additionally, daughters of teen parents are more likely to be sexually active at an early age (Levine, Emery, and Pollack 2007) and to become teen parents themselves (Meade, Kershaw, and Ickovics 2008). Sons of teen mothers are also more likely to end up incarcerated at some point in their life (Scher and Hoffman 2008). These disparities, in terms of access to opportunities compared to children born to older mothers, put these children at a great disadvantage in their attempt to succeed in school and in life.

Economic Costs to Society

The costs of early childbearing impact not only the young family, but the public sector as well. This includes the federal, state, and local governments and taxpayers who contribute to their support. In 2004, researchers estimated that teen childbearing costs U.S. taxpayers approximately $9.1 billion per year. Included in this estimate are increased health care costs ($1.9 billion), increased child welfare costs ($2.3 billion), increased costs for state prison systems ($2.1 billion), and lost revenues due to lower taxes paid by the children of teen mothers over their own adult lifetimes ($2.9 billion) (Hoffman 2006). During the 14-year decline in the teen birthrate (1991–2005), taxpayers saved an estimated $161 billion (Hoffman 2006).

The costs of a teen birth, both economically and in the subsequent life outcomes for the parent and child, are substantial and can be disheartening. Early childbearing is tied to significantly larger societal issues. It is a reality that impacts both the family and the community. Responding to the need and providing information and services to teen parents and their children can help mitigate many of these negative consequences. The focus of library services continues to evolve, as the characteristics and needs of the communities they serve grow, change, and become more complex. Meeting the needs related to teen parenting exemplifies how libraries can exist as a strong community asset.

WHY LIBRARY SERVICES?

The library serves as an institution that provides access to information, strengthens the community, and stands as the quintessential place for lifelong learning. Celebrated for their nondiscriminatory, nonjudgmental approach, libraries function as an arena where people of all ages, classes, and backgrounds can meet on equal footing. Within this context, libraries operate as a natural hub of resources and programs specifically geared toward teen parents and their children. By providing a safe and welcoming learning environment for this underserved population, library staff have the power to drastically improve quality of life and to develop the potential of community members.

Information and support services through the library for teen parents and their children help to fill the gap created by adverse life situations. Libraries serve as:

- **A free public space:** These young parents attempting to navigate life's challenges can seek refuge from a chaotic home situation in a safe, positive environment. The library can stand as a secure haven to connect with friends, study for school, look for a job, and enjoy time with their children.

- **A hub of information and resources:** Teen parents desperately need guidance, support, and accurate and reliable information as they create a better life for themselves and their children. With free access to books, magazines, newspapers, music, movies, public computers with Internet connections, and community programs, the library helps teen parents gain life and parenting skills, find a job, obtain help with schoolwork, and experience entertainment and positive social interactions.
- **A community connector:** Through information and referral services, the library links teen parents and their children to local agencies that will help them meet their basic needs and succeed in school and in life. As a community center, the library connects these young patrons to different types of people, potentially exposing them to experienced parenting styles and broadening their perspectives.

Teen parents and their children face many unique needs and challenges. By designing programs specifically geared toward these young families as separate from other traditional parent/child programs, library staff have more freedom and flexibility to hone in on their particular requirements. Providing services and support to teen parents and their families also allows for individualized rapport-building with this population, opening up opportunities for greater impact.

The multifaceted nature of a pregnant or parenting teen's needs challenges library staff to think beyond traditional roles and responsibilities. Collaborating with colleagues in an interdisciplinary approach connects the children's librarian, teen librarian, adult librarian, and outreach and literacy staff members to develop comprehensive programming. Together, the library as a unit can address the individual needs of teen parents and their children with new and existing resources.

WHAT THIS BOOK OFFERS

This book offers a practical guide on how to develop, implement, and evaluate quality services for teen parents and their children. While the book is primarily geared for use by staff at both public and school libraries, the authors believe that the majority of the content could also be useful to educators, social workers, and others wanting to create or improve programs for this population. Chapters 1 and 2 provide important background information that will help staff understand adolescent development, the demands associated with being a teen parent, and the external influences that affect many teen parents. Gaining insight into the unique needs of adolescents can help staff to recognize and accept certain behaviors as developmentally appropriate and therefore manage their own expectations. Chapter 3 offers practical suggestions on how to effectively communicate information to teen parents, including an emphasis on the importance of building relationships and utilizing a strengths-based perspective. For those staff members who have never worked with teens or may be intimidated at the thought of leading a group of teen parents, this chapter also provides valuable tips on group facilitation.

Chapter 4 offers the nuts and bolts of program development and planning for library teen parent services. This includes ideas on how to gain institutional support from library administration and frontline staff, how to identify potential client groups and build community partnerships, and how to acquire sufficient funding. Step-by-step suggestions are presented on project planning, such as a needs assessment, timeline and budget, and evaluation. The importance of training in order to develop and maintain staff competencies in working with teen parents is also discussed.

Library programs designed for teen parents and their children assume various formats and can look extremely different from one another. Chapters 5 and 6 focus on developing programs that meet the informational and recreational needs of teen parents in a setting where they are without their children. Chapter 5 offers program templates for services that build teens' literacy and life skills, including background information and resources to aid library staff on topics such as job searching, continuing education, financial literacy, and health. How to plan parenting workshops for the young mothers and fathers is also addressed. Chapter 6 recognizes the important role the library can play as a provider of recreational resources for teen parents. Program templates help staff plan for crafts, simple cooking activities, self-care advice, and leisure reading services for teen parents.

Finally, chapters 7 and 8 focus on parent and child interactive literacy and play programs, reviewing the importance of shared time between teen parents and their children. Chapter 7 offers suggestions on how to make reading part of every child's life for teen parent families, as well as providing ideas and templates for group storytimes. Learning how to effectively communicate early learning concepts to the teen parent audience and adapting the Public Library Association's (PLA) Every Child Ready to Read initiative for your teen parent program are also covered. Chapter 8 provides an overview of the milestones of early development and offers a guide to planning specific developmental play and learning activities.

Comprehensive resource lists are found throughout the book, helping staff to efficiently and effectively develop and implement programs for teen parents and their children. Best practices and professional anecdotes assist library staff to perform utilizing the philosophy that the parent is the child's first and most influential teacher.

CONCLUSION

Teen pregnancy and parenting persists as a societal concern impacting multiple facets of the community. Research demonstrates that the human and economic costs associated with early childbearing are high, and not all consequences can be measured and included in these costs. Education, employment, human development, economic independence, and psychological well-being of both the parent and the child are all impacted by a very young pregnancy and birth. While those impacts may be disheartening, research also shows that with appropriate and timely interventions, many of the negative outcomes associated with teen parenting can be alleviated or prevented altogether. Libraries have many of the necessary resources, services, and professional skills to help resolve some of the complex issues. Meeting the educational, occupational, developmental, and entertainment needs of teen parents can be a natural extension of services most libraries already offer. The library staff member serving teen parents stands as an agent of change for the parent, child, and community at present and in the long run.

AUTHORS' NOTE

As this book goes to press, there are questions as to whether federal funding will continue to some organizations and programs referred to in this text. Every effort has been made to ensure the accuracy of all websites and listings. We apologize for any inconvenience in your search.

REFERENCES

Cheng, Diana, Eleanor B. Schwarz, Erika Douglas, and Isabelle Horon. "Unintended Pregnancy and Associated Maternal Preconception, Prenatal and Postpartum Behaviors." *Contraception* 79 (2009): 194–198.

Coley, Rebekah Levine, and P. Lindsay Chase-Lansdale. "Adolescent Pregnancy and Parenthood: Recent Evidence and Future Directions." *American Psychologist* 53, no. 2 (1998): 152–166.

Constantine, Norman A., Carmen Rita Nevarez, and Petra Jerman. *No Time for Complacency: Teen Births in California.* Public Health Institute: Center for Research on Adolescent Health and Development, 2008.

Finer, Lawrence B., and Stanley K. Henshaw. "Disparities in Rates of Unintended Pregnancy in the United States, 1994 and 2001." *Perspectives on Sexual and Reproductive Health* 39, no. 2 (2006): 108–115.

Guttmacher Institute. "U.S. Teenage Pregnancies, Births and Abortions: National and State Trends and Trends by Race and Ethnicity" (January 2010), http://www.guttmacher.org/pubs/USTPtrends.pdf.

Hoffman, Saul D. *By the Numbers: The Public Costs of Teen Childbearing.* Washington, DC: The National Campaign to Prevent Teen Pregnancy, 2006.

Hoffman, Saul D. "Consequences of Teen Childbearing for Mothers: Updated Estimates of the Consequences of Teen Childbearing for Mothers." In *Kids Having Kids: Economic Costs and Social Consequences of Teen Pregnancy,* 2nd ed., edited by Saul D. Hoffman and Rebecca A. Maynard, 74–99. Washington, DC: The Urban Institute Press, 2008.

Levine, Judith A., Clifton R. Emery, and Harold Pollack. "The Well-Being of Children Born to Teen Mothers." *Journal of Marriage and Family* 69, no. 1 (2007): 105–122.

Lichter, Daniel T., and Deborah Roempke Graefe. "Finding a Mate? The Marital and Cohabitation Histories of Unwed Mothers." In *Out of Wedlock: Causes and Consequences of Nonmarital Fertility,* edited by Lawrence L. Wu and Barbara Wolfe, 317–343. New York: Russell Sage Foundation, 2001.

Martin, Joyce A., Brady E. Hamilton, Paul D. Sutton, Stephanie J. Ventura, Fay Menacker, Sharon Kirmeyer, and T. J. Mathews. "Births: Final Data for 2006." *National Vital Statistics Reports* 57, no. 7 (2009): 1:102. http://www.cdc.gov/nchs/data/nvsr/nvsr57/nvsr57_07.pdf.

Meade, Christina S., Trace S. Kershaw, and Jeannette R. Ickovics. "The Intergenerational Cycle of Teenage Motherhood: An Ecological Approach." *Health Psychology* 27, no. 4 (2008): 419–429.

National Campaign to Prevent Teen Pregnancy. "Why It Matters: Teen Pregnancy and Overall Child Welfare" (August 2010), http://www.thenationalcampaign.org/why-it-matters/pdf/child_welfare.pdf.

Scher, Lauren Sue, and Saul D. Hoffman. "Consequences of Teen Childbearing for Incarceration Among Adult Children: Updated Estimates Through 2002." In *Kids Having Kids: Economic Costs and Social Consequences of Teen Pregnancy,* 2nd ed., edited by Saul D. Hoffman and Rebecca A. Maynard, 311–321. Washington, DC: The Urban Institute Press, 2008.

Terry-Humen, Elizabeth, Jennifer Manlove, and Kristin A. Moore. *Playing Catch-Up: How Children Born to Teen Mothers Fare.* Washington, DC: The National Campaign to Prevent Teen Pregnancy, 2005.

World Bank. "People: Reproductive Health." *2006 World Development Indicators.* Washington, DC: The World Bank, 2010.

1

UNDERSTANDING
TEEN PARENTS

Adolescence is a period of significant growth, change, and transition. As teens attempt to navigate from childhood to adulthood, they experience physical, emotional, cognitive, and social transformations. Where they are within this growth process impacts their capacity to take in and interpret new information, adjust their lives accordingly, and be empathetic to others. Becoming a parent is also a stage where considerable change occurs; a mother or father is now responsible for the health and well-being of another person. These two periods, adolescence and parenthood, and their subsequent roles and responsibilities, often are contradictory and complicate the healthy development of the individual, both as a teen and as a parent. Developing an understanding of the characteristics of teen parents can guide the design and implementation of a successful program. Gaining insight into the developmental needs of adolescents can help staff to recognize and accept certain behaviors as developmentally appropriate and therefore manage their own expectations. Within this context of parallel development, an understanding and appreciation of this unique experience is critical in order to work effectively with teen parents.

"WHAT WERE YOU THINKING?" THE TEEN BRAIN IN DEVELOPMENT

The adolescent brain is not fully developed. It is actively growing as the teen takes in new information, engages in new activities, and interacts with new people and their environment. It is important to remember the dynamic nature of the teen brain and remember that adolescent growth may fall on various points on the spectrum of cognitive maturation—anywhere from thinking like a child to thinking like an adult. Teens are developing the capacity to think logically and abstractly, which impacts their emotional control, judgment, reasoning, and ability to problem solve and systematically plan for the future (Berger 2003). These are critical skills that are needed for effective parenting and take considerable time to learn. Teen parents may not be cognitively prepared to solve problems when their baby arrives.

Sommer et al. (1993) argue that there are three components that contribute to the parent's cognitive readiness to successfully fulfill her role as a parent, including her attitude about being a parent, her understanding of good parenting practices, and her knowledge base of information required for good parenting, such as child development. Most teen parents have less life experience and awareness of the principles of childrearing, and they may not know

1

how to find accurate information on the subject (Ryan-Krause et al. 2009). Additionally, the pregnancy is often an unplanned event, impacting the teen's own outlook on becoming a parent. Teen parents, therefore, may experience greater feelings of stress and frustration, as their cognitive capacity to think about and manage the demands of parenthood is limited.

"IT'S ALL ABOUT ME!" ADOLESCENT EGOCENTRISM

Teens' thinking often revolves around their own needs and lives, as adolescents are very concerned with how other people view them and how they view themselves. Their egocentric disposition, or a focus on the self as the center (Berger 2003), often hinders their rational and logical thinking and promotes a self-view where they consider themselves as much more important within society than they actually are (Elkind 1967; Berger 2003). Within this mind-set, teens often think they are invincible and that the consequences of dangerous behavior (such as unprotected sex) will not impact them (Berger 2003). They also may believe that others are very interested in their behaviors and appearance, often provoking irrational feelings of being judged or threatened.

Unfortunately, these egocentric thoughts and narcissistic beliefs starkly conflict with the need for parents to be empathetic and selfless. Babies and young children require constant attention and depend on their caregivers for love and to meet their basic needs (Parents as Teachers National Center 2005). A teen parent, who may not understand how to separate her own thoughts and feelings from those of her baby, often struggles with finding a balance between taking care of herself and taking care of her child.

"WHO AM I?" THE FORMATION OF AN IDENTITY

The changes that the adolescent experiences as he or she transitions away from childhood and attempts to gain entry into the adult world necessitate a redefining of who the teen is as an individual and her place within her family, amongst her peers, and in her community. In the process of trying to figure out who they are, what they want to do in the future, and what is important to them, it is normal for teens to experiment with different versions of themselves. Therefore, teens may behave one way when they are with their friends and behave differently when they are around their parents or teachers, often seeming to have three (or more!) different personas.

The development of a young person's identity requires significant exploration. His or her own sense of self is often defined by interactions with many different types of people and experimentation with new activities and interests. This journey is disrupted and complicated when a teen becomes pregnant and has a child (Catrone and Sadler 1984). The roles and responsibilities of parenthood are not very flexible, therefore inhibiting exploration at school, at work, and during recreation, all of which support the identity formation process. Teen parents, therefore, have two difficult tasks: they need to establish who they are as individuals and determine who they are as parents.

"I WANT TO DECIDE!" ESTABLISHING INDEPENDENCE

While teens are consumed with defining who they are as individuals, they are also struggling to assert their own independence. This quest for autonomy often results in disagreements with parents—about what teens choose to wear, how they spend their time, and which family rules they choose to follow. They often resist authority. They are negotiating and redefining their own roles and rules in the home; they want to make their own choices and exercise an increased control over decisions about their lives and their future.

This negotiation for increased freedom is disrupted when the teen has a child. The teen's need for emotional support increases because the uncertainty of pregnancy, and being a parent is often overwhelming. The question of who is in charge of the baby complicates the teen's desire for independence, as any contribution from grandparents regarding how to raise the child often results in tension (Parents as Teachers National Center 2005). It is therefore very important to consider family relationships when working with teen parents. Additionally, financial independence is difficult to achieve when a teen has a child. Teen parents have little or no time to spend in a job, yet they experience a simultaneous increase in costs. Therefore, often to the teen's dismay, the dependence on immediate family is prolonged.

"WHERE ARE MY FRIENDS?" INTERACTING WITH PEERS

Establishing meaningful relationships with peers is increasingly important for teens, as these adolescents are moving away from parental control and are seeking support elsewhere. Teens rely heavily on their peers for fun and companionship, for learning how to resolve conflict(s) within relationships, and for advice. During adolescence, peers exercise significant influence, both positive and negative, on actions and decisions made by their friends (Berger 2003). Negative pressures of peers using drugs, having promiscuous sex, or engaging in other delinquent behavior can increase pregnancy and parenting risks.

When a teen has a child, his or her time and money become much less flexible, therefore decreasing the opportunity to interact with nonparenting peers. In general, teen parents are less likely to be able to attend a traditional high school, extracurricular activities, or recreational events. Additionally, their young age makes it difficult for them to relate to older parents, which increases the teen's sense of isolation and loneliness (Feinberg et al. 2007). Social support, especially from other teen parents, is critical for the health and well-being of both the baby and the new mother or father.

TEEN FATHERS—THE TRULY UNDERSERVED

The high need for comprehensive services for teen mothers is overwhelmingly apparent, as they experience unique challenges in fulfilling their role as their child's first and most influential teacher. Yet, teen fathers have historically been overlooked, understudied, and underserved within this paradigm of serving teen parents. They remain a population with high needs and minimal access to services (Kiselica 2008). Teen fathers are plagued by stereotypes and misconceptions, such as the deadbeat dad and the absent father. It is often assumed that they do not want to be involved in raising their children. However, it is important to recognize that male teens may just need training and guidance in order to understand and assume the responsibilities of being an involved father. Individualized support can prevent the young fathers from the self-fulfilling prophecy of becoming absent fathers. Instead, they can choose to become successful parents (Lindsay and Enright 1997).

A young father faces several barriers to taking on the role of being a parent, including:

- The baby's mother may want nothing to do with him.
- The grandparents may believe he would not have a positive influence.
- He may lack access to financial resources to meet the baby's needs.
- He may not be sufficiently mature to raise a child (Schwartz 1999).

Taking responsibility often equates with taking financial responsibility. Being reliable, in this sense, is often difficult for teen fathers; they have limited earning power due to low educational levels and employment difficulties. Yet, it is important to recognize that a young father, given the opportunity and adequate assistance, has much more to offer the mother and their child than money, such as emotional support. Disregarding this fact can have serious consequences on the health, educational, and behavioral outcomes of their children. Especially for sons, the absence of a father can leave them without a male figure to identify with, and from whom to seek advice and guidance on becoming a man; dysfunctional fatherhood, therefore, often becomes cyclical (Kiselica 2008). Additionally, if a father is not engaged in raising his child, he will not understand the true responsibilities of being a parent; therefore, he may not avoid risky behavior (such as unprotected sex) again with other women.

The positive impact of an involved father on the child's well-being is becoming much more apparent, as research demonstrates that he is effective in increasing the child's academic achievement and the child's overall emotional well-being (Schwartz 1999). Additionally, when the dad is included in the child's upbringing, the chances that he or she will grow up to be a teen parent diminishes (Parents as Teachers National Center 2005). Therefore, the young father often needs to be given a chance to grow into his role as a father. Stereotypes and myths need to be challenged. Teen fathers need to be sought out and invited to participate in all aspects of programs for teen parents, including education, parenting skills, career development, and counseling.

"HOW DO I DO THIS?" MEETING THE DEMANDS OF PARENTING

Being a successful parent is often defined as loving a child unconditionally and providing a caring, safe environment that supports healthy development. Fulfilling this role is difficult at any age, but it can be especially overwhelming when the parent is also experiencing life's changes and challenges as a teen. For example, when considering what children need for the best start in life, providing a stable relationship with a caregiver is essential, as it allows the child to learn at a faster pace, develop better self-esteem, and make friends more easily (First 5 Santa Clara County 1999). Yet, when teen parents are not sure of who they are or how to manage their own stress, providing the predictable, nurturing stability that their children need can be extremely difficult. Similarly, maintaining a safe, healthy home (another key task of successful parenting) can be extra-challenging for teen parents, who may not have a stable home life. Intergenerational conflict, homelessness, or sharing a house with multiple families complicates controlling cleanliness and safety. Additionally, teens' brains may not be developed enough to problem solve about how to make reading to their children a priority, promote play as an outlet for imagination and learning, and complete their own homework assignments for class all in one day.

Teen parents are often concerned about whether they are being good parents. Prior to becoming a mother or father, they may have romanticized and glorified what having a child would be like. When the reality sets in regarding what being a parent actually entails, they may question whether they are doing the right things for themselves and for their children. Offering programs to support teens in this role and to provide them with encouragement and information on how to foster their children's healthy development will help them abandon the notion of perfection. It will also help them realize that they can successfully meet the demands of parenting and of growing up themselves.

CONCLUSION

Being a teen is extremely difficult, as the adolescent is struggling to form his or her own identity, gain independence, and move away from being a child and move toward becoming an adult. Teens' brains, bodies, and emotions are in the process of being developed. Being a new parent is also complex, challenging, and overwhelming. New parents often feel that they have to give up a great deal in order to devote the necessary time, energy, and love to their new child. When adolescence and parenthood are combined, unique challenges and conflicts arise. Program staff may feel frustrated, for example, when they see the young mother showing disinterest in her child when her boyfriend is present. Or, group facilitators may feel discouraged when there are tensions among the teen parents because of gossip or a challenge to someone's identity. When working with teen parents, it is important to have a clear understanding of their developmental needs as adolescents and as parents. Such insights will enable staff members to appropriately adjust expectations, programming efforts, and service delivery options.

Additionally, despite staff's own personal or moral viewpoints, the teen parent may not see that becoming pregnant and having a baby is an event that significantly alters her life now and in the future. Teens may actually want a baby for a variety of reasons. A teen may believe that a baby would be her only source of unconditional love, that a new child will help improve the conditions of an unhappy life, or that a baby would be a symbol of her maturity (Parents as Teachers National Center 2005). Within this context, a baby may change a teen's life for the better, potentially serving as a motivating factor to move away from risky behaviors and toward responsible actions, such as staying in school and getting a job.

Despite the developmental challenges experienced by teen parents, with sufficient guidance from family, friends, and library program staff, many young mothers and fathers demonstrate resiliency in the face of the adversity. Understanding teen parents' unique needs and strengths, as well as developing relevant programs and services, can help in supporting teen parents to manage the demands and experience the joys of growing up and raising a child.

REFERENCES

Berger, Kathleen Stassen. *The Developing Person: Through Childhood and Adolescence.* New York: Worth Publishers, 2003.

Catrone, Constance, and Lois Siebert Sadler. "A Developmental Model for Teen-Age Parent Education." *Journal of School Health* 54, no. 2 (1984): 63–67.

Elkind, David. "Egocentrism in Adolescence." *Child Development* 38, no. 4 (1967): 1025–1034.

Feinberg, Sandra, Barbara Jordan, Kathleen Deerr, Marcellina Byrne, and Lisa Kropp. *The Family-Centered Library Handbook.* New York: Neal-Schuman Publishers, Inc., 2007.

First 5 Santa Clara County. "10 Things Every Child Needs for the Best Start in Life." Adapted from *10 Things Every Child Needs DVD.* Produced by the Robert R. McCormick Tribune Foundation, 1999.

Kiselica, Mark S. *Adolescent Fatherhood in America.* New Brunswick, NJ: Rutgers University Press, 2008.

Lindsay, Jeanne Warren, and Sharon Githens Enright. *Books, Babies and School-Age Parents: How to Teach Pregnant and Parenting Teens to Succeed.* Buena Park, CA: Morning Glory Press, 1997.

Parents as Teachers National Center. *Issues in Working with Teen Parents: A Curriculum for Professionals.* Minneapolis, MN: Parents as Teachers National Center, 2005.

Ryan-Krause, Patricia, Mikki Meadows-Oliver, Lois Sadler, and Martha K. Swartz. "Developmental Status of Children of Teen Mothers: Contrasting Objective Assessments with Maternal Reports." *Journal of Pediatric Health Care* 23, no. 5 (2009): 303–309.

Schwartz, Wendy. "Young Fathers: New Support Strategies." ERIC Clearinghouse on Urban Education, Institute for Urban and Minority Education (March 1999), http://www.eric.ed.gov/PDFS/ED429143.pdf.

Sommer, Kristen, Thomas L. Whitman, John G. Borkowski, Cynthia Schellenbach, Scott Maxwell, and Deborah Keogh. "Cognitive Readiness and Adolescent Parenting." *Developmental Psychology* 29, no. 2 (1993): 389–398.

2

TEEN PARENTS WITHIN A SYSTEM: INFLUENCING FACTORS

All human beings function within a system of interrelated and interdependent factors that impact how individuals live and who they become. Whom you interact with, what environment you live in, and what opportunities you have access to, all create connections that contribute to the quality of your life. While not all teen parents fit one mold, many young mothers and fathers do confront a multitude of complex challenges within their own systems before they get pregnant and after their baby is born. They may face issues relating to poverty, community violence, mental health concerns, and a lack of a strong social support system. In addition to being a new parent and trying to navigate developmentally from childhood to adulthood, teen parents are often forced to deal with life crises in an adverse environment. They may not have fully developed the coping mechanisms and decision-making skills necessary to adequately deal with these life stressors. Pressures often influence how these adolescents act, posing unique challenges to the library staff trying to help patrons improve the quality of their lives. It is important to understand the complex ways teen parents are both a product of, and contribute to, their personal systems. An awareness and acceptance of the teen parent's complex system can assist library staff in planning and implementing programs and in developing an understanding of how the system impacts the teen parent's actions and attitudes.

THE HOME ENVIRONMENT

A teen parent may live in a nontraditional family setting with multiple key stakeholders spanning several generations, such as the teen's mother and father (or foster parents), siblings, and grandparents, and the child's other parent and the family of the other parent. Their home environments are often chaotic and may be filled with conflict, substance abuse, domestic violence, and other life experiences associated with poverty (Parents as Teachers National Center 2005). These conditions often complicate and disrupt the young parent's process of raising a new baby.

Family Dynamics

Shared Caregiving

Given the increased demands associated with being pregnant and raising a child, teen parents often turn to their own mothers for support and remain living in their parents' homes.

Parents of adolescents having babies react in various ways, ranging from excitement and joy to complete disapproval and disownment. Yet, in many cultures and communities, there is a long-standing tradition of shared caregiving. Many grandmothers provide support, guidance, love, and financial and legal stability (Black and Nitz 1996). The benefits of including the grandparent in the responsibilities associated with raising a child are significant. The young parent can have the opportunity to stay in school and therefore broaden her employment options in the future and gain financial independence (Parents as Teachers National Center 2005). The teen parent also can have more time to interact with peers, thereby decreasing isolation, as she transitions into adulthood. With shared responsibilities, the baby can develop in a less stressful environment.

Yet, shared caregiving within a multigenerational family structure can also negatively impact the healthy development of both the young parent and the baby. A power struggle over who is ultimately in charge of the child often arises. Research demonstrates that there are significant tensions related to childrearing responsibilities involving young mothers and grandmothers, especially when they live together (Black and Nitz 1996). The teen parent and her mother can disagree on the best way to raise the child and confusion can arise over obligations and roles. If the grandmother assumes the role of primary caregiver, the young parent has less opportunity to practice being a mother, which can impact her confidence and her ability to develop effective parenting skills (Black and Nitz 1996). The grandmother may neglect her role in meeting the developmental needs of her own adolescent daughter or son, as she has shifted her focus toward the baby. The quality of care given by the grandparent should also be considered; if the grandparent does not serve as a role model of strong parenting behavior, the teen may not be able to develop appropriate knowledge, and the baby suffers.

Sharing of caregiver responsibilities between the teen parent and the grandparent is common and often becomes complicated by generational differences. It is important to consider the dynamics of this relationship when working with teen parents.

The Relationship between the Child's Mother and Father

The relationship between the child's mother and father can be complex, dynamic, and unstable. As in typical teen relationships, they can love each other one minute and develop feelings of hate the next. The volatile and unpredictable nature of this relationship is further complicated by financial worries, as well as the struggle to determine how to best raise their child and who should be involved in this process. The mother's family may shun the father, limiting his participation in the child's life and his connection with the teen mom. Without the intimate support of the father, the responsibilities of childrearing fall more heavily on the mother. Simultaneously, she is struggling to understand her own personal feelings about love, trust, and abandonment in relation to the baby's father. If the young mother shares with you one day that she is madly in love with her baby's father, and then the next time you see her she screams that she can't stand him, it is because she is dealing with a multitude of complex and contradictory feelings. Offering support, without judgment, can help guide the teen through the confusion to discover what type of relationship is best for her and for her child.

The Surrounding Neighborhood

Whether the inside of the home is calm or chaotic, the surrounding community can greatly impact the quality of life and growth processes of both the teen parent and her child. Young families may live in neighborhoods plagued by high rates of poverty, low literacy skills, community violence, and a deficit in nutritional knowledge and practices. Gang activity and experiences with neighborhood crime, either as a victim or a witness, negatively affect the social and emotional development of the teen and her baby. If the teen parent feels unsafe to walk to and from school, for example, or lives in constant fear of gang violence, the associated stress and anxiety create an adverse environment for the family. It is important to consider the implications of the local neighborhoods when talking with teen parents about developmentally appropriate activities, such as going on a nature walk (see chapter 8) with their children. If they seem hesitant or resistant to engage in such a beneficial learning activity, open up the discussion by asking whether they feel safe doing this activity in their neighborhood. If they do not, brainstorm alternative ideas.

In addition to having concerns surrounding community violence, teen parents often do not have access to reliable transportation, resulting in feelings of isolation and possibly hindering their ability to access quality health care and child care. Neighborhoods with higher rates of poverty and with more minority residents have fewer grocery stores with fresh fruits and vegetables and have more liquor stores (Moore and Roux 2006). The minimal access to low-cost healthy food impacts dietary issues, such as obesity, and is important to consider when discussing nutrition with teen parents.

Homelessness

The lack of a stable home and the subsequent concerns about shelter and safety increase stress levels for young parents and have negative outcomes for both the mother or father and the child. Unfortunately, homelessness is a reality faced by too many teen parents. Whether it was because they were escaping some type of abuse, they were thrown out of their own home because of the pregnancy, or they left home due to conflict with family members (Meadows-Oliver 2009), teen parents can be confronted with housing instability. They may live on the streets, live in shelters, or move from couch to couch at the homes of distant family members or friends. The transient nature of this lifestyle results in increased feelings of isolation and alienation from peers at a time when, developmentally, interaction and support from friends is so important to the adolescent's growth process.

Young children feel comforted by predictability, and consistent routines help them learn about the world and develop a sense of security. Homelessness causes frequent changes in their living environment and disrupts important household routines. This can result in the child acting out and being disobedient, making it extra-difficult for the teen parent, who has minimal parenting skills to manage behavior (Meadows-Oliver 2009). Additionally, in transitional housing facilities, such as shelters, the young parent has a lack of control over what the child is exposed to, such as vulgarity, hostility, and negative health factors. The teen parent, in these types of stressful living conditions, can easily become overwhelmed and tired, hindering her ability to adequately care for herself and her child.

Sexual Abuse

Research indicates that a strong link exists between prior sexual abuse and teen pregnancy (Parents as Teachers National Center 2005). Victims of such maltreatment and exploitation at a young age often suffer from low self-esteem and impeded social and emotional development. Subsequently, risky sexual behavior, promiscuity, and the inability to determine appropriate relationship boundaries are common reactive behaviors of those who suffered such childhood traumas (Parents as Teachers National Center 2005). The teen parent may never have identified, acknowledged, or dealt with the abuse. Yet evidence suggests that parents need to heal from any kind of sexual, domestic, or other violent abuse in order to adequately foster healthy development for their own children (Leiderman and Almo 2001). Without awareness of this connection between abuse and adolescent pregnancy, there are often misconceptions about the teen's choices or reasoning behind engaging in sexual activity. It is important not to underestimate the implications of sexual abuse and trauma and to ensure that teen parents are connected to community resources designed to support victims of abuse.

Mental Health Concerns

Mental health issues, such as low self-esteem and depression, can seriously impact quality of life for both the teen parent and her child. These issues can compromise the parent's ability to sufficiently and consistently care for her children. Often, maternal self-esteem is dependent on experiencing meaningful, positive interactions that bond the parent and the child together (Cox et al. 2008). If the young mother or father has numerous successful exchanges with her or his child, then she or he will start to believe, "I can do this!" Yet, when faced with adversity within his or her own system (conflict at home, health and safety concerns, financial issues, sexual or domestic abuse, emotional immaturity) it is difficult for a teen parent to overcome problems, find balance, and develop that strong sense of self as an individual and as a parent.

Depression is common in both pregnant and parenting teens; according to recent research, 42 percent of pregnant teens demonstrated mental health problems including depression (Cox et al. 2008). Adolescents with depression, anxiety, and conduct disorders are more likely to have babies when they are in their teens (Harvard Medical School 1997). Whether the onset of the mental health issues occurred before, during, or after the pregnancy, the existence of these serious problems can significantly compromise the young parent's self-efficacy and competence, and therefore can result in negative outcomes for the children. If the mother is too depressed to get out of bed, who will care for her children, and who will care for her? While mental health concerns are beyond the scope of the role of library staff, linking the young families to appropriate services in the community will positively impact all other facets within their system.

EDUCATIONAL EXPERIENCES AND ISSUES

The joys, challenges, and additional demands associated with a pregnancy and becoming a parent often interfere with teen parents' educational experiences. They struggle with academics, may not have time to attend classes and do homework, and navigate parenthood and adulthood at the same time. Young parents often have poor basic academic skills, and learning disabilities may go undiagnosed. The younger the parent is at the time her child is born, the greater the educational setback. Low educational attainment and a high dropout rate result in difficulties obtaining a job; therefore teen mothers and fathers often have lower earning power and lower job satisfaction (McDonell, Limber, and Connor-Godbey 2007). As a result, it becomes increasingly difficult to meet the financial demands of being parents on their own and to gain financial independence. Additionally, the level of academic achievement of parents is strongly correlated with their children's future success in school. Therefore, the cyclical nature of lower academic achievement and socioeconomic status can be passed on from teen parents to their children.

Hurdles at School

Challenges faced by young parents at school are major contributing factors to a high dropout rate. They often feel isolated, alienated, and uncomfortable among their peers, teachers, and staff at school. School may not seem relevant to their current situation, such as when a pregnant teen is experiencing morning sickness or when finding child care for the baby is a problem (Lindsay and Enright 1997). Without sufficient support and guidance from school personnel in creating a safe and accommodating learning environment for young parents, school attendance decreases and dropout rates increase.

Title IX of the Educational Amendment Act of 1972 protects teen parents from discrimination in the educational system based on gender, pregnancy, and marital or parenting status (Center for Assessment and Policy Development 1999). Teen parents cannot be excluded from extracurricular activities. They cannot automatically be assigned to separate schools or programs unless those schools offer the same educational experience accessible to other students (Center for Assessment and Policy Development 1999). Additionally, the school cannot fail students because of excessive absences related to pregnancy (Ducker 2007). The school administrators, school staff, and the teen parents themselves may not realize that actions taken by the school directly violate this law. It is important to help these young parents understand their rights and options in their educational experiences.

INFORMATION AND REFERRAL

Gaining an understanding of teen parents' systems and the associated challenges will help you to better design and implement programming for this underserved population and improve their quality of life. However, many of the complex problems faced by these young parents are beyond the scope of what library professionals can offer in terms of programs. A crucial service you can provide is information and referral, connecting these patrons with the appropriate resources to meet their needs. Becoming aware of what local community agencies have available for those in need in terms of housing, health, child care and support, and education will allow you to link the teen parents in your program to services when issues arise.

Housing

If a teen parent in your program is struggling with finding a place to live, this unmet basic need can impact all other facets of his or her life. Most cities and towns have some type of homeless shelter or transitional housing facility. To locate a place that will keep these young families safe and off the streets, contact the National Runaway Switchboard at 1-800-RUNAWAY (1-800-786-2929) or visit their website. This 24-hour crisis line will refer young parents to shelter, food, and medical/legal assistance, while maintaining confidentiality.

Another housing assistance option in some states is connecting the teen parents with Second Chance Homes. This federally funded program helps states and local governments establish adult-supervised, supportive group homes that provide a safe, stable, and nurturing environment for pregnant and parenting teen mothers and their children. With comprehensive programming, the Second Chance Homes generally include requirements to finish high school or obtain a GED, attend parenting and life skill classes, and participate in some type of job training. Mentoring and development of a transition plan for the teen parent's independent living in the future are also offered. Nationwide, at least six states have made a commitment to Second Chance Homes, including Massachusetts, Nevada, New Mexico, Rhode Island, Texas, and Georgia. Additionally, there are many local Second Chance Homes operating in at least 25 other states. More information about this program can be found on the U.S. Department of Housing and Urban Development's website.

Health

Medicaid

If the teen parent's employer does not provide health insurance, there are alternatives to accessing quality health care at a low cost. While private health insurance can be costly without financial contributions from the employer, the government does offer public health-care coverage for qualifying individuals and their families. Medicaid is a state-run health program that receives federal money and provides health care to people with low income and minimal resources (Lawton 2007). To qualify to receive Medicaid benefits, you must be a U.S. citizen or a lawfully admitted immigrant. Eligibility requirements are specific to each state. For more information, call 1-877-267-2323 or visit Medicaid's website.

Children's Health Insurance Program (CHIP)

Another health-care option for low-income families is the Children's Health Insurance Program (CHIP). This is a state and federal program that provides low-cost health insurance coverage for children in families that earn too much to qualify for Medicaid but that cannot afford to pay for private health insurance coverage. Eligibility requirements and care coverage vary by state. To learn more about this program, and to locate state-specific information, visit the Insure Kids Now website or call 1-877-KIDS-NOW (1-877-543-7669).

Women, Infants, and Children Program (WIC)

WIC is a federally supported program that provides those in need with nutritional education, funds to purchase healthy supplemental food, and help finding health care and other needed services. To be eligible to receive WIC benefits, you must meet income guidelines and be pregnant or the mother of a child younger than age five. Through this program teen parents can also receive support and helpful information about breastfeeding their babies. For more information about WIC, including the location of the WIC office in your community and state-specific eligibility requirements, visit the Women, Infants, and Children website of the USDA's Food and Nutrition Service.

Vaccines for Children (VFC) Program

The VFC program is federally funded and provides free vaccination to children who may not otherwise have access because of inability to pay. Children 18 years old and younger are eligible to receive the VFC vaccines if they qualify to get Medicaid benefits, are uninsured or underinsured (e.g., they have private health insurance, but coverage does not include vaccines), or are American Indian or Alaska Native (Lawton 2007). VFC vaccines are administered by any enrolled VFC Program provider, such as a private doctor, a private or public health clinic, a hospital, or a school. To locate a VFC-enrolled provider in your community, visit the Vaccines and Immunizations' "VFC: State/Territory—VFC Coordinators" website of the Centers for Disease Control and Prevention.

Mental Health

Accessing quality mental health services is critical for the teen parent in distress to be able to sufficiently care for herself and her child. To connect a young patron with the appropriate services, try visiting the Substance Abuse and Mental Health Services Administration's (SAMHSA) "Mental Health Services Locator" website. Here you can access a mental health services directory and facilities locator by state.

Child Support

In order to ensure that the child is properly supported, teen parents may need assistance in getting child support. Library staff members can refer them to the Child Support Enforcement (CSE) program, where federal, state, and local agencies work collaboratively to try to collect child support payments for the parent (Lawton 2007). The CSE provides assistance in locating noncustodial parents, establishing paternity, establishing support orders, and making sure child support payments are made. If the teen parent is already receiving financial assistance through Temporary Assistance for Needy Families (TANF) or Medicaid, he or she may qualify to receive free services through the CSE program. If not, then he or she may have to pay a small fee (Lawton 2007). For more information and to locate your state's child support agency, visit the Office of Child Support Enforcement's webpage.

Child Care

If the teen parents in your library program are working or in school, they will likely need assistance in locating quality child care at a low cost. The child-care resource and referral (CCR&R) center in your community will help teen parents select child care and identify sources of financial assistance. Child Care Aware is a program of the National Association of Child Care Resource Referral Agencies that helps parents locate affordable, quality child care and evaluate providers to ensure that their children are safe. For more information, call 1-800-424-2246 or visit their website.

Most states have subsidies to assist low-income, working families to pay for child care. Additionally, many states now offer free or low-cost pre-kindergarten for three-and four-year-olds to improve school readiness. All states have Head Start or Early Head Start programs, which are federally funded programs that provide free early child education and care to low-income families. To locate the Head Start office in your community, visit the Early Childhood Learning and Knowledge Center's website or call 1-866-763-6481.

Local Community Referrals

Navigating the complexity of community agencies and services can be overwhelming. Funded by federal and local governments, local United Way organizations, and various community foundations, 2-1-1 centers have been established nationwide to connect callers to information about critical health and human services, both public and private, available in the community. For example, searching the Maine 2-1-1 resource directory for the term "teen parents" results in a list of parenting, health, and education programs that serve teen parents. The information can also can be limited by geographic area. As funding for government-supported services waxes and wanes, use of the 2-1-1 network may offer the most accurate information possible. As of August 2010, 2-1-1 covers all or part of 47 states, plus the District of Columbia and Puerto Rico (www.211us.org/status.htm). To access free and confidential information and referrals, call 2-1-1 or visit the 211.org website.

CONCLUSION

As library staff working with young families, it is important to be aware of the environmental stressors in a teen parent's system and how these are interrelated. This understanding of the challenges confronted by teen parents in their daily lives can help staff predict feelings, needs, and behaviors. Staff can also gain a greater awareness of the underlying causes of teen parents' actions, priorities, and concerns. However, while it is critical to recognize the complex nature of their systems, you must to be careful not to make assumptions that will lead to lowering your expectations for teen parents. Keep in mind that not all young mothers and fathers face the same challenges. Creating an environment in which teens feel safe to share, and you feel comfortable asking questions, will foster the creation of programs that best meet the needs of young parents and their children. Be wary of taking on the role of a social worker. Instead, connect teen parents with critical information and referrals in the community; this will help to drastically improve their quality of life. A deeper understanding of the complexities, challenges, and confusions shared by teen parents will enable staff to more effectively create a healthy climate where teen parents and their children can learn and grow together.

REFERENCES

Black, Maureen M., and Katherine Nitz. "Grandmother Co-Residence, Parenting, and Child Development among Low Income, Urban Teen Mothers." *Journal of Adolescent Health* 18, no. 3 (1996): 218–226.

Center for Assessment and Policy Development. "Helping the Education System Work for Teen Parents and their Children" (October 1999), http://www.capd.org/pubfiles/pub-1999-10-06.pdf.

Cox, Joanne E., Matthew Buman, Jennifer Valenzuela, Natalie Pierre Joseph, Anna Mitchell, and Elizabeth R. Woods. "Depression, Parenting Attributes, and Social Support among Adolescent Mothers Attending a Teen Tot Program." *Journal of Pediatric and Adolescent Gynecology* 21, no. 5 (2008): 275–281.

Ducker, Brittany. "Overcoming the Hurdles: Title IX and Equal Educational Attainment for Pregnant and Parenting Students." *Journal of Law and Education* 36, no. 3 (2007): 445–452.

Harvard Medical School. "Adolescent Psychiatric Disorders Linked to Teen Parenthood." *ScienceDaily* (October 4, 1997), http://www.sciencedaily.com/releases/1997/10/971004091829.htm.

Lawton, Sandra Augustyn, ed. *Pregnancy Information for Teens: Health Tips about Teen Pregnancy and Teen Parenting.* Detroit, MI: Omnigraphics, 2007.

Leiderman, Sally, and Cari Almo. *Interpersonal Violence and Adolescent Pregnancy: Prevalence and Implications for Practice and Policy.* Washington, DC: Healthy Teen Network, 2001.

Lindsay, Jeanne Warren, and Sharon Githens Enright. *Books, Babies and School-Age Parents: How to Teach Pregnant and Parenting Teens to Succeed.* Buena Park, CA: Morning Glory Press, 1997.

McDonell, James R., Susan P. Limber, and Jennifer Connor-Godbey. "Pathways Teen Mother Support Project: Longitudinal Findings." *Children and Youth Services Review* 29, no. 7 (2007): 840–855.

Meadows-Oliver, Mikki. "Adolescent Mothers' Experiences of Caring For Their Children While Homeless." *Journal of Pediatric Nursing* 24, no. 6 (2009): 458–467.

Moore, Latetia V., and Ana V. Diez Roux. "Associations of Neighborhood Characteristics with Location and Type of Food Stores." *American Journal of Public Health* 96, no. 2 (2006): 325–331.

Parents as Teachers National Center. *Issues in Working with Teen Parents: A Curriculum for Professionals.* Minneapolis, MN: Parents as Teachers National Center, 2005.

RESOURCES

General

Lindsay, Jeanne Warren, and Jean Brunelli. *Your Pregnancy and Newborn Journey: A Guide for Pregnant Teens.* Buena Park, CA: Morning Glory Press, 2004.

2-1-1. "Find Your Local 2-1-1 Service." http://211us.org/.

Housing

National Runaway Switchboard. http://www.1800runaway.org/.

U.S. Department of Housing and Urban Development. Home and Communities. "Second Chance Homes." http://www.hud.gov/offices/pih/other/sch/.

Health

Department of Health and Human Services. Centers for Disease Control and Prevention. "Vaccines and Immunizations." http://www.cdc.gov/vaccines/programs/vfc/contacts-state.htm.

Insure Kids Now. http://www.insurekidsnow.gov/.

U.S. Department of Health and Human Services. Centers for Medicare and Medicaid Services. "Medicaid." http://www.cms.gov/home/medicaid.asp.

U.S. Department of Health and Human Services. National Mental Health Information Center. "Mental Health Services Locator." http://mentalhealth.samhsa.gov/databases/.

USDA Food and Nutrition Service. "Women, Infants, and Children." http://www.fns.usda.gov/wic.

Child Support

U.S. Department of Health and Human Services. Administration for Children and Family. "The Office of Child Support Enforcement." http://www.acf.hhs.gov/programs/cse/.

Child Care

Early Childhood Learning and Knowledge Center. "Head Start Locator." http://eclkc.ohs.acf.hhs.gov/hslc/HeadStartOffices.

National Association of Child Care Resource Referral Agencies: Child Care Aware. http://www.childcareaware.org.

3

COMMUNICATING WITH TEEN PARENTS

Communication is the process of conveying information in order to establish a shared understanding between people. How the information is presented, how it is interpreted by an individual, and the body language used all contribute to how meaning is delivered and received. Library staff working with teen parents always want to find the best way to communicate, connect with, and assist these younger patrons; yet they may feel frustrated when it appears that the teen parents are not listening or engaging in an activity. Working and interacting with teen parents becomes more effective when you understand the developmental factors and life experiences they face in their daily lives. In chapters 1 and 2, we discussed how teen parents experience many physical, emotional, and social changes as a teen and as a new parent, and how they face many challenges within their lives. Adolescent self-consciousness, for example, may hinder a teen parent from fully participating in a group discussion. A young mother may be worrying about where she and her child will sleep that night, and therefore may not be focused on storytime. Understanding these internal and external struggles helps library staff to not take the teen's behavior or comments personally.

Teen parents, as well as teens in general, need positive adult role models. This chapter will guide you to exercise that positive influential power through effective communication and facilitation of group meetings, programs, and storytimes. By showing respect to these young patrons, offering words of encouragement, and providing useful information for them and their children, you will leave a lasting impact far beyond the walls of the library.

WORKING WITH TEEN PARENTS

Building Relationships

Offering storytimes, workshops, and other programs as a library service provides opportunities for teen parents to learn literacy skills, to develop self-esteem, social skills, and a sense of belonging, and to help one another grow. It is important to establish a safe learning environment where the young mothers and fathers feel comfortable sharing and exploring. As the program facilitator and as a representative of the library, it is crucial that you continually build rapport and establish respect with each individual; this is necessary in order to ensure an enjoyable learning experience for everyone. Below are a few tips on how to successfully create a positive atmosphere for productive interactions with your teen parent patrons (Carney 2007; Small and Day 1990).

1. **Reserve judgment:** Teen parents come from many different walks of life. They may not have the same value set as you, and their decision-making process may not be fully developed. You may not agree with the choices they have made and continue to make. Regardless of these differences, it is important that you convey a sense of compassion and that you reserve judgment. Try to see past a person's negative behavior and understand that actions may come from internal confusion or pain and external pressures. Recognize that no matter what they do, these teens are doing the best they can, considering how they see the world at any given time.

2. **Establish ground rules:** When your group of teen parents meets for the first time, setting ground rules is a good way to create a safe space for learning and sharing. As teens sometimes react negatively to authoritative ways, it is generally most effective to jointly establish these rules ("Community Agreements"). Invite the young parents to generate this list, asking them what they need to feel safe in order to discuss potentially difficult topics. This allows them to have ownership of the process and establishes accountability. Write down these rules and post them in the room where your group meets; this way you can easily refer to them if conflict ever arises. When new teen parents join the group, ask the other participants to go over the community agreements with the newcomers. Examples of commonly used ground rules are:
   - Respect one another. This includes active listening.
   - Speak for yourself and from your own experiences; use "I" instead of "we" and you."
   - Refrain from personal attacks.
   - What is shared in the group stays in the group; respect confidentiality.
   - Be mindful of what you say through body language and other nonverbal responses (Gorski 2010).

3. **Take them seriously:** Although adolescents may developmentally be somewhere between childhood and adulthood, as parents and as individuals, they deserve to be recognized as equal to adults in their self-worth. It is important to not brush off something that they are going through with comments like "You are too young to really understand this" or "You are only going through a stage—you'll grow out of it." It is critical to validate their experiences and feelings instead of minimizing them.

4. **Be authentic:** Young adults generally do not like being told what to do; it is often helpful for library staff to take a more relaxed and informal approach when conveying information. Yet, it is important that you don't try to act too "cool" or "in" with teen parents. They will see right through you! If you don't understand a slang word or a pop-culture reference, do not pretend that you do or try to integrate it into your own repertoire. Being yourself helps to establish genuine relationships with the teen parents and models openness and the importance of being okay with who you are.

5. **Recognize their strengths and their efforts:** Teen parents have a lot to offer in terms of life experience, perspective, and knowledge—if they are given the chance. Don't assume that they know you think they are doing a good job—spell it out for them. Honest, specific praise demonstrates to the teen parents that you respect them and what they do. It also helps build their self-esteem as individuals, and as parents. Positive reinforcement that emphasizes good behavior often helps to minimize negative behavior. Recognizing and giving feedback on their talents, abilities, and efforts are powerful tools in helping teen parents realize their potential.

6. **Listen to them:** Communication has been considered 80 percent listening and 20 percent speaking. Teen parents are confronted with many complex issues in their daily lives; the programs you provide can offer the teens an opportunity to discuss and discover new ways of looking at these challenges. As the group facilitator and adult, listening, and not imposing your own values, will show the teens that you accept, respect, and value them. It also encourages healthy exploration in a safe environment.

7. **Have a sense of humor:** When working with teen parents, try to remember not to take yourself too seriously. A sense of humor is a great way to alleviate tension, and it shows the young adults that it is okay to be a little silly—especially when they are interacting with their children. Your enthusiasm and positive energy will be contagious within the group and will allow for a more enjoyable learning environment. If you are relaxed and calm, your teen parent group will be put at ease. Establishing relationships will more readily happen under these conditions.

8. **Be patient, persistent, and flexible:** Patience and persistence are of particular importance when you are trying to communicate library, literacy, and learning information to teen parents. Remember, they are still growing cognitively, socially, and emotionally, so not all activities will be warmly received. Being flexible with your program or storytime plan will allow you to try an activity a different way if the original strategy did not work with your group. Be patient with yourself as you explore and discover the best ways to meet the needs of the teen parents in your group.

Establishing that safe learning environment in your library or at your partner agency's site is critical in keeping teen parents active, engaged, interested, cooperative, and returning again and again. Icebreakers (see chapter 5) are a great way to get to know one another and to build rapport. As the group facilitator, remember to be nonjudgmental and to not take anything personally. Be flexible, adaptable, and authentic, and have patience with yourself and with the teen parents you are working with in your community.

Utilizing a Strengths-based Perspective

Everyone has unique strengths, talents, assets, knowledge, and capacities. Honing in and focusing on these assets call for library staff to think about what the teen parents know and can do, rather than focusing solely on their needs and deficits. Utilizing a strengths-based perspective empowers these young patrons to help themselves, which is a sustainable strategy that will carry them long after the library program is completed.

During a program or storytime, you can build on the strengths you observe in the teen parents. If nothing else, the young parents showed up to the workshop, signifying the desire to create a better life for themselves and their children. Begin by activating prior knowledge; bring up topics or ideas that the teen parents have some familiarity with, and exposure to, in their own world. This gives them a context for the information introduced in the workshop. For example, if you want to talk about the importance of play for their child's healthy development, start by brainstorming as a group the fun activities they enjoyed when they were younger. This illustrates for the teen parents what they already know; the rest of the workshop can be spent building on that knowledge by introducing and exploring new ideas and expanding the teens' perspectives.

Utilizing this strengths-based approach encourages the teen parent in her role as her child's first and most influential teacher. Brazelton Touchpoints Center is an organization dedicated to strengthening the systems of care that serve young children and their families. Many libraries and child-care centers utilize the Brazelton Touchpoints Center's approach. Core to their methods is a focus on strengths, functioning under the assumption that the parent is the expert when it comes to his or her child, that all parents want to do what is best for their child, and that all parents can contribute to the healthy development of their child (Brazelton and Sparrow 2003). Recognizing that the parent is the expert on his or her child is a great place to start in your workshops or storytimes. It emphasizes that the relationship you build with them is a partnership, rather than a teacher-student affiliation, where both parties are contributing to learning and growing.

Teen parents face many challenges before, during, and after the birth of their child. Yet, in the face of adversity, many young families are resilient and are able to live healthy lives. Recognizing this strength of resiliency is often the driving force that keeps many library staff members motivated to continue their important work with teen parents, appreciating growth and changes, both small and large.

Effectively Communicating Information

Every person has his or her own individualized learning style, or a preferred mode of receiving and processing information. While everyone utilizes a mix of learning styles, some people may prefer to learn by seeing and looking (visual), while others function best by hearing and listening (auditory). Further, there are many people who take in information best when they have hands-on experiences (kinesthetic). Therefore, it is not surprising that many library staff members working with teen parents have found that in general, just talking at teens, or lecturing on a specific topic, is not very effective. It is difficult for many people, including teen parents—whose brains are still developing—to stay focused for an extended period of time while someone is giving them information. Instead of just sharing facts about your chosen topic, try to prepare a program where teen parents are actively engaged in the learning. This will generate deeper learning and greater lasting interest in the topic, as well as create a more positive attitude toward the library in general.

When introducing a topic, first set the stage for learning. Share what you will be doing, why it is important, and how it applies to the teens' lives. Be as enthusiastic as possible, as your excitement is often contagious. Next, model what you want participants to do. For example, if you are giving them a book to read to their child, show them how to read it by using animated voices, asking questions, and pointing out pictures (see chapter 7). Finally, guide the teen parents in practicing the new skill or activity that they will do with their children. Let them explore in a hands-on way while you support and encourage them in their efforts. Within this framework, a sample workshop on making playdough with their children could be structured in the following way:

1. **Introduce the what and why:** "Today we are going to learn how to make playdough at home with your child. This is a fun, simple, and inexpensive way to help your child learn. Playdough is great because it helps your child build the muscles in their fingers and hands, which will allow them to hold a pencil when they are a little older. It also strengthens their hand-eye coordination and helps them learn about colors, simple math concepts, and so on. Plus it's just plain fun!"

2. **Model:** "Making playdough is pretty simple, even if you aren't a cook! All you need is flour, salt, water, and food coloring. See how I measure the ingredients and stir everything together? You can guide your child to do this too. I'm putting only a little bit of food coloring in, but you and your child can experiment with the colors; there is no wrong way to do this!"

3. **Guided practice:** "Now let's try this together. You all have the materials in front of you. Look at the playdough recipe. Is this something you think your child would enjoy? Can you see yourself doing this activity with him or her at home?"

By your providing the purpose of the program, making sure it is relevant and applicable to their lives, showing them how to do it, and offering them the opportunity to practice, the teen parents will gain a deeper understanding and feel more confident integrating the skills or information learned into their daily routines.

Depending on how your library program is set up, utilizing a discussion-based format can be an engaging, fun way to build on the teen parents' prior knowledge and strengths. While it may be intimidating for the group facilitator to lead a discussion, dialogue allows the teen parents to be more active participants in their learning. It also gives feedback to you in terms of what the teen parents already know, need to know, and want to know. Remember to allow enough time for response after asking a question during a discussion. Some teen parents, particularly if English is their second language or if they have learning disabilities, need more processing time to think about the question posed and to develop a response that they feel comfortable sharing. Also, remember to encourage discussion by giving positive feedback and reinforcement to those who participate. For example, try saying, "That's a really great idea. What do the rest of you think about that?" This way, it opens up the discussion to the entire group while providing praise to the contributor.

Integrating discussion into your program and encouraging participation, as opposed to simply talking at the teen parents, is usually a more effective approach. Below are a few techniques to optimize learning and engagement.

- **Think, pair, and share:** Introduce a topic or question. Ask the teen parents to think about their response for at least 10 seconds. Then pair up the group participants (this could be as easy as turning to the person next to them), and have the two parents share with each other their ideas. After a few minutes, ask for volunteers to share their best responses.

- **Brainstorm:** As a group, focus on a topic and encourage the free flow of ideas from the teen parents. Pose a question or a problem, and ask everyone to contribute possible answers or thoughts. Write down the list of responses (or ask for a volunteer from the group to be the recorder) and include every idea, without judgment. Once the list is generated, review the responses together.

- **Role-play:** In role-playing, teen parents act out a predefined situation or incident. For example, in a pair, one person can be a child misbehaving in a grocery store, and the other person can be the parent helping the child calm down. This can help both parents broaden their perspective by seeing a problem or situation from a different viewpoint.

- **One thing I learned and one thing I can use:** At the end of the workshop or storytime, ask the teen parents, either in pairs or as an entire group, to share a few things they learned and a few things they feel they can use at home. This is a great review and provides feedback to you about what worked.

- **Thumbs up or thumbs down:** In every group, there will be some people who feel too shy to talk. In order to encourage participation from everyone, try sharing a statement, and then ask the group if they agree or disagree. Instead of people shouting out the answers, they can voice their opinions by giving a thumbs-up for agreement or a thumbs-down for disagreement. Allow time for the group to observe everyone else's opinions.

- **Stand up if you agree:** As a variation on the thumbs-up/thumbs-down exercise, have the teen parents stand up if they agree with a statement you read. This will get them out of their seats and moving, while remaining focused on the topic.

- **Values line:** This is another great activity that gets the teen parents moving. Place a sign that says "Strongly Agree" at one end of the room, and place a "Strongly Disagree" sign at the other end of the room. Read off value statements and have the teen parents go stand somewhere on the spectrum (the middle of the room is neutral). For example, read, "It is okay to hit your child." Have the teens move to the side of the room that they feel matches their beliefs. You can pair up people from opposite sides of the room to discuss their differing opinions.

Before beginning any type of discussion or activity, remind the teen parents of the community agreements, or ground rules, that they as a group established at the beginning of the workshop. Some of these activities, such as the Values Line, generally work better when the participants know each other and feel comfortable sharing opinions on sensitive topics. When choosing which activity to try, consider group dynamics, cultural and language factors, individual learning styles, and your own comfort level in leading the exercise. Don't be afraid to try something new. If an activity doesn't work, evaluate why, see what you can change, or try something else next time. Interactive learning activities where teens feel respected help to keep the parents engaged, motivated, and returning to the library program for more!

FACILITATING A GROUP

Group Dynamics

Working individually with teen parents who come into the library is always beneficial, as the librarian can focus on the patron's individual needs or interests. Yet, there is something very powerful about bringing teen parents together as a group, whether it's for a storytime, meeting, or other type of program. When gathered with one another, these young moms and dads discover that others have similar experiences, problems, concerns, and feelings. It is often reassuring to the teen parents that they are not alone; sometimes the challenges they face on a daily basis are less frightening and easier to deal with when they are shared. A teen parent group offers an opportunity for mutual aid and support; it is so valuable for these young patrons to be able to receive help as well as give it to others in the group.

Group dynamics can be complex. In every group, individual members bring their own personal histories, biases, perspectives, experiences, and culture, which influence interactions and processes (Hunter, Bailey, and Taylor 1995). The varying perspectives and opinions may not be shared by all group members, contributing to the nature of how the group functions together. Other factors that influence group dynamics include how familiar members are with one another, how much or how little trust exists between members, communication skills, whether group members feel comfortable and safe, and how open minded the group members are to differences (Rees 1998). Especially among adolescents, where cliques often exist within groups, it is critical to establish and review those community agreements, or ground rules, at the beginning in order to maintain a respectful learning environment.

The nature and structure of the group also contributes to dynamics. Most library-based programs have open groups where teen parents may come to one program or storytime and never attend again. This constantly changing setting influences the group's interactions. New people often disrupt the established cohesiveness of the group. However, they also bring new energy and new ideas that everyone, including the facilitator, can benefit from.

The dynamics of the group, including how comfortable people feel contributing to a discussion, play a part in the roles teen parents assume within the group. Usually without fail, roles such as "the shy one" or "the monopolizer" emerge as you get to know the members of your group. It is always important to encourage comments and contributions; but, if you find that one or two people are dominating the discussion, there are tactful ways to redirect the dialogue. Say something as simple as "Thank you for sharing your great ideas. Now let's see what other people think." This is a good technique to invite others to participate. Similarly, when there is a quiet teen parent who rarely speaks up, the facilitator can use a direct but gentle approach and ask, "Janet, what do you think about this?" If that doesn't work, you can always try including everyone by posing a question and going around the group asking each person to respond. Although you want to be inclusive, it is important to be respectful of the teen parent's comfort level and always give the option of passing on answering a question or contributing to an activity.

When leading any kind of group program for teen parents, including storytimes, it is important to consider your own role as the facilitator and your purpose in bringing the group together. As a library staff member, your job is often to assist patrons in obtaining requested information by locating written materials, using electronic resources, or connecting patrons with similar interests and needs. While you are facilitating the acquisition of knowledge, it can be most effective to stay away from the teacher role, especially with teens, who often resist being told what to do. Think of this as a partnership in learning, where you bring research-based ideas and the young parents bring their experiences and their openness to improving their lives and the lives of their children.

Room Configuration and the Group

When considering group dynamics, it is important to take into account the utilization of space within your meeting room and how the space is configured. While options may be limited, there are small steps that can be taken to maximize comfort and efficiency. Having the group sit in a circle, rather than in the rows found in a traditional classroom setting, is optimal and helps everyone see each other's faces, which encourages both participation and accountability. Whether the room is big or small, creating a tight circle where everyone is close together enhances the intimacy of the group and the program. Consider what may be distracting in the room; if there are windows that display busy activity, it may be best to have the teen parents sit with their backs facing the windows.

Your place within the room is also important. Sit with the teen parents rather than at the head of the room or table, reinforcing the partnership in learning between the facilitator and the participants. If there are two facilitators within the group, it may be best to sit opposite one another; as being able to read each other's facial expressions and to give nonverbal cues to one another can be helpful. Additionally, if you notice two teen parents having side conversations throughout the program, try sitting between them. While they may not like this diversion at first, the program and discussion will run more smoothly with less distraction.

CONCLUSION

Reaching out to young mothers and fathers through library services benefits the parent, the child, and beyond. Effectively communicating information to the teens, connecting them to community resources, and serving as a positive adult role model contributes to the healthy development of the family. Recognizing that adolescence and new parenthood are periods of significant transitions and challenges is critical to move beyond frustrations you may feel during program development and implementation. To reiterate, when working with teen parents, be nonjudgmental, try not to take comments or attitudes personally, and be flexible, patient, adaptable, and authentic. Most important, enjoy observing these young parents and their children as they grow and learn together.

REFERENCES

Brazelton, T. Berry, and Joshua Sparrow. "The Touchpoints Model of Development." Brazelton Touchpoints Center (2003), http://www.touchpoints.org/nwsltrs_flyers_forms/Touchpoints_Model_of_Development_Aug_2007.pdf.

Carney, Susan. 2007. "Building Trust with Teens: Ten Ways to Improve Your Relationships with Kids" (March 2007). Youth Development. http://youthdevelopment.suite101.com/article.cfm/building_trust_with_teens.

Gorski, Paul. "Guide for Setting Ground Rules." EdChange (2010), http://www.edchange.org/multicultural/activities/groundrules.html.

Hunter, Dale, Anne Bailey, and Bill Taylor. *The Art of Facilitation*. Tuscon, AZ: Fisher Books, 1995.

Rees, Fran. *The Facilitator Excellence Handbook: Helping People Work Creatively and Productively Together*. San Francisco: Jossey-Bass Pfeiffer, 1998.

Small, Stephen, and Patricia Day. *What Teenagers Need From Parents, Teachers and Other Adults*. Madison, WI: Cooperative Extension Publications, University of Wisconsin-Extension, 1990.

4

PROGRAM DEVELOPMENT OF SUCCESSFUL TEEN PARENT SERVICES

The old adage "It takes a village to raise a child" is particularly relevant and applicable when it comes to developing successful teen parent services. While it may necessitate the navigation of a web of institutions, personnel, and obstacles, the results benefit the population the library seeks to serve, the library itself, and the library staff who create and manage the project. The results offer enrichment and improvement of the lives of young families through library use and literacy education, and higher visibility for teen and school library services within the institution and the community. Lasting partnerships are made that will position the library as a participant in civic youth development. Additionally, the creation of successful teen parent services will support youth librarians' acquisition of skills and knowledge that will aid in their own personal and professional growth. The creation of successful teen parent services requires the following components:

- Institutional support
- Identification of client groups and community partners
- Program and services planning and development
- Evaluation
- Staffing and staff training
- Funding

The priority of importance of these core areas depends upon the context and circumstances of your library environment; it is highly likely, however, that eventually all components will come into play. The metaphorical question "Which came first, the chicken or the egg?" reflects the sometimes complex process of teen parent program development. You need support from your library or school administration to pursue the project, but you also need to identify a client group in order to generate a program proposal to gain support. Program development determines staffing and funding needs, but there may be a funding opportunity that motivates program development. Evaluation helps improve program success, satisfies your funder's expectations, and justifies an ongoing commitment to the new services. Wherever the cycle starts, it is important to keep all of these interconnected factors in mind.

INSTITUTIONAL SUPPORT AND ISSUES

To begin, depending on your library environment, include exploration of the development of teen parent services as part of your library's annual work plan. Start thinking and talking about what costs might be involved (staff time, gift books, and program materials) and potential sources of funding. Because services to teen parents may potentially involve staff from other areas (children's services, literacy, adult services, circulation, fundraisers, and even technical services in public libraries, or teachers, counselors, and administrators in schools) make sure that everyone you need is on board. Touch base with other staff members to see what programs may have been offered in the past, and what worked and didn't work. Don't be discouraged by anything you hear—just take note and try to anticipate solutions should problems arise. It may be prudent as the project proceeds to form a small committee of key staff to brainstorm, plan, and implement. Even if it is not feasible to formally convene as a committee, keep the key staff members in the loop, especially when the time comes to make major decisions or take action steps. Make sure that news of your successes filters up, bringing credit to your superiors as well as to yourself. When the powers that be in your organization, your funders, or your state want some type of report, always be sure to generously give credit where credit is due.

Addressing Challenges

In both public and school libraries, there can be larger institutional issues complicating support for teen parent programs; library policies and staff attitudes can be deterrents to offering quality services to pregnant or parenting teens in the community.

Public Library Challenges

Public libraries may require minors (those under the age of 18) to have a parent's signature on their application to be issued a library card. Some teens may not be on good terms with their parents and cannot obtain permission from them to get a card. Also, verification of address may be impossible for a teen who does not have a state-issued identification or is not living at home. More often, the teen parent has existing fines for overdue and lost materials leftover from childhood and quit using the library once the debt limit was reached and the card was suspended. Even if they have a card, teen parents can also be at a higher risk of losing library materials. For the teen who is a couch surfer (moving from one friend's house to another) or lives in a group home, keeping track of a library book or DVD can prove difficult. Often without reliable transportation, and sometimes without easy access to a phone or computer, the teen parent may have problems returning or even renewing library materials.

Potential conflict between library staff and pregnant and parenting teens can also be a deterrent when developing teen parent services. The teens may be hypersensitive about the responses they get when interacting with unfamiliar adults in positions of authority, and they may take the slightest hint of firmness to heart. Library staff may not be equipped, especially on a tough day, to exhibit the tact, patience, and empathy necessary for a productive discussion of library policies with teen parents. Additionally, some teen parents are not aware of the library's expectations of parents' responsibilities regarding their children's behavior. Frequently, they are not very skilled at controlling their young children's actions. This detrimental combination of staff attitudes, lack of awareness of expectations, and minimal parenting skills can result in a bad experience that prompts the teen parents to avoid the library.

Public Library Answers

Circulation policies. In even the most supportive library environments, there are bureaucratic limits to making policy changes, but it never hurts to ask. Verification of a teen's address might be possible through his or her school or social service agency. It could be feasible to lower the age minimum for issuing cards without parental consent to 16, when teens can get a driver's license or state identification card. Fines and fees are the stickiest wicket. Institutional bean counters are highly unlikely to waive fines under any circumstances. Libraries do exist that do not levy fines on special categories of materials, such as paperbacks or children's books; it might be possible to create special teen parent collections of this type.

Alternatives to traditional services. When working with underserved populations, librarians often develop alternative programs to avoid problems and accept the realities of less than full-service use of the library by these patrons. Keep in mind that the top priorities are getting books into the hands and homes of teen parents and enabling access to information. Consider partnering with institutions, such as group homes and high school classes, and purchase on-site depository collections of relevant materials. Or, try purchasing materials to give teen parents: age-appropriate board and picture books to create home libraries for their children and informational and recreational reading for themselves. Try whatever means possible to get library cards in the hands of teen parents because, in most libraries, library cards are the gateway to free library computer use of word processing software and the Internet, which can compensate for disadvantages of their financial or family situation in relation to technology. Additionally, to alleviate the potentially difficult transportation logistics of visits to the library, consider planning programs at partner sites, make these locations a bookmobile or outreach delivery stop, or offer subsidized access, such as bus passes, to public transportation.

Successful library visits. It is crucial that library visits for these young families are consistently positive experiences. Set up all key players, including both the library staff and the families, to facilitate successful visits. Make sure that all public service staff are given notification in advance when a teen parent group is coming to the library. This is especially helpful when teen parents visit with their children; be sure to sympathetically explain to staff that behavior might be rowdier than usual. In an equally sensitive and low-key manner, discuss with the teen parents in your program what the library's behavior expectations are prior to their visit. Especially if children are accompanying their parents, reserve your library meeting room, or another space where everyone can gather and spend time without worrying about disturbing other library patrons. Make yourself available as an intermediary when a staff member must apply library policies with a teen parent, because your joint connection will be helpful to both parties.

School Library Challenges

High school libraries may have their own spectrum of restrictions to offering quality services to teen parents. Funding may be limited and not allow for the development of services to a small population. Limited staff time and a lack of expertise in the services needed by teen parents, such as early literacy education, can also be challenging. The lack of facilities or space creates challenges for program logistics; teen parent classes may be held at continuation high schools that do not have an on-site library facility, or the facility size may not allow space for additional materials or activities. Additionally, school library collections often do not include critical materials, such as books on parenting and child development, needed by teen parents.

School Library Answers

Functioning under the "many hands make light work" philosophy, a consortium of school librarians could seek grants or foundation funding to develop teen parent services throughout a county or wider geographic area or could support funding of a model project in one jurisdiction as the basis for replication in others. High school library staff can partner with an elementary school librarian, preschool teacher, or youth, literacy, or children's librarian from a public library to develop a teen parent program that includes the component strengths, expertise, and knowledge that each partner brings to the table. Installing deposit collections and visiting teen parents' classrooms on a regular basis is a nontraditional, but effective, program idea. Try coordinating learning projects with teen parent instructors, and purchase a core collection of relevant materials.

IDENTIFYING POTENTIAL CLIENT GROUPS AND PARTNERSHIPS

While teen parent families can be reached and touched on an individual basis, in the public library they can be hard to identify in your general population of users. Additionally, many teen parents may not be frequent library users to begin with, making it difficult to identify and establish contact with this population. Many young families, however, are utilizing school and community social services; making connections with these types of organizations may be your best bet for identifying a client group and for establishing community partners. (Note for funding: grant funders are very partial to projects that incorporate partnerships; in fact, a community partnership is often required). Staff within your own institution, including the public library's adult and children's services staff, literacy coordinators, or high school counselors and administrators at schools, may have knowledge to share regarding local programs that involve teen parents.

WebJunction, an online library community founded by OCLC (Online Computer Library Center) with funding from the Bill and Melinda Gates Foundation, offers a primer, "Communication and Partnerships—Tools," on what to consider when starting a community partnership. Among the useful tools are the list of "Compatible Partners," "What to Consider When Entering into a Collaborative Process," and the list of "Tips and Techniques for Creating Strong Partnerships" (WebJunction n.d.).

Teen parents who receive public assistance are required to attend high school and other support programs. The current thinking is that it is in the best interests of both teen parents and their children to give the young parents comprehensive support, including health benefits, child care, and financial assistance, while educating the parents to become employable and self-sufficient. The state health and public assistance programs targeting teen parents are usually administered through county and city agencies, which give you a local connection.

The 2-1-1 information and referral centers discussed in chapter 2 also can serve as resources for locating potential community partners (2-1-1 Service, n.d.). Searching the term "teen parent" within your geographic locale will lead to listings of health and human services organizations to contact.

(Note: In the context of fundraising, the term "partners" is often used to describe the business or organization that funds a project. For the purposes of this discussion, we are defining "partners" as community, school, and social service agencies that have established collaborative partnerships with the library. We use the term "funders" for those providing financial support.)

Local Connections

When establishing partnerships within your community, begin by contacting your local school district. Inquire about district-sponsored teen parent programs. If there is a district continuation high school, the staff there may also be able to provide leads. High school librarians may need to locate the site of the teen parent education program within their district. Other community organizations providing services for teens, such as teen centers, hospitals, and health clinics, may also run or be aware of local established programs. For example, a hospital-based program in Kansas City, Missouri, is the Truman Medical Centers' StartRight/Teen MOMS, which offers a mentoring and life skills curriculum. Often there is overlap between organizations, and teen parents being served by one may also be clients of another social service agency.

Government Agencies

Check your state's human services division website. Look for its version of the federal Temporary Assistance for Needy Families (TANF) program. Each state's name for this program varies a little. For example, it is known in New Mexico as NMWorks, in California as CalWORKs, and in Ohio as Ohio Works First. From the TANF website, it is possible to locate a field office or coordinator contact for your area. Often using the obvious search term "teen parents" on state and county websites will lead you to the appropriate agencies and programs. County and city agencies bring you closer to your local jurisdiction. Look for listings for programs under both health and human services divisions. For example, when you search the San Mateo County (California) website, the Adolescent Family Life Program, San Mateo County's version of a statewide program, shows up in the results. This program sponsors youth development groups for teen parents and would be a great contact for an outreach visit. Searching under the same keywords under "Community Services" on the Santa Fe, New Mexico, website leads to the Teen Parent Center at Santa Fe High School. Contacting the local county welfare office could also provide potential leads.

Private Nonprofit Organizations

Private nonprofit organizations throughout the country, including some faith-based agencies, also serve teen parents. Among those are Catholic Charities, the Salvation Army, YWCA, United Way, Planned Parenthood, and the Family Service Agency. For example, in San Francisco, the Family Service Agency is the local provider for the Adolescent Family Life Program, which the agency calls the Teenage Pregnancy and Parenting Project (TAPP) (Family Service Agency of San Francisco, n.d.).

Transitional Housing Agencies

Nonprofits and government agencies that provide supervised group housing for homeless teen parents and their children are also potential partners and client groups. In Chicago, New Moms, Inc. offers a Cooperative Living Program in addition to outreach and educational programs for teen moms (New Moms n.d.). The U.S. Department of Housing and Urban Development funds Second Chance Housing, for teen parents who are unable to live with their families, through community public and private organizations (U.S. Department of Housing and Urban Development 2000). Contact the local HUD or public housing authority office in your jurisdiction to see if any programs are offered (see chapter 2). Also contact groups that offer transitional housing and crisis counseling for teens, as they may have or know of a teen parent group home. The National Crittenton Foundation (n.d.) is the umbrella organization for Crittenton agencies working in 24 states. Once known for their "maternity homes" for unwed mothers, today's Crittenton organizations provide strength-based family and education support services and transitional housing for girls and young women.

Community Meetings and Coalition Building

Inquire about and attend meetings of collaborative groups of community agencies that provide services to low-income families and work on child/family-related issues. Among the attendees there may be representatives of an agency working with teen parents or those who have knowledge of local programs. Additionally, *The Family-Centered Library Handbook* (Feinberg et al. 2007) suggests these strategies for developing partnerships.

- Establish relationships with local agency representatives. Keep them updated on library services, get on their mailing or e-mail lists, and touch base occasionally.
- Encourage staff to volunteer for, or serve on, the boards of potential partner agencies.
- Make library meeting rooms available for partner events and distribute their literature.
- Develop resource lists of library materials for agency staff and clients that support the partner's activities.

Making Contact

Establishing contact with potential partners is an opportunity for you to build the teen parent program while simultaneously marketing library services and resources. Developing a prepared introduction of yourself and your ideas for collaboration will help the outreach process run smoothly. Make an outline for yourself of what you want to say (Pfeil 2005). Consider including these details in the description.

1. Your name, the library's name, and your position.
2. Your purpose. You are exploring opportunities to develop library services for teen parents in your community and are interested in finding out about organizations that work with teen parent groups to try to identify potential groups to work with.

3. What type of program you might develop. This depends on the needs of the group and the community. It could focus on early literacy and the notion that the parent is a child's first teacher, library resources for life skills (e.g., employment and parenting), or lifelong learning.
4. Where the programs would be held and how often. Again, this depends on the group's needs and situation and on the library's capacity.
5. Be sure to give contact information at the close of your conversation.

Remember, the person answering the phone may not be the person in the organization who knows the answer to your query. If you receive a negative response, always ask, "Is there anyone else in your office who might know?" or "Is there anyone in your office who might suggest somewhere else for me to contact?" Persistence is critical when conducting initial outreach efforts.

Alternatives for Smaller Communities

For many smaller communities across the country, the options for connecting with local social service agencies or schools in the direct service area may be limited. Additionally, there may be only a few noticeable teen parents in the local vicinity. If this is the case, and if it is geographically feasible, try connecting with other libraries to coordinate a joint teen parent program. Further, isolation is a key challenge faced by many young mothers and fathers. If there are only a few teen parents in your library's community, reach out to them individually, connect them with one another, and actively encourage them to attend the mainstream library programs (such as job hunting for teens or a regularly scheduled storytime).

You may find that there is a cluster of teen parents outside the immediate vicinity of the library's service area. If possible, make arrangements with your library's administration for you to travel to where the teen parents are located to offer workshops or storytimes. This is usually more feasible than arranging for the transportation of the teen parents (and children!) to the library. Smaller communities with limited potential collaborative partners will have to think outside the box in order to serve teen parents and to figure out how to successfully integrate this population into mainstream library programming. While this may pose a challenge, the outcomes will be significant and will align with your library's mission and core values.

Happily, on some occasions, the teen parents take the initiative and approach the library. This was the case at the Borrego Springs branch of the San Diego County Library in California. Teen parents in this isolated community asked for storytime training, and the children's services staff were able to fulfill their request. The teen parents used this learning to lead an infant storytime at the library, which was open to all families in the community, and gained knowledge of early literacy, new parenting skills, confidence, and a connection to the library in the process (Smart and Maciel 2009).

SERVICE AND PROJECT PLANNING

Preparing a project proposal is a good idea, even if there is no grant seeking involved, because it forces you to hone your thinking into a well-thought-out, specific set of ideas. Utilize the following components for designing a project, adapted for teen parent services, from *Grants for Libraries* (Gerding and MacKellar 2006) and the *Nuts-and-Bolts Guide to Nonprofit Program Design, Marketing, and Evaluation* (McNamara 2002).

Form a Project Team

Put together your project planning team. Include key staff at the library or school and community partners. The team members, with their varying perspectives and expertise, can be invaluable assets for establishing efficient and effective services for teen parents. For optimal initial input, consider starting with an inclusive advisory meeting, and pare down the committee into a smaller work group after the direction of the project is clarified.

Assess the Needs of the Teen Parent Group

With your planning team, assess and prioritize the needs of your teen parent group(s) based on their circumstances, situation, logistics, and interests, and the library's ability to dedicate resources to the project. Adults working directly with the teen parents at a partner agency are one of your most valuable information sources. They can explain their organization's goals, the environment and characteristics of the group, and what they perceive as the group's needs based on their interactions with the teen parents and their children. Be prepared to explain what the library can offer, giving concrete examples to demonstrate how the library is a vital resource for this population. Visit your partner site, meet some of the teen parents, and observe their established services. Be aware that the emphasis of your program may be different depending upon the demographics of your teen parent group; some groups may be exclusively pregnant teens, some may be just parents with children, and some may be a combination of the two.

Doing a direct needs assessment with the teen parents can be challenging because they may not have enough information to offer opinions. For example, they might not know the importance of reading to young children, and therefore would not voice the need of how to pick out age-appropriate books. Additionally, it can take time to develop a relationship with the teen parents to the point at which they feel safe and comfortable enough to express their opinions.

Many teens enjoy filling out questionnaires about themselves, so it can be worth a try to utilize a needs assessment tool. If you decide to do a direct needs assessment with the teen parent group, keep your questions brief and specific. It is best to not include more than 10 questions, and make them easy to answer, with check boxes and multiple choices for the teen parents to quickly select. There can be an added open-ended question or comments section if appropriate, but don't expect to get detailed responses. The fact that you will most likely be surveying a small, cohesive group makes it easier to devise something relatively simple. A reproducible Library Needs Survey is included in the appendix at the end of chapter 5. If you are planning on using outcome-based evaluation (see the "Evaluation" section below), design your needs assessment to be used as an initial and a concluding evaluation tool.

The materials from Gail McGovern's (2007) Infopeople Workshop, "Needs Assessment: Asking Significant Questions," covers effective needs-assessment techniques. Although geared to the library as a whole, it provides background knowledge that can be applied to assessing the needs of teen parents.

Another strategy is to offer a buffet of activities during the early months of the project, all of which meet your objectives, and see which activities the teen parents seem to respond to and learn the most from. At the very least, once you have established a rapport with the teen parents, engage them in a simple discussion of what they would like to know more about. Again, it does not hurt to try.

Developmental Assets, Maslow's Hierarchy of Needs, and the Needs of Teen Parents

The Search Institute's 40 Developmental Assets for Adolescents are widely used as a planning and evaluation tool for youth services in libraries. The Search Institute is an independent nonprofit research organization whose mission is "to discover what children and adolescents need to become caring, healthy, and responsible adults" (Search Institute 2010). The Developmental Assets comprise the relationships, positive environments and experiences, and personal traits that teens need to avoid high-risk behaviors and succeed in life. They apply across the board to all teens, no matter their socioeconomic or personal situation. The greater number of assets a teen has, the less likely he or she is to engage in problem drug or alcohol use, be sexually active, suffer from depression, or have problems in school (Search Institute 2010).

Of the 40 assets, only two, "religious community" and "time at home," are beyond the scope of what school or public libraries can offer teens (Gorman and Suellentrop 2009). The clearly identifiable assets that libraries can provide for teens to support their healthy development include the following.

- Support from other adults
- A caring neighborhood and school environment
- A sense of being valued by the community, especially when teens are offered useful roles and service opportunities
- Safety, and clear rules and boundaries at school and in the neighborhood
- Adult role models
- Creative activities
- Youth programs
- Active learning, motivation to achieve in school, and homework support
- Reading for pleasure
- Valuing helping others and taking personal responsibility
- Planning ahead and making choices
- Self-esteem and sense of purpose

When examining the status of many (but not necessarily all) teen parents, it is painfully obvious that their tally of developmental assets is at the lower end of the scale. While there should be no more important goal than to do whatever is possible to support their healthy development, the 40 Developmental Assets do not begin to address what sometimes can be the dire needs of teen parents. As many teen parents are struggling to survive and often living in unstable environments, the perspective of Maslow's hierarchy of needs may be a better fit for their situations.

One of the leaders of humanistic psychology, Abraham Maslow came up with a list of human needs. This list is commonly depicted as a pyramid, a hierarchy of human motives, with those at the bottom being more critical to survival than those higher up. At the base of the pyramid are a person's physiological needs, including the basics like air, water, food, and sleep. Following those basic needs is safety, such as the need to experience stability and security in a chaotic world. Next is love, in this context the feeling of acceptance as part of a group or family. Above love is esteem: self-esteem stemming from a sense of personal competency and from recognition by the outside world for achievement. At the apex of the pyramid is self-actualization, or the desire to reach one's full potential as a person (Anderson 2004).

Teen parents commonly are working on the first two to three lower levels of Maslow's hierarchy, the physiological and safety needs. One could even conjecture that having a child at a young age is an attempt to achieve the third level, love, through independent choice. Keeping in mind the list of Developmental Assets, but focusing on helping teen parents acquire the tools they need to climb Maslow's pyramid, creates a hybrid rationale for teen parent services, which is a stronger vision than either alone.

Define the Project

Like all library users, teen parents can benefit from the wide range of resources libraries can offer. But, experience has shown us that there are two main areas involving the greatest needs for teen parents. First, teen parents often are in need of life skills (including information literacy and skill at locating career and health information). Second, they often lack an understanding of children's early learning, especially related to language and intellectual development, the important role a parent plays in a child's development, and how to be their child's first teacher. In addition, exposure to library environments and programming can provide teen parent families with unanticipated benefits.

- It can enhance teen parents' quality of life and give them a personal connection to the library.
- It can provide a safe and stimulating haven for them and their children.
- It can reduce stress.
- It can promote bonding with library staff, open avenues of communication, and strengthen a connection to the community.

From your needs assessment, professional knowledge, and collaborative discussions, ideas about the direction for your teen parent services are sure to emerge. The *Nuts-and-Bolts Guide to Nonprofit Program Design, Marketing, and Evaluation* (McNamara 2002) suggests exploring programs that could be replicated from work done by other libraries. In addition to the information you will find in chapters 5 through 8 of this book, excellent sources for ideas include the "Inventory of Current Early Literacy Activities Undertaken by Oregon's Public Libraries" (Multnomah County Library 2005), *The Family-Centered Library Handbook* (Feinberg et al. 2007), and the field-tested programs from libraries across the United States listed at the end of this chapter. McNamara's book also suggests getting recommendations from experts in the field. In this case, on the topics of early literacy and teen services at the library, look to entities such as the Association for Library Service to Children; the Young Adult Library Services Association; Zero to Three: National Center for Infants, Toddlers, and Families; the Healthy Teen Network; and books like Paula Brehm-Heeger's *Serving Urban Teens* (2008). Additionally, seek advice or guidelines from (potential) funders during the process of defining your teen parent project.

Formulate a Plan

It's time to bite the bullet and decide what can realistically be done with your available and potential resources. Addressing your program/service development through the following sequence takes your planning from the inspirational big picture to the nitty-gritty details.

1. **Vision:** How will your teen parent families' lives be changed by your program or services? What impact will your project have on their knowledge, behaviors, attitudes, or values? Example: children of teen parents will start elementary school with the same early literacy skill set as children from middle and upper socioeconomic group families.
2. **Mission:** What is the purpose of your program? Example: to help ensure that the children of teen parents succeed in school and that they use the library to support their successes.
3. **Goals:** What are the specific accomplishments you hope to achieve? Example: develop teen parents' early literacy knowledge and motivate them to use early literacy practices with their children.
4. **Strategies:** What are the methods used to achieve your goals? Example: teach teen parents how to read aloud interactively with their children.
5. **Objectives:** What are the specific, achievable results used to implement your goals? Objectives are expected to be SMART (Specific, Measurable, Achievable, Realistic, and Time-Bound). Example: between January and April, a children's librarian will hold four monthly read-aloud sessions with teen parent participants in small groups to introduce, model, and practice early literacy techniques.
6. **Activities:** What will you specifically do to achieve your goals and objectives? Example: during each read-aloud session, a different aspect of early literacy (rhyming, singing, text recognition, and parent-child communication) will be explored through age-appropriate books.

During the planning process, it is important to also keep other important questions in mind. Are your goals directly related to meeting the needs of teen parents that you seek to address? Do they cover everything you want to accomplish, and can you accomplish them? Are your activities realistic, effective, and related to your goals (McNamara 2002)?

Determine a Timeline and Budget for the Project

Creating project timelines does not have to be a very difficult task. They are usually either fiscally or calendar driven (e.g., they will run the length of the funded time period), or they are based on the academic calendar (usually from September through June) if you are working with a high school class. Budgets, on the other hand, can be an intimidating endeavor until you have done a few. To quantify staff time, work out the components of each staff person's responsibilities, the amount of time they will take during the project, and the cost of the salary (and benefits) for those hours (Gerding and MacKellar 2006).

For operational costs, estimate the amounts needed for books, materials, and supplies. Those numbers might include calculating 25 board books per month, for 9 months, at an average of cost of $8.00 each, which comes to $1,800. Or, for a craft project, estimating 20 5-inch by 7-inch wooden craft frames at $1.50 each, plus 3 pounds of dried pasta shapes at $2.00/pound, plus one package of food coloring at $5.00 per package, plus 10 small bottles of craft glue at $1.50 each, adds up to $56.00. After doing several of these calculations, you may be able to approximate a fairly reliable cost for each of the program's components. Do not underestimate; be conservative but realistic.

Evaluation

As you are developing the program, you should also be planning how you will evaluate it. In the same way that a librarian would advise a student to be smart and research a topic on which there is plenty of available information, you want to set objectives for which it is possible to be accountable and consciously try to build indicators of success into your project.

Why Evaluate?

Evaluation is an important part of the project development and implementation process. Consider the following reasons to incorporate evaluation into your plan.

- Evaluation helps you understand and confirm the impact that your program is having on the teen parent group.
- Evaluation can help improve, expand, or reconfigure your program and services.
- Evaluation can verify for you that you are doing what you think you are doing.
- Evaluation can help other stakeholders understand what you are doing and produce data that can be used to attract additional support.
- Evaluation examines and describes the substance of successful programs and encourages their duplication by others.
- If you are seeking outside funding, almost all funders require that an evaluation component be built into your project proposal (McNamara 2002).

Designing the Evaluation Component

When designing the evaluation component of the program, consider the following questions to guide your evaluation plan.

1. Who will your audience be? Is it the library or school administration? Is it your school board or jurisdiction management? Is it a funder, such as your state library, a community organization, or a nonprofit foundation?
2. What decisions will be made on the basis of the evaluation? Will it be a renewal of the funding or a replication at other sites? Is there a possibility of cessation?
3. What questions need to be asked to make these decisions?
4. What information do you need to answer the questions?
5. How, when, and where will the information be collected?
6. How will the data be analyzed, interpreted, and reported?
7. Who will conduct the evaluation (McNamara 2002)?

Types of Evaluation

There are different perspectives for evaluating a project, and the one you choose to use depends upon what specific information you want to gather. In contrast to the project planning steps, which descended from a vision and mission to the goals, objectives, and activities, these evaluation types start with the concrete factors and ascend into the abstract. If you want to know whether you are doing *what* you said you were going to do, try an *implementation evaluation*. Ask questions about what actually goes on, including activities and logistics. Also ask whether changes have been made from the original plan; if so, what are the changes and why were they made? For example, you find that few families turn up for an afternoon early literacy program at a transitional housing site for teen parents. What might motivate more families to come? Perhaps providing a snack? So, library staff decide to offer a light meal for all attendees, and the audience triples.

If you want to know *how* your project is achieving results, try a *process evaluation*. This type of evaluation shows accurately how the project does what it does, revealing its strengths and weaknesses, and offers suggestions for improvement. What is the process that participants go through in the project? Use process evaluation if participants and staff are unhappy with how the project functions, or if it seems inefficient. This type of evaluation is also helpful for other groups that wish to replicate your program. For example, the children's librarian has early literacy presentations that have worked well for parent groups at local preschools and the library. With the teen parent group, their lecture format bombed. She switches to an interactive format where she briefly mentions several things to observe during the activity, the teen parents then do the activity, and afterward the teens discuss their impressions of the experience. During the third phase, the librarian is able to share a few more relevant early learning concepts. Implementation and process evaluation are usually ongoing. Discussing and assessing how each program or presentation went, and tweaking the content and format, are essentially these forms of evaluation.

If you want to know whether you are *achieving* the goals and objectives that you started with, do a *goals-based evaluation*. In addition to determining whether the project goals have been achieved, consider the following questions. Are your goals realistic? Does it seem that additional resources are needed to achieve them? Should they be changed? Should new goals be added? For example, one project goal is to issue library cards to all teen parents attending the partner agency's program. During the registration process, it becomes clear that about ⅓ of the teen parent group already have cards but cannot use them because they owe too much for overdue and lost materials. Library policy does not allow any exceptions to the rules regarding payment of fines. The program goal is amended to apply to new cardholders only. An additional goal is added of creating a "no fine or fee" deposit collection of teen and children's materials at the partner agency's site.

If you want to know whether your project is *changing the lives* of your teen parent participants, plan to do an *outcomes evaluation*. The United Way has defined outcome measurement as: "Outcome: not how many worms the bird feeds its young, but *how well the fledgling flies*" (Higgins and Mittelman n.d., slide 9). Outcomes evaluation has become almost standard for grant reporting in nonprofit and government organizations. This type of evaluation seeks to capture the heart and soul of your activities in a measurable way. It benefits greatly from the inclusion of personal stories to support your numbers. Human anecdotes tell the "real" story of the benefits of your program. For example, at the start of a teen parent–only discussion, the mother of a three-year-old said, "I don't know what to do about this. Dominic wants me to read to him all the time. He wants me to read to him in the morning, and after school, anytime that we are together. I hate to tell him that I can't read to him right then, but, especially in the morning, it makes us late getting ready for school." The librarian is elated that the "problem" is reading too much. She responds to the mother, "Children love it when you read to them because you are totally focused on them; and there is nothing that they love better than to have their parents' attention. There are a couple of things you can try. See if you can establish specific times of the day when Dominic knows that you will be reading together. Then you can remind him that you always read after lunch, and that you can hardly wait. Or, you can tell him that you don't have time for a book right then, but that you can sing a song together while you get ready for school, and have a big hug. Or, you can make the effort to reorganize your morning schedule a little bit, in order to have some time for reading."

This anecdote illustrates a significant behavioral change in that family, which can be documented by a simple pre- and post- survey asking the questions "Is your child interested in being read to?" and "How often do you share books with your child?" Harking back to your vision and mission statements and goals, an outcomes evaluation systematically tracks the degree to which participants actually experience the program's intended changes or benefits (United Way of Greater Richmond and Petersburg n.d.). The goal is to make the abstract concrete—to figure out observable measures that will suggest that you are achieving a desired outcome. Be smart when creating the mission, vision, and goals for your program, and make sure that they are written to be measurable.

Outcome-based evaluation requires the most unbiased feedback possible from program participants. Stephanie Gerding and Pamela MacKellar, in *Grants for Libraries*, suggest employing the following measurement practices.

- **Questionnaires or surveys:** Crafting thoughtful questions that ask what you need to know and emphasizing the importance of honest answers is the key. It is especially important to use these measurement tools pre- and post-project (both before and after your programming) to demonstrate behavior changes. For example, query teen parents at the beginning of your project and at different points along the way to track these types of changes: (1) How many times each week do they read to their child? (2) Does their child ever ask them to sing a special song or read a special book? (3) Has the teen parent used any library books or Internet resources in the last month?

- **Interviews and focus groups:** These methods provide more in-depth information but also may be more subjective. If the focus group kindles group discussion, it can elicit more meaningful information than individual interviews. Both can be quite time consuming, but either can create stronger ties with partners and participants.

- **Observation:** With many of the program activities that are used with teen parents, such as early literacy education and use of library electronic resources, it is certainly possible to use observation to gauge the program's progress. It might be helpful to have the observations done by a qualified staff member who is not directly involved with the project.

Helpful documents for the development of outcome evaluation are "Excerpts from *Measuring Program Outcomes: a Practical Approach*" (United Way of America n.d.) and the more detailed "Outcomes Toolkit Version 2.0," which is designed specifically for libraries from IBEC (Information Behavior in Everyday Contexts), a research project of the Information School of the University of Washington. The latter document offers a step-by-step approach to the outcomes evaluation process (Information School of the University of Washington / IBEC n.d.).

Privacy Concerns

The participation of teen parents, especially those under the age of 18, in surveys, evaluations, photographs, or interviews may be limited. Partnering agencies may restrict access for reasons of confidentiality and privacy, or parents of teens may not grant permission. It goes without saying that you must always follow your partner's guidelines. For purposes of both needs assessments and evaluation, be prepared to be creative about how to garner the information you need. In the best-case scenario, you will find that your partnering agency will generally try to be as flexible as possible. In one instance, a school district allowed interviews and photos of teen parents who were over 18, which does not require parental approval, but stipulated that the teens' names could not be used. For outcomes evaluation, observations or anecdotal responses from partner agency staff may be the best method for assessing your program if privacy restrictions exist.

A Shorthand Planning Process

Try using this 10-step project planning list adapted from Infopeople's "Getting Started in Library Grant Writing" (Hinman 2007), to jumpstart your thinking. Follow this step-by-step guide.

1. Write one sentence to describe the project.
2. State the target audience.
3. Explain the problem that your project will focus on and how it will be documented.

4. Identify your community partners.

5. State the goal of your project.

6. Name at least two project objectives. Are they SMART (Specific, Measurable, Achievable, Realistic, and Time-Bound)?

7. What are the action steps that will realize your objectives?

8. How will the project be evaluated?

9. Make a list of the staff and other resources that will be needed. Determine how they will be funded (In-kind? Grants? Monetary or resource contributions?).

10. Work out the costs of all resources in question number nine.

If you have answered all 10 questions, then you are ready to launch your project!

Program Frequency, Scheduling, Location, and Attendance

While a one-time workshop, either at the library or at a partner site, is beneficial, it has been our experience that an ongoing series of programs over time makes a far greater impact on encouraging teen parents' early literacy interactions with their children. Ongoing programs also improve the participants' perceptions and increase their use of the library. Consistent, repeated meetings are more effective because it takes time to build the rapport that teen parents need to feel comfortable participating. Often at first, the activities you ask them to engage in, such as singing during a storytime, are outside their comfort zone. Additionally, the constituency of teen parent groups tends to be very fluid; attendance can be irregular and members' lives may be apt to change (someone will be gone after the baby is born, coming back after four to six weeks, or someone will leave suddenly and move away, and then reappear two months later). Repetition is important for teen parents to recognize the value that library resources can offer them and their children, from browsing the collections to seeing the pleasure their children get from interacting with a book.

Teen parents who are in high school parenting classes, or are attending regular meetings sponsored by community agencies, are a ready-made audience. The only drawback may be that the day and time slot for your visit is predetermined and beyond your control. Having a regular audience is well worth the inconvenience of adapting to someone else's schedule. Public library–sponsored programs that are open to all teen parents will require promotion through local agencies serving teen parents to draw an audience.

Program location must be seriously considered. Programs at the library offer the obvious benefits of giving your teen parents an in-depth library experience, allowing them to really see what the library has to offer. Attendance at a library program by teen parents and children together is dependent on having safe transportation for the children. Young families may rely on walking, public transportation, or a private car to get to and from the library. Transportation to the library, especially at a specific date and time, can often be a barrier for teen parents. There are creative ways to address transportation issues. For example, members of the Young Moms Club at Stark County Library in Canton, Ohio, are given bus passes to use for their trip home and for their return trip to the next monthly meeting.

Offering library services at community sites is generally more logistically feasible; it's easier to get one or two library staff members somewhere than to transport the teen parents and their children. If the site provides child care, it is possible to divide your visit time between a session and activity for parents only and a parent-child activity time. Ellin Klor's monthly programs at the Young Parents' Center in Santa Clara, California, alternate locations between two library branches and the school site, giving the teen parents both types of experiences.

If your program takes place outside the structured schedule of the school day or during an ongoing group meeting time, teen parents' many responsibilities can complicate their program attendance. A staff member, from either the library or the partner agency, needs to contact the teen parent group members to remind them of the meeting date, time, and, if it varies, location (Feinberg et al. 2007). The communication method, which can be phone, e-mail, text message, or a printed flyer, should depend upon the teen parents' preference.

STAFFING AND STAFF TRAINING

Youth librarians in public libraries should look to their colleagues in literacy and children's services for cohorts for teen parent services. Adult services librarians can be tapped when developing life skills resource presentations and for help with collection development. High school librarians can do the same with teachers and administrators who are involved with the district's teen parent and vocational education programs. Elementary school librarians and district preschool teachers, especially those working with low-income children, could potentially be strong collaborators if you decide to make early literacy a component of your services. School librarians and youth service librarians at public libraries can be excellent resources for one another. Collaborative efforts among different library-based disciplines are critical in developing effective and comprehensive services for teen parents.

Staff Competencies

The multifaceted nature of teen parent services requires competencies that draw from children's, teen, and adult services, with a strong component of literacy integrated throughout. The goals are to have the right people in place to share their expertise and to expose each participating staff member to new proficiencies for their own professional growth, thereby creating a stronger library as a whole. In high schools, the emphasis is on collaboration with faculty, reaching out to teen parent instructors and their support staff to provide literacy skills acquisition for both the parents and their children.

Drawing from the Association for Library Service to Children's (ALSC) "Competencies for Librarians Serving Children in Public Libraries" (American Library Association, "ALSC" 2009), the Young Adult Library Services Association's (YALSA) "Competencies for Librarians Serving Youth: Young Adults Deserve the Best" (American Library Association, "YALSA" 2010), Patrick Jones's "Core Competencies for Outreach" in *Going Places with Youth Outreach* by Angela Pfeil (2005), and *Connecting Young Adults and Libraries* (Gorman and Suellentrop 2009), the qualities relevant specifically to teen parent services include these competencies.

1. Be familiar with adolescent, infant, and toddler learning, development, and developmental needs.
2. Understand and appreciate diverse cultural and ethnic values, especially in the area of parenting philosophy, and be nonjudgmental, patient, and empathetic.
3. Understand the stresses and challenges of teen parents' lives, recognize the obstacles they may face to using the library, and use library services to support the improvement of their quality of life, encouraging them as lifelong library users.
4. Create programming and interpersonal environments that make library experiences enjoyable for teen parents and their children.
5. Design programs for teen parents that speak to their interests and needs, especially in the areas of their own development and parenting.
6. Have the knowledge of library resources and ability to provide quality impromptu library instruction, reference, and readers' advisory assistance whenever necessary.
7. Educate teen parents about information literacy, especially using electronic resources, in an engaging and relevant manner.
8. Understand adolescent and family literacy issues, recognize their implications for teen parents and their children, and develop strategies and collections to address them.
9. Know quality popular literature for young children, sources of parenting information that are accessible to teens, and popular young adult materials of interest to teen parents, which may vary depending on their cultural and ethnic background.
10. Have skill and experience presenting story programs for children under five of mixed ages that incorporate early literacy principles, and encourage participation from both the parents and the children.

11. Involve teen parents in planning programs and projects by learning their interests and concerns.

12. Collaborate with other community groups and agencies serving teen parents and their children, and be a cross-pollinator, recruiting resource people to share their knowledge with teen parent groups.

13. Plan and manage all the components of a complex project, including the assessment, setting goals and priorities, critical thinking and prioritizing, evaluation, creativity, and flexibility.

14. Feel comfortable communicating with groups who may not initially be receptive, and be able to win them over through actions and words.

15. Conduct realistic evaluation of programming efforts, and revise and improve them.

16. Advocate for teen parent families with administrators, funders, and community groups.

If you are feeling overwhelmed, keep in mind that comprehensive services to teen parents are a team effort. One individual is not expected to know everything; remember to reach out to all key stakeholders.

Suggestions for In-house Collaborations

There are various ways to establish in-house collaborations to work together to achieve the goals of the teen parent program at your library. The teen librarian and family literacy coordinator could pursue grant funding for an early literacy workshop for a teen parent group. A children's librarian knowledgeable about early literacy could work with a teen librarian and literacy coordinator to plan and present a program consisting of a literacy-based storytime, library tour, lunch, and craft/play activity for parents and children. A reference librarian and teen librarian could create a job search workshop. The family literacy coordinator and children's librarian could develop a play-based early learning event with activity stations for teen parent families. At a school-based library, the high school media specialist and classroom teacher could develop lessons together on early literacy to present in child development, teen parent, or English classes. Topics could include how young children learn and brain development, family literacy, reading aloud, and how to choose appropriate books for infants, toddlers, and preschoolers (Klingler 2008). These are only a few suggestions on how to create a cohesive group of staff members, each with his or her expertise to share, where the working result is synergy.

Staff Attitudes

A study of the helping qualities that adolescents prefer in adults determined that among the traits teens most desired from adults were respect, time shared, and openness (Martin et al. 2006). Committed youth librarians more or less naturally fall into line with these values; but working with teen parents may be an intimidating endeavor for other staff, especially if they have a limited understanding of adolescent development. The social stigma that can be attached to teen parents, despite their sometimes glamorized portrayal in the media, can be a deterrent for staff buy-in and participation in program development and implementation.

Lead Personnel

Outreach programming demands a flexible mind-set. Community members who may have had limited, and possibly negative, experiences with libraries may be wary of any outreach efforts. It is up to library staff to explore opportunities to connect with teen parents on a more personal level that may reach beyond the scope of a traditional job description. This could mean participating in fun activities for a shared enjoyable experience, disclosing personal anecdotes that help to build rapport and bond, or allowing teens to take a more active role in the planning of programs and activities. The more they come to trust you and know what to expect, the more receptive teen parents will be to important information. Be prepared, at first, to give without expecting much response, but know that your relationships will build over time. You may feel as though you are giving 80 percent and getting only 20 percent in return, but this may be more interest than your teen parent group has ever demonstrated to anyone else. Never underestimate the positive influential power that a trusting and caring adult can have in a teen parent's life.

Frame everything in the most positive light possible. If the teen parents do not like something you have planned for them to do, ask them what they would like to do instead, and get their input for the next program's activity. Understand that your purpose is to provide them with information and resources to improve their quality of life; set aside your ego, and plunge in.

Public Service Staff

The youth or school librarian is not the only personnel with which a teen parent will have contact. It is important to educate all public service staff about the status and circumstances of teen parents in your community. A presentation about the teen parent groups you are working with, and their challenges and struggles, can be eye-opening for library staff. People who work in libraries usually have a commitment to the betterment of society at large, and you will find that personal stories and photographs can be powerful public relations tools. Sharing the successes and failures of your own teen parent activities is a tactful way to educate other staffers on how to interact and engage with teen parents.

Utilizing the Developmental Asset perspective. Teen parents may have a long way to go to possess the Search Institute's 40 Developmental Assets, but they can be powerful concepts to use with library staff to improve their perspective on working with teens. In *Serving Urban Teens* (2008), Paula Brehm-Heeger suggests that all staff who interact with young people in the library need to hear the following messages.

- Everyone on the staff, not just youth services, has an active part to play in promoting positive youth development; you don't have to be a professional librarian to do it.
- Strong relationships between teens and library staff are the basis for youth development, and library staff can be positive role models for teens.
- The future of the library depends upon teens (including teen parents) growing up to be library users and supporters.

Reach staff at an all-staff meeting, visit individual branch staff meetings, or schedule an informal discussion session to get the ball rolling. Incorporate the following steps as you share information at these meetings.

1. Use information from chapters 1 and 2 to explain the dynamics of teen parents' development, behavior, and life circumstances, making your presentation specific to the members of your group.
2. Move on to explain the concept of developmental assets, and share copies of the "40 Developmental Assets for Adolescents" list from the Search Institute.
3. Ask staff to circle the assets that they feel they, as the embodiment of the library, can offer to teen parents and their children.
4. Discuss and compile everyone's choices; brainstorm ways to implement youth asset building as part of everyone's daily interactions and activities.
5. Ask everyone to write themselves a private note about one thing they will do differently at work to boost youth development (especially within the context of teen parents).

"Teens @ Your Library" training. Sara Ryan of the Multnomah County Library and her colleagues on the Teen Action Team have created a training presentation, "Teens @ Your Library" (Ryan 2010), which all staff members in her library system are required to view. The topics covered in the presentation include:

- Adults' stereotypes about teens—teens are disrespectful unpredictable, loud, and so on
- The reality behind these behaviors—they are connected to teens' developmental tasks

- Defining teens' developmental tasks—adapting to their maturing bodies and feelings, developing their identities and roles in the world, taking on increasing life responsibilities, acquiring skills in abstract thinking, decision making, problem solving, and deciding on personal values and beliefs
- Teen brain development and its influence on behavior
- The development stages (early, middle, and late) of adolescence, and how librarians should respond
- Teen development risk and protective factors
- Program and service attributes that contribute to teens' developmental assets
- Types of library youth participation
- Strategies for dealing with difficult situations and confronting challenging behavior—the four R's—Relationships, Rules, Reactions, and Respect

A PowerPoint version of the presentation may be accessed for use through the Multnomah County Library website. For staff with minimal experience working with teens, this will deepen their understanding of, and sensitivity to, adolescent patrons. Augmenting this presentation with information from chapters 1 and 2 creates a powerful vehicle for staff training about teen parents.

Behavior challenges with children of teen parents. A significant issue for staff in relation to teen parents is helping the teens understand the library's expectations for young children's behavior in the library, and supporting them as they try to manage their children's behavior. A sensitive approach to this challenge can make expectations clear while encouraging return visits to the library. Unfortunately, the majority of library staff is not always trained to effectively cope with disruptive children in a way that leads to a constructive outcome.

When talking to staff about your teen parent programs, it is important to also address this issue. Hopefully, some knowledge and tools will help library staff effectively intervene with teens to help support them in their role as parents. When working with staff, the following concepts need to be understood and remembered.

1. Teen parents, like many newcomers to the library, may have limited knowledge of the library rules for behavior. They may not realize that expectations of appropriate behaviors of children vary in different venues.
2. Teen parents, working on their own self-control and judgment skills, often lack confidence in their parenting skills. Limited in their parenting knowledge, the young parents can have difficulty setting the consistent limits that young children need in order to learn appropriate behaviors. The parents may veer from doing nothing to overreacting in anger.
3. Teen parents, like all teens, can be extremely sensitive to even the slightest hint of criticism, especially from an authority figure, and may feel the need to "save face."
4. Young children are works in progress; they are still learning acceptable behaviors and limits. It is unrealistic to expect behavior that is beyond a child's age and developmental level.
5. Children's behavior becomes unpredictable when they are tired, hungry, or overwhelmed by their environment. Teen parents often have a hard time modifying their reactions to their child's changing needs while they are managing other responsibilities.
6. The word discipline has its origins in the ancient Greek word for teach. Conveying the behavior you want positively, calmly, and with empathy makes both parent and child feel respected. Keep the big picture in mind; you want this family to enjoy their library visit and want to return while helping them understand what behavior is expected.
7. Let the parent know that you are a partner, not an adversary. Try putting a positive spin on the issue. Instead of saying, "You need to stop . . ." or "You can't . . . ," offer alternatives or a distraction to shift the child's focus.

8. If a child is crying or having a temper tantrum, suggest a quiet, out-of-the-way place for the parent and child to go for a minute until the child calms down. If a child is running, evenly say to the child, "I can tell that you're a good runner, but the library is not a running place," and to the parent say, "She has got a lot of energy. What can we do to help her quiet down while she's in the library?" If a child has food, say, "I'm really sorry, but we can't let people eat in the library. Would you like to go outside until you finish?"

9. Reinforce the behaviors that you want with sincerity. If a child calms down and is looking at a book the next time you walk by, comment, "I can see that you're doing a really good job looking at books. I'm glad that you are enjoying the library." This is also an effective way to communicate the library's behavior expectations.

10. Always make the family feel welcome. Ask the age of their child and tell the family about the library's programs that are appropriate for that age (adapted from Parents as Teachers 2005 and Lindsay and McCullough 1998).

Perhaps the most effective way to convey these ideas is through discussion of actual problem situations that staff have experienced. They need not be limited to incidents with teen parents. Suggest several weeks in advance of your discussion that staff document situations as they occur. Use them as examples, applying the suggested ideas to develop better solutions that the staff are comfortable applying.

FUNDING

Youth or school librarians may or may not have direct involvement in fundraising or grant seeking for their project. Yet, staff members who implement the program are often called upon to develop data and the project's elements, estimate costs and expenses for budgeting purposes, demonstrate need, and explain the value and rationale of their project to potential donors. The funding needed to support your teen parent services or program is, of course, dependent on its scope. The two basic considerations when planning for funding are:

- Can current library staff absorb these services into their workload, or will additional staff hours be required?
- What will be the source of funding for books and supplies?

Staffing will always have the biggest price tag, and it is the most challenging to fill. If staff are not able to absorb the hours into their current activities, it may be prudent to seek grant funding to jumpstart the project. Large library systems will typically have more bandwidth when it comes to juggling staff responsibilities, and they will be better able to utilize existing staff. Identifying potential funding sources for materials and supplies can be much less daunting. Library Friends groups, local businesses and service clubs (such as Rotary International), and even individual donors may be able to contribute money for books and programming activity materials. In fact, one can never anticipate where funding might come from. In the heart of Silicon Valley in California, a work group at Hewlett-Packard Corporation, seeking to support a worthwhile cause at holiday time, donated children's books and funded the purchase of children's music CDs and CD players for teen parents at the Santa Clara Unified School District's Young Parents Center. The donation was made through the Santa Clara City Library's LSTA-funded Early Learning for Families program.

Contacting groups and individuals for donations is usually done through specific channels within the library system. Is there a staff person who generally focuses on fundraising efforts and can identify possible funders and coach you through the process? Does your library director or top administrator like to be the point person when it comes to funding requests? Is there another individual in your larger institutional framework who knows whom and how to ask? Is there someone who has contacts in local community service groups and foundations? Finding the right person to work with, both within your institution and with potential funding contacts, is important for success.

Fundraising and Grants

Over the past several decades, with shrinking tax dollars dribbling into their coffers, libraries have looked more and more to fundraising and grants as the way to kick-start new projects, programs, and services. Teen parent families, whose needs are well documented, can be an easier "sell" to funders than many other constituencies. It is straightforward to make the case that services for teen parents can make a measurable difference in their lives and the lives of their children and can benefit our communities and society as a whole.

At first glance, fundraising and grant seeking can look like a complex and daunting process. To begin, a distinction should be made between fundraising and grants. Grants are a subset of fundraising. While fundraising can run the gamut from mailing in cereal-box coupons to courting an individual donor to fund a new research wing for the library, a grant is generally a more formal request, often in response to a "request for proposals," and requires a specific form of application and accountability. In general, grants come from government agencies, corporations (sometimes through their nonprofit foundation arm), private nonprofit foundations, and family foundations. Grants usually fund specific programs or projects, the substance of which are clearly defined and explained in the requisite grant proposal. A good starting place for the neophyte is the Mid-Hudson Library System (New York State) website, which has created an extensive primer for fundraising and grant seeking. While somewhat centered on system member libraries, much of the information is applicable to all public and school libraries. Included are links to sample grant proposals, fundraising plans, corporate sponsor appeal letters, and other fundraising informational websites (Mid-Hudson Library System n.d.).

The scope of your project determines where to find a funder. Holly Hinman, of the Infopeople Project, a library training project funded by the California State Library, recommends the following guidelines.

- Look to local foundations and corporations to fund projects that meet local needs.
- Look to state programs and foundations for projects that can be a model for other libraries in your state.
- Look to federal and national foundations for projects that can be replicated in other states (Hinman 2007).

With the help of the many readily available resources, some mentoring, and a little experience, the grant-seeking path will be clearer. Find an experienced grant-writing mentor among your library's staff, such as those directly involved in fundraising (e.g., the library's Friends/Foundation). Seek advice from your partner organization or another agency in your community, and don't forget to query knowledgeable colleagues at other libraries.

Grantsmanship Training and Information

Some state libraries offer leadership institutes and other grant-writing training for library staff. Examples include the California State Library's Eureka! Leadership Institute and Infopeople training. Infopeople and WebJunction make materials from their past workshops and projects available to everyone through their websites without cost. Infopeople has training materials on the topics of "Getting Started in Library Grant Writing," "Library Fundraising Basics," and "Needs Assessments: Asking Significant Questions." Check the Library Management page of WebJunction for articles on funding, including the topics "grants and grant writing" and "fundraising."

Also consider exploring The Foundation Center, which maintains the most extensive database on grantmakers and their grants in the United States and provides a variety of useful tools to help identify funding sources and learn to effectively pursue grants. Their website includes a section devoted to RFPs (Requests for Proposals) and news for adults in youth service. In addition to five regional Foundation Centers (in Atlanta, Cleveland, New York, San Francisco, and Washington, DC), which offer classes, resources, and advice, the Foundation Center supports a network of libraries and nonprofit information centers across the country. Network members also make available to visitors fundraising information and funding-related assistance, public access to the Center's online databases, a collection of Foundation

Center publications, and free funding research guidance. It is also possible to subscribe to the Foundation Center's e-newsletter and e-mail discussion list, which will periodically announce grant opportunities.

The Grantsmanship Center offers access to local funding sources with listings by state, including community foundations, corporate giving programs, grantmaking foundations, and government homepages. It also offers training workshops, podcasts of presentations by grantsmanship experts, and informational articles like "One Program Officer's Candid Tips for Grantseekers" and "A Basic Guide to Program Evaluation," all of which are extremely useful to both neophyte and experienced grantseekers.

Types of Grant Funding

Library Services and Technology Act (LSTA) Grants

Commonly, government-funded grants received by libraries are funded through the federal Library Services and Technology Act, and managed by state libraries, which set the funding priorities for grants based on statewide long-term library development goals. LSTA's priorities include targeting library services to underserved communities in both urban and rural areas and specifically mention children from families whose incomes are below the poverty line (California State Library n.d.). Many teen parent services would fall under this category. LSTA grants are available to both public and school libraries. Some statewide library initiatives, such as family literacy, are appropriate programs in which to posit teen parent services. Check your state library's website for further information about LSTA grants in your state. Consultants from your state library may be available to provide information and advice and also make available resources to assist you (LSTA-specific grant-writing webinars, tip sheets, grant-writing workshops, etc.).

Corporate and Private Nonprofit Grants

Corporations, including sports franchises, often like to support the communities where they are located. Start by compiling a list of both national and local corporations in your community. Many large companies have established nonprofit foundations to facilitate their philanthropic giving and post grant opportunities and applications on their websites. For example, Target has Early Childhood Reading Grants that are funded up to $2,000. Others may require digging to locate a specific contact person for "corporate giving." A friendly phone call to a local company is sometimes all it takes to reach the right person. Often they are in the company's human resources department. Again, finding the right contact can take persistence, but doing so can be a huge benefit to your funding chances in the long run. Getting out to corporate-sponsored events in your community is another way to meet contacts. And, once your project is funded, it is very important to give visibility to your corporate and business donors through library media and events.

Writing a Grant Proposal

There are many valuable resources containing information on writing grant proposals. Stephanie Gerding and Pamela MacKellar's *Grants for Libraries: A How-to-Do-It Manual* explains the process within the context of library organizations. Gerding's 2005–2006 articles for the journal *Public Libraries* offer an abbreviated summary of the process. In her article "Writing Successful Library Grant Proposals" (Gerding 2006b), she offers the following guidelines.

1. Follow the grant proposal guidelines religiously—submit on time, use the correct format, and fulfill all stated requirements.
2. It's okay to share the work of writing the proposal among staff.
3. Your summary statement should be individual and persuasive; write it last and make sure it mentions all aspects of your project.
4. The "statement of needs" describes how your grant project will solve a problem in your community. Explain why your approach is best. Use statistics, stories, and facts to validate your assumptions.

5. The project description explains everything—what you want to do, how you will do it, what the outcome will be, and what you will need to implement the project.

6. Be specific and accurate with your budget numbers.

7. Don't forget to evaluate—think outcome-based evaluation.

Advice for Successful Grant Seeking

No one wants to waste time and energy tilting at foundation windmills. This advice from grant-funding experts, Dr. Joel Orosz, a former program officer at the Kellogg Foundation, and Bonnie McCune, a consultant for the Colorado State Library, tells it like it is from the grant giver's perspective:

1. Make sure that your grant is a good fit with the funder's areas of interest. In addition to what they may state, verify what sort of projects they have actually been funding.

2. Be very clear about what they *will not* fund; this could include food, staff time, books to give away, and more.

3. Foundations look for innovation; they want to fund something that sounds new and promising; either present them with something new, or give them a great existing program with a new slant or approach.

4. Involve your client group in your project from day one. Do it with them, not to them.

5. Make it clear what your institution is contributing to the project. If it is not cash, then offer some type of in-kind contribution, such as staff time, volunteers, or collections.

6. Skip the library-speak in your written proposal; avoid using acronyms or technical (services) terms. Have a non-library friend read your proposal for clarity.

7. Take a collaborative approach with those community partners you connected with when preparing the grant proposal.

8. State how the project will be evaluated, and do it. It doesn't have to be complicated.

9. Explain your plans for sustaining the project after the grant ends.

10. State how you will give your funder public visibility and credit for their support.

11. Design your program for potential replication in other jurisdictions, giving your funder more possible bang for the buck.

12. If your proposal is rejected, contact the organization and ask for feedback about the decision (Orosz 2002 and McCune 2007).

Program Sustainability

Full grant funding, which adequately covers all staff and material needs through a one- or multi-year cycle, affords the opportunity to establish a teen parent outreach program on a firm foundation. This depth of funding gives library staff time to cement relationships with the partnering agency and the teen parent participants, gain an understanding of what are the most effective methods of working with the young families, and develop a precise idea of the time and costs involved. After the ambitious, well-funded grant initiative is finished, however, the moment comes to establish a sustainable level of service that can be maintained over time.

It may be most feasible to develop a plan of services that will require a lower level of grant funding, which may be obtained in increments from different sources. This might mean cutting back to quarterly visits to a transitional teen parents' group home after a year of monthly visits. For example, the Santa Clara City Library's Friends and Foundation group and family literacy staff have supported visits to the Bill Wilson Center's teen parent group home over the past two years through a patchwork of small grants from Target, the Kaiser Medical Center, and the Library Friends and Foundation. Teen parent programs can also be bundled as part of a broader grant initiative; they are a good fit with family literacy outreach services. It is always important to remember that any impact you have is better than none.

ALIGNING ESTABLISHED SERVICES WITH TEEN PARENT NEEDS

Teen parents' life experiences and situations decidedly impact their needs, interests, and activities. However, their response to, and participation in, traditional teen library services is far more wedded to their educational, cultural, and social backgrounds than to the fact that they are teens with children. Lack of familiarity with libraries, potential low literacy skills, and discomfort opening up in a group situation may all be barriers to participating in standard teen services, such as booktalking and book discussion groups.

Booktalking

Tread carefully when it comes to booktalking. Get to know your group, and make sure they know and trust you. Walking in and delivering a dramatic booktalk may fly, but it may also crash and burn. The general rules of booktalking apply—your booktalk should be like a movie trailer, a teaser to grab their attention. But be as authentic as possible; teens can sense a phony a mile away. Booktalking will be most useful to introduce a deposit collection of materials that you are leaving at a teen parent group site or classroom. If the deposit collection includes read-alouds for the children, don't forget to promote them as well. When helping teen parents at the library, you will find yourself often "shelftalking," which is what Paula Brehm-Heeger describes as briefly pitching a book in a sentence or two when in the stacks doing readers' advisory (Brehm-Heeger 2008).

Book Discussion Groups

The success of a book discussion group hinges on positive group dynamics, a book selection that everyone connects with, and a discussion leader who facilitates with the right touch for the group. Again, we suggest getting to know your group before launching a formal book discussion. In fact, sharing a few books, then casually checking back at your next visit to see how they were received might yield a better result or potentially lead to interest in a more formal book discussion.

Teen Parent Volunteers at the Library

Youth participation is a core value of best practices for youth services in libraries. There is no question that teen parents, just like their nonparenting counterparts, would benefit from library volunteer opportunities. Once again, the other demands in teen parents' lives tend, out of necessity, to take precedence. However, in light of community service graduation requirements at many high schools, it is important to make the teen parents aware of opportunities for volunteering at the library.

Author Diane Tuccillo, in *Teen-Centered Library Service: Putting Youth Participation into Practice* (2010), suggests creating a drop-in volunteer program for teens who cannot make an ongoing commitment. Volunteering in a library environment, even for only a few hours, will enable teens to gain insight into how libraries operate and what they offer, increase their personal comfort level in the library, and offer a possible employment option. Consistently scheduling specific drop-in hours and having ongoing task lists available maximizes efficiency (Tuccillo 2010). Another option is to bring a teen parent group to do a service project at the library during your regular meeting time. Examples of potential jobs include book and CD cleaning, stamping books for discard, shelf reading, and creating and mounting displays. As parents themselves, they might do well helping with activities related to storytimes, such as preparing or distributing information packets or helping with post-storytime craft activities.

Low-maintenance Teen Parent Services

While it may not be possible to provide comprehensive services to teen parents, there are low-maintenance methods that offer young families the library's support.

Public Libraries

- Offer community groups that are working with teen parents free use of library meeting-room space for teen parent group meetings.

- Save discarded board books and give them to teen parent classes or groups.
- Purchase infant and toddler board books, parenting books, and young adult titles of interest to the specific teen parent group, and leave them as deposit collections at their organization or housing site.
- Arrange for teen parent groups to attend regularly scheduled infant lapsits and toddler programs.
- Supply your partner organization's staff with a perpetual quantity of library card application forms, and ask them to establish library card registration as a component of their intake procedure. Allow address verification through the organization's official records, and arrange for pickup and drop-off of forms and cards.

High School Libraries

- Create small collections of appropriate parenting books and DVDs and infant/toddler board and picture books for use by teen parent families. House them either in the school library or in the teen parent classrooms.
- Partner with an elementary school or public library children's librarian for an early literacy-based storytime for teen parents and children in your school library.
- Offer tutoring for high school exit exams.

Both Public and School-Based Libraries

- Create a section of your website for teen parents. List community services and vetted websites on topics such as health and nutrition, parenting, careers, and job searching. Include topics and links covered in presentations to teen parent groups, teen and early literacy booklists, and links to other helpful and pertinent parts of your library's website. Make sure that announcements for relevant library programs, including children's storytimes and Internet usage classes, are promoted on your teen parents' pages. If your library maintains a community information database, don't forget to highlight that as well.
- Offer annual (at least) tours of your library to teen parent groups. Try using a library scavenger hunt.
- Mount displays in the library of projects made by teen parents at library programs. Especially appropriate are bookmaking projects that they have done

A display at the Santa Clara City Library of books made by teen parents at the Young Parents Center in Santa Clara, California. (Vickie Shelton)

Creating Collections for Teen Parents

Materials collections for teen parents need to address their personal needs and the needs of their children. Along with the annotated list at the end of this chapter, scattered throughout chapters 5, 6, 7, and 8 are many suggestions for titles and resources on these relevant topics:

- Parenting and early child development books and media for teens
- Board books, picture books, and recorded music for infants and toddlers
- Popular fiction
- Nonfiction books on life skills and recreational activities
- Program and services planning guides for youth librarians

Teen parents also will be interested in the same kind of current teen culture and entertainment as their nonparenting peers in your community, especially popular movies and music.

Public libraries will most likely already have many of the suggested titles and resources in their collections; it is just a matter of making teen parents aware of where to find them in the library. It is as simple as pulling together a sample of materials for a display that the teens can browse during a library visit. Also add recreational reading to the display as you learn what the teen parents enjoy reading.

High school libraries may want to invest in small collections of infant and toddler books, parenting books, and a popular parenting magazine to support teen parent classes on their campuses. Creating a new school collection geared specifically toward teen parents might be an attractive funding opportunity for a local private donor, nonprofit or corporate giving program. Existing popular reading collections also will appeal to teen parents, especially in genres that they enjoy. One addition might be to strengthen the vocational and job preparation material collections.

When selecting adult nonfiction books for teen parents, purchase items that are easy to use, with a clear layout, with lots of topic headings and instructive graphics. Teen parents who are infrequent book browsers need accessible texts to easily find what they are seeking. The following adult literacy and specialty parenting resource distributors are excellent sources of appropriate and relevant materials.

- Child Development Media, Inc. has a diverse collection of DVDs and books, including Spanish-language versions, for parents, parenting education, and childhood development instructors.
- Destination Learn, Inc. offers family literacy materials in multiple formats, available in Spanish and English.
- Films Media Group has DVDs and streaming video on parenting and child development topics such as basic baby care, nurturing, and fathering for young dads.
- InJoy Birth and Parenting Education, Inc. has a print and DVD catalog that features "Healthy Steps for Teen Parents" (2nd Edition), a three-volume DVD set that is also available in Spanish.
- Morning Glory Press is a top publisher of resources written specifically for pregnant and parenting teens, in English and Spanish, including curriculum workbooks and DVDs.
- New Readers Press has quality adult education and ESL materials, including life skills and family literacy resources.
- Parenting Resources by Glazebrook and Associates offers an extensive selection of books and DVDs, categorized by subject, including child development, effective parenting, learning in the home, fun parent-child activities, and teen parents.

CONCLUSION

Taking the time to plan and design efficient and effective library-based programs for teen parents is critical in order to offer quality services that have a lasting impact on this population and the community at large. Gaining institutional support from the library and library staff, thoroughly understanding teen parents' needs, establishing community partners, and conducting timely evaluations will promote accountability in meeting the program's objectives. It is time to take the big step and make your service plans a reality. In the following four chapters, you will be introduced to a raft of ideas and strategies for improving the quality of life of teen parents and their children and supporting them to become lifelong library users. So, gather your "village," and move forward.

REFERENCES

Partnerships

County of San Mateo. Family Health Services. "Adolescent Family Life Program (AFLP)." http://www.co.sanmateo.ca.us/portal/site/health/menuitem.e61f1c321415a767a181dda7917332a0/?vgnextoid=63d479a5a91a0210VgnVCM1000001d37230aRCRD.

Family Service Agency of San Francisco. "Teenage Pregnancy and Parenting Project (TAPP)." www.fsasf.org/svc_childrenyouthfamily.html#tapp.

Community agencies are such as these are examples of potential partners for libraries developing teen parent services.

Feinberg, Sandra, Barbara Jordan, Kathleen Deer, Marcellina Byrne, and Lisa G. Kropp. *The Family-Centered Library Handbook*. New York: Neal-Schuman, 2007.

A detailed description of the "Family Place" service philosophy and how to implement it in the public library setting. A valuable resource for parent-child programming ideas, including an excellent chapter on services for limited-literacy, low-income, and teen parent families.

National Crittenton Foundation. The Crittenton Family of Agencies. (n.d.). www.thenationalcrittentonfoundation.org/crittenton-family-of-agencies.

Crittenton agencies provide prevention and intervention services to at-risk young women and their families. Teen mothers have historically been a focus of their efforts.

New Moms, Inc. "Cooperative Living Program." www.newmomsinc.org/new-moms-cooperative-living.php.

An example of a supportive community housing project for teen mothers that would be perfect as a library community partner.

Pfeil, Angela. *Going Places with Youth Outreach: Smart Marketing Strategies for Your Library.* Chicago: American Library Association, 2005.

Santa Fe, New Mexico, Official Website. Community Services. Santa Fe Public Schools. "Teen Parent Center at Santa Fe High School." http://www.santafenm.gov/index.aspx?NID=2093.

An example of a high school based program for teen parents, and potential library partner.

Smart, Margo, and Veronica Maciel. "Teen Mom Baby Storytimes @ Borrego Springs Library: A New Model for San Diego County Libraries." Presentation as part of "Serving Teen Moms: From Life Skills to Literacy" Workshop, California Library Association Annual Conference, Pasadena, CA, Oct. 30–Nov. 2, 2009.

Truman Medical Centers (Kansas City, Missouri). "StartRight/Teen MOMS," http://www.trumed.org/truweb/corporate/patients_visitors/family_services/family_services.aspx.

2-1-1. "Find Your Local 2-1-1 Service." http://211us.org/.

Glean the names of potential community partners, both public and private, from your local 2-1-1 database.

U.S. Department of Housing and Urban Development. "Second Chance Homes: Providing Services for Teenage Parents and Their Children" (October 2000), http://www.hud.gov/offices/pih/other/sch/sch-paper.cfm.

A HUD program that provides housing and other supportive services to teen mothers, with the goal of giving them the skills to succeed as parents and as independent adults, goals in line with those of library teen parent services.

WebJunction. "Communication and Partnerships—Tools." Planning for Success Cookbook. WebJunction. http://www.webjunction.org/partnerships/articles/content/36821786#tools2e.

Valuable insights and considerations to enable libraries to establish strong and rewarding partnerships with other organizations.

Service and Project Planning

Anderson, Sheila. "How to Dazzle Maslow: Preparing Your Library, Staff, and Teens to Reach Self-Actualization." *Public Library Quarterly* 23, no. 3–4 (2004): 49–58.

Brehm-Heeger, Paula. *Serving Urban Teens.* Westport, CT: Libraries Unlimited, 2008.
> This book addresses many library service concerns that are applicable to teen parents, whether or not they are in an urban environment, especially programming, volunteering, and staff attitudes and training.

Child Development Media. http://www.childdevelopmentmedia.com/.
> A vendor of parenting books and DVD's, including a dozen or so specifically for teen parents, some of which are available in Spanish.

Destination Learn. http://www.destinationlearn.net/.
> Family literacy materials in English and Spanish.

Films Media Group. http://ffh.films.com/.
> Streaming video and DVDs on parenting and early childhood topics.

Gorman, Michelle, and Tricia Suellentrop. *Connecting Young Adults and Libraries: A How-to-Do-It Manual.* 4th ed. New York: Neal-Schuman, 2009.

Healthy Teen Network. http://www.healthyteennetwork.org.

Higgins, Margaret, and Mary Mittelman. "Models of Program Outcome Measures." (n.d.) www.alz.washington.edu/NONMEMBER/FALL08/higmit.pdf.

Information School of the University of Washington. IBEC (Information Behavior in Everyday Contexts). "Outcomes Toolkit Version 2.0." (n.d.). http://ibec.ischool.washington.edu/toolkit.php.
> An outcome measurement planning guide that is specifically designed for libraries.

InJoy: Birth and Parenting Education. http://injoyvideos.com/.
> InJoy produces its own multiple series of films, including a series available in English or Spanish for teen parents.

McNamara, Carter. "A Basic Guide to Program Evaluation." The Grantsmanship Center (2002), http://www.tgci.com/magazine/A%20Basic%20Guide%20to%20Program%20Evaluation.pdf.
> An excerpt from the author's book, *Field Guide to Nonprofit Program Design, Marketing and Evaluation,* listed in the "References" section of this chapter.

McNamara, Carter. *Nuts-and-Bolts Guide to Nonprofit Program Design, Marketing, and Evaluation.* Minneapolis, MN: Authenticity Consulting, 2002.
> A comprehensive guides whose concepts are directly applicable to establishment of teen parent programs, in particular the program development and evaluation components.

Morning Glory Press. http://www.morningglorypress.com/catalog/.
> Publishes teen parent materials exclusively.

Multnomah County Library. "Inventory of Current Early Literacy Activities Undertaken by Oregon's Public Libraries." Library Development Services. State of Oregon. (Fall 2005). http://www.oregon.gov/OSL/LD/youthsvcs/earlylit/doing/current_activities.pdf.
> An inspiring compilation of ideas, some familiar and some new.

New Readers Press. http://www.newreaderspress.com/.
> Source for life and family skills materials for limited-literacy adults which are appropriate for teen parents, including titles like *Your Home Is A Learning Place* and *Control Your Money.*

Parenting Resources. http://www.parenting-resources.com/.
> Extensive backlist, including books and DVDs, specifically for teen parents.

Search Institute. "Mission, Vision, and Values." (2010) http://www.search-institute.org/about/mission-vision-values.
> As originators of the Developmental Asset philosophy and approach to youth engagement the Search Institute website provides extensive detail on the topic.

Tuccillo, Diane. *Teen-Centered Library Service: Putting Youth Participation into Practice.* Westport, CT: Libraries Unlimited, 2010.

United Way of America. "Excerpts from *Measuring Program Outcomes: a Practical Approach.*" (n.d.). http://www.unitedwayslo.org/ComImpacFund/10/Excerpts_Outcomes.pdf.

United Way of Greater Richmond and Petersburg. "A Guide to Developing an Outcome Logic Model and Measurement Plan." (n.d.). http://www.yourunitedway.org/media/Guide_for_Logic_Models_and_Measurements.pdf.
> An informative primer on outcome-based evaluation.

Zero to Three: National Center for Infants, Toddlers, and Families. http://www.zerotothree.org/.
> *The* source for up-to-date information on early childhood development topics.

Staffing and Staff Training

American Library Association. Association for Library Service to Children. "Competencies for Librarians Serving Children in Public Libraries." (2009) http://www.ala.org/ala/mgrps/divs/alsc/edcareers/alsccorecomps/index.cfm.

American Library Association. Young Adult Library Services Association. "Competencies for Librarians Serving Youth: Young Adults Deserve the Best." (2010) http://www.ala.org/ala/mgrps/divs/yalsa/profdev/yacompetencies2010.cfm.

Klingler, Susan. "Low Literacy: Breaking the Family Cycle." *Indiana Libraries* 27, no. 2 (2008): 36–39.
> Suggestions for school librarians that apply to teen parents.

Lindsay, Jeanne Warren, and Sally McCullough. *Discipline From Birth to Three: How Teen Parents Can Prevent and Deal With Discipline Problems with Babies and Toddlers.* Buena Park, CA: Morning Glory Press, 1998.
> Written for teen parents, this book is a springboard for the development of strategies librarians can use to help teen parents teach their children behavior appropriate in the library.

Martin, June, Michael Romas, Marsha Medford, Nancy Leffert, and Sherry L. Hatcher. "Adult Helping Qualities Preferred by Adolescents." *Adolescence* 41, no. 161 (Spring 2006): n.p.

Parents As Teachers. *Issues in Working with Teen Parents Curriculum.* St Louis, MO: Parents As Teachers, 2005.
> A worthwhile investment for in-depth strategies and understanding of working with teen parents.

Pfeil, Angela P. *Going Places with Youth Outreach: Smart Marketing Strategies for Your Library.* Chicago: American Library Association, 2005.

Ryan, Sara. "Teens @ your library: Training by and for Staff at Multnomah County Library; Portland, Oregon." (2010) Mulnomah County Library. http://www.multcolib.org/products/mclpresents.html.
> A model presentation for deepening understanding of teen patrons.

Search Institute. "40 Developmental Assets for Adolescents (ages 12–18)." http://www.search-institute.org/developmental-assets/lists.

Funding

California State Library. "Library Services and Technology Act." http://www.library.ca.gov/grants/lsta/.
> A brief explanation of how the LSTA grant funding system works in one state. Check with your state library for information on your locale, and potential grant seeking possibilities.

California State Library and Infopeople. "Eureka! Leadership Institute." http://eurekaleadership.org/.
> An example of a professional development training program that includes a grant-seeking component.

Foundation Center. http://foundationcenter.org/.
> A major resource for information on grant seeking, supported by over 500 U.S. philanthropic foundations.

Gerding, Stephanie. "A Common Purpose: Community Foundations and Libraries." *Public Libraries* 45, no. 1 (2006a): 32–36.

Gerding, Stephanie. "Ten Terrific Tips for Library Grants." *Public Libraries* 44, no. 6 (2005): 336–338.

Gerding, Stephanie. "Tips and Resources for Finding Grants." *Online* 32, no. 6 (2008): 16–21.

Gerding, Stephanie. "Writing Successful Library Grant Proposals." *Public Libraries* 45, no. 5 (2006b): 31–33.

Gerding, Stephanie, and Pamela MacKellar. *Grants for Libraries: A How-to-Do-It Manual.* New York: Neal-Schuman, 2006.

Hinman, Holly. "Infopeople Workshop—Getting Started in Library Grant Writing." Infopeople (2007), http://www.infopeople.org/training/past/2007/grants07/.
> A beginner's tutorial on the anatomy of a grant proposal, how to write a good grant and find the right funder.

McCune, Bonnie. "10 Tips for Getting Grants to Keep Your Library Afloat." *Computers in Libraries* 27, no. 7 (2007): 10–14.

McGovern, Gail. Infopeople Workshop, "Needs Assessment: Asking Significant Questions." Infopeople (2007), http://www.infopeople.org/training/past/2007/needs/.

Mid-Hudson Library System. "Resources: Funding—Basics." (n.d.). http://midhudson.org/funding/main.htm
> Examples, templates, and links to documentation of all aspects of fundraising.

Orosz, Joel. "One Program Officer's Candid Tips for Grantseekers." The Grantsmanship Center (2002), http://www.tgci.com/magazine/One%20Program%20Officer's%20Candid%20Tips%20for%20Grantseekers.pdf.
> Advice and secrets that only grant program managers know. Most are applicable to library grant-seeking environments.

Field-Tested Teen Parent Services

Pima County Library. "Project L.I.F.T. (Literacy Involves Families Together)." WebJunction (2007), http://www.webjunction.org/spanish-families-teens-and-kids/articles/content/453752.

Tucson-Pima Public Library. "Library Services: Project L.I.F.T." Tucson-Pima Public Library (2009), http://www.library.pima.gov/services/literacy/projectlift.php.

Willis, Colleen. "Infopeople Workshop: Simply Irresistible: Storytimes for Newborns to Two Years." Infopeople(2008), http://www.infopeople.org/training/past/2008/simply/.

RESOURCES

Anderson, Sheila. *Extreme Teens: Library Services to Nontraditional Young Adults*. Westport, CT: Libraries Unlimited, 2005.

Anderson, Sheila. *Serving Older Teens*. Westport, CT: Libraries Unlimited, 2004.

Benson, Peter, Judy Galbraith, and Pamela Espeland. *What Teens Need to Succeed: Proven, Practical Ways to Shape Your Own Future*. Minneapolis, MN: Free Spirit Publishing, 1998.

Dresang, Eliza, Melissa Gross, and Leslie Edmonds Holt. *Dynamic Youth Services through Outcome-Based Planning and Evaluation*. Chicago: American Library Association, 2006.

Fader, Ellin. "Everyone Serves Youth: Developing 21st Century Skills to Serve Today's Children and Teens." PLA 2010 Conference. http://www.placonference.org/session_handouts.cfm.
   Tested strategies for improving staff service to youth in the rapidly changing library environment.

Gilton, Donna. "Information Literacy as a Department Store." *Young Adult Library Services* 6, no. 2 (2008): 39–44.

International Federation of Library Associations and Institutions. "Guidelines for Library Services for Young Adults. IFLA Professional Report." (n.d.) http://archive.ifla.org/VII/s10/pubs/ya-guidelines-en.pdf.

McNamara, Carter. *Field Guide to Nonprofit Program Design, Marketing and Evaluation*. Minneapolis, MN: Authenticity Consulting, 2006. (Order directly from the Authenticity Consulting website http://www.authenticityconsulting.com/pubs.htm.)

Miller, Donna. *Crash Course in Teen Services*. Westport, CT: Libraries Unlimited, 2008.

Mondowney, JoAnn. *Hold Them in Your Heart: Successful Strategies for Library Services to At-Risk Teens*. New York: Neal-Schuman, 2001.

O'Dell, Katie. *Library Materials and Services for Teen Girls*. Westport, CT: Libraries Unlimited, 2002.

Salpeter, Judy. "Make Students Info Literate: How to Develop a New Generation of Knowledgeable Digital Citizens Who Can Operate in the Unregulated Online World." *Technology and Learning* 28, no. 10 (2008): 24–28.

Walter, Virginia. *Twenty-First-Century Kids, Twenty-First-Century Librarians*. Chicago: American Library Association, 2010.

YA-YAAC Electronic Discussion List. http://www.ala.org/ala/mgrps/divs/yalsa/electronicresourcesb/websitesmailing.cfm.
   Join the discussion and receive e-mail messages about teen programming. Send in your own queries to receive thoughtful responses from the teen librarian community. This listserv connects committed and innovative librarians from across the United States.

APPENDIX: FIELD-TESTED TEEN PARENT SERVICES AND PROGRAMS

These are examples of library teen parent programs and services from throughout the United States. Most descriptions are based on responses to a questionnaire from the authors.

EVERY CHILD READY TO READ® (ECRR) WITH PREGNANT/PARENTING TEENS

   Maryann Mori, Director, Waukee Public Library, Iowa (current position)

   Evansville Vanderburgh Public Library—Evansville, Indiana

   Des Moines Public Library—Des Moines, Iowa

Group: Pregnant or parenting teens in mixed group formats, including some with fathers, some with babies, and others with mothers only.

Duration and Frequency of Program: Weekly programs of 30 to 45 minutes or monthly one-hour programs.

Community Partners: The YWCA, Planned Parenthood, local schools, corporations, and a hospital that sponsored the local women's shelter.

Location(s): At the library, women's shelters, alternative high schools, or nonprofit community organizations like the YWCA and Planned Parenthood.

Program Content: Presented early childhood literacy programs and information to pregnant/parenting teens, usually with their babies present. The programs consisted of an overview of ECRR and the importance of reading to infants, as well as demonstrations of lapsit programs for infants. Sessions focused on various topics, such as why reading is important, how to select a book for infants, how to use books with infants, and how to modify those aspects as the child grows. Some locations were given depositories of both young adult titles and books for babies.

Staff: Teen Specialist Librarian or Outreach Services Coordinator.

Funding: Included in library budget.

Evaluation: No formal evaluations were conducted, but plenty of positive, observable outcomes were noted. Teen parents visited the library and specifically checked out board books for their babies, partnering groups' coordinators saw teen moms reading more to their babies, and parents and children became more comfortable with participating in storytime activities. In one instance, a teen mom commented that it was while watching her baby's response to a storytime presentation that she (the mom) became convinced of the power and importance of reading to her child.

TEENS WITH TOTS

Becky Schaade, Coordinator of Library Services

Fairfield County District Library—Lancaster, Ohio

Group: Teen mothers and their family members (fathers, grandparents, etc.) in the "Help Me Grow" program.

Duration and Frequency of Program: Once a month during the school year; twice a month during the summer.

Community Partner: Help Me Grow, Ohio's community-based services for expectant parents, infants, toddlers, and their families.

Location: At the library.

Program Content: Teen parent families and relatives came to the library every month for a special storytime geared specifically toward infants and young toddlers.

Staff: One professional library staff member (usually Coordinator of Library Services), and one Help Me Grow Service Coordinator.

Funding: Included in library budget (for library staff) and Help Me Grow funding for snacks and door prizes.

Evaluation: No formal evaluation method, but teen parents stated that they are reading more to their babies and visiting the library more often.

YOUNG MOMS CLUB

Diane Stroud, Programming and Literacy Coordinator, and Marianna DiGiacomo, Children's Librarian

Stark County District Library—Canton, Ohio

Group(s): Parents in their teens and early twenties from the following organizations:

- The Mother Mentors, a group that matches mothers under the age of nineteen with an adult mentor
- The GRADS program at Timken High School for students who are parents or expecting a child

- The "Keep It Real" young moms group at Skyline Terrace, a private HUD housing development
- The Aultman Hospital Physicians Center "Centering Program" for young expectant mothers
- Teen parent library patrons

Group Size: 15 parents and children, plus some grandparents.
Duration and Frequency of Program: Monthly, ongoing.
Community Partner(s): Friends of the Library, the Stark County District Library Foundation, Community Services of Stark County, the Mayor's Literacy Commission Timken High School, Skyline Terrace Apartments, and Aultman Hospital Physicians Center.
Location: Stark County District Library and at community sites.
Program Content: The Young Moms Club programs include a storytime integrating the Every Child Ready to Read® (ECRR) pre-reading skills, along with tips for using them at home, and recommendations for books that will reinforce pre-reading skills. Dinner is provided, as well as a craft, activity, or speaker. Members are given books to build a personal library, funded by the Mayor's Literacy Commission. Incentives are an important component of this program. Each month club members can complete a reading incentive form to enter a drawing for a prize basket filled with necessities such as diapers, wipes, and clothing that these young parents struggle to provide for their children. Speakers from local community service organizations have proved a valuable resource for teen parents in the program.
Outreach: The library also makes outreach visits to Timken High School's GRADS program, the "Keep It Real" moms' group at Skyline Terrace, and the Centering Program for young expectant mothers at Aultman Hospital Physicians Center. The children's librarian presents literacy programs to encourage the young parents to read to their children and visit the library, provides storytime and literacy tips, and promotes library resources and services, including the Young Moms Club. At Skyline Terrace, bus passes are distributed for those in need of transportation to the library. At Aultman Hospital, children's and teen books donated by the Friends of the Library are distributed to program participants. The library also takes part in community events that promote services to at-risk families, offering information about the services and resources available at Stark County District Library, and working to educate families about the importance of literacy for all ages, especially preparing children for kindergarten.
Staff: One coordinator oversees the planning and budgets, and one librarian implements the program and the outreach in the community.
Funding: Funding has come from a Library Foundation Grant, the library's programming and literacy budget, and the Friends of the Library. An LSTA grant has helped pay for some of the literacy materials.
Evaluation: No formal evaluation, but monthly program attendance has increased from 15 participants in 2008 to 26 in 2009. Anecdotally, the positive results include:

- Increased social interaction between the parents. Parents share stories about their children and discuss common issues in their lives while working on their crafts and enjoying their meal. The group has remained constant for almost one year, and friendships have grown.
- Children are benefiting from library visits and storytimes. They are now familiar with the routine of storytime, and children have evolved from a group who didn't really know how to respond to books and songs to a group that is actively engaged and participates.
- Participants are gaining knowledge about the importance of early literacy while enjoying activities that they may not have the resources to do at home. They are making the library a routine part of their children's lives and are starting them on the road to reading success.

FLORENCE CRITTENTON BOOK CLUB

Padraic McCracken, Teen Services Librarian
Lewis and Clark Library—Helena, Montana

Group: Residents of the Florence Crittenton Home for Pregnant and Parenting Teens, young women ages 14 to 22.

Duration and Frequency of Program: Monthly, ongoing since 2007.

Community Partner: Florence Crittenton Home for Pregnant and Parenting Teens.

Background: The Florence Crittenton Home made the initial contact with the library. They were removing televisions from the girls' living space and wanted to do something to encourage more reading. The teen librarian suggested a book club.

Location: At the partner organization's site.

Program Content: A monthly book club for the residents of the local Florence Crittenton Home for Pregnant and Parenting Teens. They have done book and movie combos, read in conjunction with the community's Big Read program, and had an author visit with Brent Hartinger after the group read his book, *The Last Chance Texaco*. Through a grant from Target, new mothers at Florence Crittenton receive a baby book bag with information on the importance of reading to babies and several vinyl board books.

Staff: Teen services librarian; staff and volunteers at the Florence Crittenton Home; a children's librarian prepares the baby book bags.

Funding: The library budget, an ALA Great Stories CLUB grant Round IV, and a Target grant for baby book bags.

TEEN PARENT BABY LAPSIT PROGRAM AT BORREGO SPRINGS LIBRARY

Veronica Maciel, Bilingual Specialist and Margo Smart, Youth Services Librarian II

San Diego County Library (SDCL)—San Diego, California

Group: Teen moms in the Borrego Springs community.

Duration and Frequency of Program: Program lasted about six months. Librarians met with teens twice a month for lapsit training, and storytimes were held once a month.

Location: Borrego Springs Library, a branch of the San Diego County Library.

Program Content: SDCL staff taught teen moms baby lapsit techniques, and teen moms led a regularly scheduled Baby Lapsit storytime at the library, which was open to all families in the community. Inspired by components of Meg Schofield's Library S.T.A.R. (Sure They Are Ready) and Colleen Willis's "Simply Irresistible" (available on the Infopeople website) baby storytime training programs, Margo Smart designed a Baby Lapsit training manual for San Diego system-wide training that was also used to train the Borrego teens. A musical CD included in the manual coordinates the rhymes and fingerplays and made it easier for the teens to lead their own storytime. Besides the obvious early literacy education benefits, preparing for the baby storytime built self-esteem for the teens as they took ownership of the program.

Background: Borrego Springs is an isolated community, located in the 600,000-acre Anza-Borrego Desert State Park in northeastern San Diego County; the nearest stoplight is 50 miles away. The teen moms approached the library and asked for the lapsit training.

Staff: One bilingual (Spanish-English) children's librarian and one youth services librarian.

Funding: Included in the library budget.

PROJECT L.I.F.T. (LITERACY INVOLVES FAMILIES TOGETHER)

Tucson-Pima Public Library—Tucson, Arizona

Group: Teen parents in Tucson and Pima County who are enrolled in parenting programs in local school districts, in alternative education programs, and through social service agencies.

Duration and Frequency of Program: Ten 60- to 90-minute sessions. The program has been offered for 10 years at 46 different sites.

Program Content: Participants learn songs and rhymes to share with their children and learn how to choose books for their children. They also make their own baby books through workshops, library tours, and bookmaking activities. Additionally, they receive a baby memory book, which includes pages to record favorite language development activities. Those activities are also rewarded with prizes through the Baby Reading Club, an incentive program.

Location: At agency, school sites, and the library.

Funding: Originally funded in 1997 by the Barbara Bush Foundation for Family Literacy. Currently, the program is funded on an ongoing basis through the library's budget, the Friends of the Pima County Public Library, and other grants.

(Tucson-Pima Public Library 2009, Pima County Library 2007)

TEEN PARENT OUTREACH

Ellin Klor, Children's Librarian II, and Priya Mascarenhas, Family Literacy Coordinator

Santa Clara City Library—Santa Clara, California

Group: Teen parents enrolled in the Santa Clara Unified School District's Young Parents Center and residents of the Bill Wilson Center's Teen Parent Transitional Housing Program.

Duration and Frequency of Program: The Young Parents Center program is held monthly during the school year. The Bill Wilson Center programs are dependent on the level of grant funding and usually occur quarterly.

Community Partner(s): Santa Clara Unified School District and the Bill Wilson Center.

Location: At partner sites and at two library branches, on an alternating basis.

Program Content: Visits are structured around interactive participation in two areas: early learning for children and life skills for teens. Activities include parenting discussions, crafts for teens, making a children's book, storytimes and playtime, and library visits focusing on use of library resources and children's programs.

Staff: Children's Librarian II and Family Literacy Coordinator.

Funding: Originally funded by an LSTA "Early Learning for Families" grant through the California State Library. The YPC program is currently supported by an "Even Start" LSTA grant through the school district. The Bill Wilson programs are funded by short-term grants. Grantors have included Target Stores, the Kaiser-Permanente Health System, and the Friends and Foundation of the Santa Clara City Library.

Evaluation: No formal evaluation. Occasional feedback surveys from participants, and regular post-program discussions with teen parent group teachers and social workers.

YOUTH LITERACY PROJECT (YLP)

Sarah Lapin, Adult and Family Literacy Services Specialist, and Pamela Bilz, Youth Outreach Coordinator

San Mateo County Library—San Mateo County, California

Group: Pregnant or parenting teens participating in two community-based teen parent programs.

Duration and Frequency of Program: Monthly, ongoing.

Community Partner: Coastside Mental Health, with San Mateo County Mental Health Department, and New Creations Home Ministries, a nonprofit organization that offers residential programs for young mothers and their children.

Location: At partner sites, with annual library visits.

Program Content: The YLP functions in two formats. At Coastside Mental Health, young parents and their children are together and engage in meaningful parent-child interactions that focus on literacy development. It is a designated time for them to learn and play together. At New Creations Home Ministries, the Youth Outreach Coordinator leads a storytime with the children in one room, while the parents build their literacy, parenting, and life skills in a separate room through discussion and interactive activities.

Staff: Adult and Community Literacy Services Specialist and Youth Outreach Coordinator.

Funding: Originally funded by a three-year "Youth Literacy Project" grant, which was supported by the U.S. Institute of Museum and Library Services under the provisions of the

Library Services and Technology Act, administered in California by the State Librarian. The YLP is currently funded on an ongoing basis through the library's budget.

Evaluation: No formal evaluation. Feedback mostly comes from informal discussions with both the teen parents and the partner agency staff. One pre- and post- survey demonstrated an overall increase in library card use, reading time with their children, and interactive discussion between parents and children during reading time.

APPENDIX: RECOMMENDED FOR TEEN PARENT COLLECTIONS

Books

Davis, Deborah. *You Look Too Young to Be a Mom: Teen Mothers Speak Out on Love, Learning, and Success.* New York: Perigee, 2004.

A collection of first-person stories of real teen mothers' experiences, which emphasizes their efforts to succeed and make a life for their child(ren).

Fields, Denise, and Ari Brown. *Baby 411: Clear Answers and Smart Advice for Your Baby's First Year.* Boulder, CO: Windsor Peak Press, 2010.

Fields, Denise, and Ari Brown. *Toddler 411: Clear Answers and Smart Advice for Your Toddler.* 2nd ed. Boulder, CO: Windsor Peak Press, 2008.

Easy-to-read and access parenting information for those critical early years.

Haskins-Bookser, Laura. *Dreams to Reality: Help for Young Moms: Education, Career, and Life Choices.* Buena Park, CA: Morning Glory Press, 2006.

Practical and supportive advice to help young mothers make good choices, utilize available resources, and continue their education.

Haskins-Bookser, Laura. *Softer Side of Hip-Hop: Poetic Reflections on Love, Family, and Relationships.* Buena Park, CA: Morning Glory Press, 2008.

A collection of direct and heartfelt poems that will resonate with teen moms. The author was a teen mother herself.

Lindsay, Jeanne Warren. *The Challenge of Toddlers: For Teen Parents: Parenting Your Child from One to Three.* 3rd ed. Buena Park, CA: Morning Glory Press, 2004.

Lindsay, Jeanne Warren. *Discipline from Birth to Three: How Teen Parents Can Prevent and Deal with Discipline Problems with Babies and Toddlers.* Buena Park, CA: Morning Glory Press, 1998.

Lindsay, Jeanne Warren. *Mommy, I'm Hungry!: Good Eating for Little Ones.* Buena Park, CA: Morning Glory Press, 2007.

Lindsay, Jeanne Warren. *Teen Dads: Rights, Responsibilities, and Joys.* Buena Park, CA: Morning Glory Press, 2008.

Lindsay, Jeanne Warren. *Your Baby's First Year: A Guide for Teenage Parents.* Buena Park, CA: Morning Glory Press, 2004.

Lindsay, Jeanne Warren, and Jean Brunelli. *Nurturing Your Newborn: Young Parents' Guide to Baby's First Month.* Buena Park, CA: Morning Glory Press, 2005.

Lindsay, Jeanne Warren and Jean Brunelli. *Your Pregnancy and Newborn Journey: A Guide for Pregnant Teens.* Buena Park, CA: Morning Glory Press, 2004.

These titles from Morning Glory Press are designed specifically for teens. They are written at a basic literacy level and use a mix of first-person narratives and facts. Formatted with large typeface, photos, and an unambiguous table of contents, they are books that teen parents will readily read and consult. Many of these titles are also available in Spanish.

Mayer, Gloria G., and Ann Kuklierus. *What to Do When Your Child Gets Sick.* La Habra, CA: Institute for Healthcare Advancement, 2008.

Mayer, Gloria G., and Ann Kuklierus. *What to Do When You're Having a Baby: Easy to Read—Easy to Use.* 3rd ed. La Habra, CA: Institute for Healthcare Advancement, 2004.

Both of these titles are comprehensive but easy to read and use. In some hospitals, *What to Do When Your Child Gets Sick* is given to parents as a gift.

Morris, Jon. *Road to Fatherhood: How to Help Young Dads Become Loving and Responsible Parents.* Buena Park, CA: Morning Glory Press, 2002.

This book is based on the author's ROAD (Reaching Out to Adolescent Dads) program in Roanoke, Virginia, and helps young men cope with the responsibilities of fatherhood rather than walk away from them. This book presents the life scenarios of a variety of teen dads and details the help and support they were given to succeed as parents. It is designed to enable the reader to establish a similar program in any community.

Odes, Rebecca. *From the Hips: A Comprehensive, Open-Minded, Uncensored, Totally Honest Guide to Pregnancy, Birth, and Becoming a Parent.* New York: Three Rivers Press, 2007.

Pregnancy and parenting advice in a tone and format that will be palatable to teens. Includes resources related to teen pregnancy.

Students at South Vista Educational Center. *Daycare and Diplomas: Teen Mothers Who Stayed in School.* Minneapolis, MN: Fairview Press, 2000.

First-person stories of struggles, challenges, and achievement from teen moms who are enrolled in a model high school program that enables them to graduate but also helps them be good parents.

Williams-Wheeler, Dorrie. *The Unplanned Pregnancy Book for Teens and College Students.* Virginia Beach, VA: Sparkledoll Productions, 2004.

An unbiased primer to help a young woman cope with an unanticipated pregnancy. This book can help with decision making, and it provides information and referral resources for whatever choice the individual makes.

Magazines

To date, there are no parenting magazines published specifically for the teen parent audience. Although the following titles are targeted to an older demographic, they do offer easily digestible information in an attractive format.

American Baby. www.AmericanBaby.com. An informational website with free subscriptions to straightforward articles on baby care and concerns.

Parenting: Early Years. www.parenting.com. A specialized edition of *Parenting* for parents with babies and toddlers. Information is also available by age on the magazine's website.

5

PARENT-FOCUSED PROGRAMS: LITERACY AND LIFE SKILLS

Library programs designed for teen parents and their children may assume a variety of formats and can look extremely different from one another. They can take place inside the library or at a local community agency. One program may be for parents and their children together to engage in storytimes, another may be for parents learning to create a resume. Regardless of how the program looks, it is important to tailor the style, focus, and content to meet the individualized needs of the teen parents you work with, taking into account their culture, language, socioeconomic status, interests, and goals. This chapter highlights teen-focused programs that recognize the duality of the teen parent's roles as both teen and parent, and it emphasizes that the parent is the child's first and most influential teacher. While it is extremely beneficial to provide an opportunity for parents and children to interact together in a literacy-rich environment, facilitating learning with only the parents is equally as valuable. Without the distraction of children in the same room, you can work with focused individuals, providing the opportunity for more in-depth discussion on a specific topic, more self-exploration, and more growth as a parent—and as a teen.

PROGRAM PLANNING TEMPLATE

Simultaneously faced with responsibilities that can challenge even mature adults, and often functioning as little more than children themselves, the teen parent population frequently necessitates thinking outside of the box for library services. The duality of teen parents as parents and as teens is never more evident than within the context of program planning.

Meeting the informational and recreational needs of teen parents requires considering a few important factors:

- Teen parents do not necessarily fit the same profile as their nonparenting peers who frequent libraries. Their interests, needs, and availability may be different from those of your mainstream teen population. Many have been forced to mature far beyond their years. Yet, they may also delight in simple activities that more sophisticated teens would resist.

- Many teen parents are functioning in survival mode, and it is unrealistic to expect teen parents to be able to plan or coordinate their lives in order to participate in regularly scheduled public library teen programming. Between school and work schedules and the need for child care, turning up on a whim is usually not possible for them. This is another indicator that the easiest way of reaching teen parents is through collaboration with agencies and schools that have established teen parent groups.

- The content of programs must be considered in light of the demands of their lives. For example, while a teen mom might enjoy a Mehndi hand-decorating program, Mehndi designs must be left untouched for several hours, which is impractical for someone who is changing diapers and feeding an infant or toddler.

Learning through engaged involvement, a basic precept of almost all teen programming, is also fundamental to programs for teen parents. The adages about experiential learning definitely ring true for this population. Providing enjoyable experiences goes a long way toward giving you the credibility you need to connect with the teen parents and to gain their attention when sharing valuable information for them and their families.

Child Care

Programming exclusively for parents can occur only when child care is secured. If you are collaborating with a community agency already working with a teen parent group, explore the child-care options that they have used in the past or currently use. Often, existing teen parent groups at a school or agency have some type of established child care. If library staffing is possible, ask a colleague to do a storytime with the children in a separate room while you work with the parents, transforming what was just child care into an early learning experience. If there is no established child care, incorporate the cost of hiring child-care professionals into the budget during the planning phase of the project. This can be an expensive option. Utilizing volunteers may be a viable alternative, yet it will take a little legwork to investigate requirements for volunteers working with children at the partner agency or at your library (e.g., fingerprinting).

If the teen parents do bring their children to a program that was designed specifically for mothers and fathers only, adaptability and flexibility is the name of the game. The priority is the attendance and participation of the teen parents; they may not have alternative child-care options or feel comfortable being separated from their children. It might be helpful to have some materials and toys on hand for the children to use. If you notice that the teen parents are regularly bringing their children, it might be time to reevaluate the type of teen parent program you are offering (i.e., plan to include children) in order to better meet their current needs.

Preliminary Planning

Begin planning by consulting with the partnering agency staff member who has been facilitating the group. Find out what has worked (or hasn't worked) with the group, and what he or she views as the group's needs. Discuss the topics you view as high priorities, and ask for suggestions and feedback, as well as goals that the agency has set for the teen parents. Prepare a brief needs assessment for the teen parents to fill out. Make sure it is simple and specific. Assume that none of them have ever been introduced to the library or its services before, and avoid using library-specific terminology like "circulation" or "reference." Questions might include the following:

1. Which of these topics would you like to know more about? (a) parenting and child-care; (b) personal health and fitness; (c) cooking; (d) great books to read; (e) craft projects; (f) personal computing; (g) job search techniques and resume writing.
2. What are your future career goals? What types of jobs interest you?
3. How old is your child?
4. Which of the following topics interest you? (a) good books to read with your child; (b) how to play so that your child has fun and learns too; (c) learning songs and rhymes to sing.

An example of a simple teen parent needs assessment is appended to this chapter.

Based on what you learn, create a game plan that incorporates everyone's goals and interests into a program idea list. Refine it into a series of program outlines that combine activities, learning opportunities, and discussion. Review it with the group leaders from the agency. They can help you organize and schedule your programs so that impact is maximized.

Ellin Klor, a children's librarian at Santa Clara City Library in California, has collaborated closely with the teachers at the Young Parents' Center, a program affiliated with the local school district. During the preliminary planning discussion, their group's enjoyment of craft activities was mentioned. These activities, which afford the teen parents time to relax, be creative, and express themselves, have become a key component of Ellin's programming. In a 5-to-10-minute meeting or via e-mail, Ellin and the agency's teachers discuss the logistics of each month's program. Ellin attributes much of her program's success to the input and guidance of the Young Parents' Center's staff, who know the teen parents best.

In addition to the big ideas for teen parent programming, the nitty-gritty basics of program planning must also be considered. The Infopeople Project (Infopeople.org) in California offered a workshop in 2007, "Beyond the Bookshelf: Teen Programming." Kelley Worman, the workshop presenter, compiled a YA Program Planning Guide, which is available on the Infopeople website. While not all aspects of this guide may apply directly to planning teen parent programs, utilizing it will help avoid any oversights. Key points to consider include audience (age group and interests), purpose (what you want to accomplish), implementation (staffing, space, time, supplies), and evaluation (including feedback).

Icebreakers

At the beginning of every meeting with teen parents, it can be extremely beneficial to start with an icebreaker, a facilitated game or activity that warms up the group. Often teen parents are hesitant to contribute to a discussion, share personal information or thoughts, and interact with participants they do not know. Icebreakers can raise the comfort level, encourage openness to self-understanding and an appreciation of others, and create an atmosphere where it is safe to share. Icebreakers also aid in the development of group cohesiveness and allow individuals to establish mutual trust with their peers. Plus, they're just good fun.

An icebreaker can be as simple as going around in the group circle and asking everyone to share their name and answer an exploratory question or request, such as "What is your favorite food?" or "Please tell us one thing others do not know about you." It is best to always start the group off by answering the question yourself, demonstrating that you feel comfortable sharing with everyone and modeling an appropriate response.

Depending on time constraints and size of the group, a warm-up can be more involved and interactive. It should not be more than 10 or 15 minutes, as you do not want it to take over the planned discussion topic and learning activities of the session. Below are a few classic examples of icebreakers that you can try with your group.

- **Two Truths and a Lie:** This is a fun way for members of your group to get to know one another. Tell participants to introduce themselves by sharing two truthful statements about their life, and one lie. The rest of the group will guess which statement is the lie. Encourage the teen parents to try to trick one another by thinking of little-known facts about themselves.

- **Human Bingo:** This is a great interactive activity that gets everyone up and moving and talking to everyone else in the group. Before the meeting, create a bingo sheet. At the top of each square, put a short description of characteristics about a person, such as "Speaks more than two languages," "Likes to play a sport," or "Has broken a body part." Every participant gets a copy and is directed to circulate around the room to ask other members to sign a square that is a true statement about themselves. Each person can sign their name only once on another participant's bingo sheet. The first person to get bingo wins a prize (something small: a children's book, candy bar, etc.). If you enter "Human Bingo" into your favorite Internet search engine, there are many websites that offer free templates to download.

- **Telephone:** As the group facilitator, whisper a random statement into the teen parent's ear next to you. Have that person pass on the message to the person next to her, and so on until the statement has gone around the entire circle. When the last person hears the message, she will share with the rest of the group the statement that was whispered into her ear. It's fun to see how the message has changed. This is a great way to begin a discussion about the importance of building clear communication skills.
- **The Toilet Paper Game:** The group facilitator takes a roll of toilet paper and tears off a few squares before handing the roll to the next person and asking him or her to do the same. When everyone has toilet paper, tell the teen parents to count the number of squares they have, and then they tell everyone in the room that number of things about themselves (i.e., if they took four squares of toilet paper, then they share four things about themselves). Don't tell the group in advance of the activity what the toilet paper is for—inevitably you will get at least one teen who takes a lot of toilet paper without knowing that he or she will then have to think of many personal things to share with the group! This is a fun way to get to know each other.
- **Stand Up/Sit Down:** Before the group meeting, create a list of statements that may describe some of the participants. During the meeting, read the list, and have the teen parents stand up if the statement applies to them or remain seated if it does not. This is a great opportunity for the teens to see how much they have in common—in ways they may have never guessed. Depending on the comfort level of the group, this activity can be used in a light way (e.g., by reading statements such as "Stand up if you have an older sister") or in a more serious way (e.g., "Stand up if you have ever felt like you could be a better mother").

Never underestimate the importance of building rapport and establishing a comfort level among group participants. Breaking the ice will influence your participants to be open, share, and feel comfortable about trying new activities with each other and with their children at home. Not all icebreakers will work with every group; it often depends on a range of variables that contribute to group dynamics, such as size, energy level, and pre-established relationships within the group. There are many resources online that offer diverse warm-ups that can be used in your group. The book *201 Icebreakers: Group Mixers, Warm-Ups, Energizers, and Playful Activities*, by Edie West (1997), also has a comprehensive list with guidelines on how to best incorporate the activities into your workshop. *Team Challenges: 170+ Group Activities to Build Cooperation, Communication, and Creativity*, by Kris Bordessa (2006), is another great icebreaker resource. As the group leader, be open to trying different icebreakers in order to develop cohesion among the teen parents and, again, to have some fun together.

Program Session Format

Programs that include a mixture of activities are most effective for keeping teen parents engaged. Depending on the activity, the number of people in your group, and the total length of your meeting time, the time frame for each activity can range from about 15 to 60 minutes. Typical formats include programs at the library for parents only, programs at the library with parents and children together, programs at the site of a partnering community agency with only the parents, and programs for parents with their children at the community site. These formats are based on public library programming components, but some aspects (in particular, the life skills topics) can be readily adopted by high school librarians.

1. **Library visit (parents only):** A program in the library without children is a great way to share the information and diverse resources that libraries can offer teen parents. Typical programs include an introduction and icebreaker, an informational activity (such as a tour or Internet/library website presentation), a break with a snack, a hands-on activity (such as a craft project or library scavenger hunt), and an opportunity to browse collections. The following is a sample library visit program plan for teen parents only.

Topic: Website Orientation and Library Exploration

    a. Register teen parents for library cards.

    b. Review the library's website.

        i. Discuss the teen component of the library's website, including topics such as emergency help and advice, health, homework help, jobs and money, relationships and style.

        ii. Look at research databases (if available), including topics such as education and careers, language learning, practice tests for GED and high school subject tests, and job search and workplace skills.

        iii. Visit children's databases, highlighting where to locate children's program schedules.

        iv. Browse local information for newcomers, including topics such as transportation, health, and legal information.

    c. Tour the library with the teen parents, highlighting the locations of picture and board books, picture books in Spanish (if relevant to your group), the teen sections, parenting and early learning collections, the health/wellness collections, and subject requests from group participants.

    d. Observe a preschool storytime, utilizing a checklist to evaluate the parents' role during storytimes. Discuss with the teen parents their reactions to the storytime.

    e. Introduce a gift book, such as *Wiggle Wiggle* by Jonathan London.

    f. Enjoy a snack together.

2. **Library visit (parents and children):** A structured visit to the library with their children is a meaningful and enjoyable learning experience for parents and children to share. A typical format of this type of program can include the following components.

    a. Welcome the group and introduce key staff members.

    b. Offer a brief tour of the library, pointing out key sections.

    c. Have the children's librarian provide an interactive, special storytime for the teen parents and their children.

    d. Guide teen parents in helping their children with a prepared craft activity related to the storytime topic.

    e. Coordinate a library scavenger hunt. This can be done with the children in tow, or half the teen parents can do the Scavenger Hunt while the other half of the group helps the children with the craft. The parents can then rotate.

    f. Enjoy a snack together.

3. **Community site visit (parents only):** Providing library services at a community site is an optimal way to reach teen parents who may not be able to regularly attend library programs. These programs can be educational (such as discussing the importance of reading to their children) or recreational (offering a craft activity) or both. Typically, the format for this type of program includes an introduction and icebreaker, an introduction of the program topic, a group discussion, an interactive activity, a demonstration of a free giveaway book, and a snack. The following is a sample community site visit program format for parents only.

Topic: Communicating with Your Children

    a. Introductions and Icebreaker: Play the "telephone game, where you whisper a sentence in a person's ear and the sentence goes around the room until the last participant says what she heard out loud. Discuss the communication skills used during the game.

    b. Activity: Participants draw a picture of a child. The group leader reads a story of a mother who yells at her child. Have participants tear off a piece of their drawing every time the boy in the story is hurt by words. Ask participants to describe what it would take to put the pieces back together (e.g., kind words, big hugs, and an apology).

  c. Discussion: How do words hurt or help a child grow?

  d. Read *The Chocolate-Covered-Cookie Tantrum* by Deborah Blumenthal and discuss how the story relates to the teen parents' children.

  e. Enjoy a snack together.

4. **Community site visit (parents and children):** Partnering agencies often offer some type of child care during teen parent programs. If this is the case, utilize the time with parents only by doing an icebreaker activity and a brief discussion or activity on a parenting topic. Then invite the children to join the program for a storytime and early learning activity related to the parent discussion. The following is a sample community site visit program format with parents and children learning together.

Topic: Book Sharing with Young Children

  a. Introduce the morning's activities and present the gift book (*The Everything Book* by Denise Fleming).

  b. Model reading the book to parents and offer ideas for creating an interactive experience, including making animal sounds, naming the foods and asking your child which one he likes best, naming the fruits and colors, singing the ABC song, counting eggs and crocodiles, and playing peekaboo.

  c. Hold a group storytime with the children, including reading the gift book.

  d. Offer an interactive activity, such as fingerpainting with pudding (see chapter 8).

Program planning is a dynamic process that will evolve over time. It is all about trial and error, as some ideas and activities will work with some teen parents, and others will not. Don't be afraid to try something new, and don't be discouraged if it doesn't work. Especially during programs with children, expect chaos, as the young parents are still learning effective behavior management skills. Try to be as adaptable as possible during the program because things don't always go as planned (and that's okay!).

Informational Content Planning

Select a Topic

Surveying the teen parents you work with and giving them topic choices to vote on encourages interest and buy-in from the start. Query them for needs and challenges that they have experienced, and consider topics that come up during your time with them. If you are connecting with an already established teen parent group, talk to the group leader about possible relevant topics.

Educate Yourself on the Topic

It is not necessary to become an expert on every topic discussed in your program or workshops. Learn enough so that you feel comfortable answering questions and applying the knowledge you have to situations that teen parents may bring up. Utilize key Internet resources to gather timely information efficiently. If you want, discuss your program plans and ideas with another colleague or knowledgeable professional. And remember, it is always okay to say to a teen parent that you do not know the answer to a question and that you will find the information for next time.

Communicate the Topic

Understand that you will not be lecturing to an audience that hangs on your every word. Determine the most important issues and select a few key concepts to cover. It may also be necessary to consider how to simplify concepts, breaking them down into digestible bits. Remember that teens' brains are not fully matured; teens need concrete examples to make sense of complex ideas. Discussion of a particular topic may move beyond your specific focus for the program—don't consider that a problem! A successful program is one in which the teen parents are involved and learning. Your flexibility is crucial.

Present the Topic

Source format may, in part, determine the structure and logistics of your presentation. Topics of personal interest and/or humor make information memorable for teens. When introducing websites, search for topics that will inform and amuse them, such as articles from the eHow (2010) and Instructables (n.d.) websites on cutting hair, preventing pimples, and do-it-yourself pedicures.

Discuss the Topic

Consider what will be the most effective way to engage the group to promote thought and discussion on your topic. Knowing that teens respond best when they are actively engaged, possibilities might include completing a questionnaire, playing a game, and writing responses to a prompt that are then shared and read aloud (for more ideas, see chapter 3).

Record the Details

Meticulous recording of activities, supplies, content, and resources will make everything a breeze the second time around (and there will be a second time). Make notes of what worked and where there is room for improvement.

Mainstream Teen Program Ideas to Consider

Books and websites on teen programming present many ideas that are suitable for teen parents. It is essential, however, to make sure there is a good fit between your teen parent group's interests and the topics selected. Here is a list culled from current resources that offer great possibilities for programs with young parents.

- *More Teen Programs That Work*, by RoseMary Honnold (2005), has many life skills programs that will be helpful to teen parents. Job and education events like "Career Night" and "How to Go to College for Almost Free" can be adapted to meet your group's requirements. "Club Tech," a computer skills series, "Emergency," focusing on child safety and first aid, and "Feeling Safe: Tips for Teens and Parents" all address relevant issues. Teen moms, with limited opportunities for self-exploration, will enjoy "For Girls Only!!" devoted to personal safety, body image, and creativity, and "This Is Me," a program about understanding personality types that uses personality tests. It also makes a tidy segue into discussing children and temperament.
- Ideas from *Teen Library Events: A Month-by-Month Guide*, by Kirsten Edwards (2002), include "Getting a Summer Job," offering tips from local employers who hire teens (which for teen parents probably means year-round employment, not just in the summer), and "Urban Legends;" be sure to keep the little kids in another room while you share examples of bizarre but untrue folklore. The latter could tie in with a program about website evaluation and information literacy.
- Among the suitable ideas from *Teen Programs with Punch: A Month-by-Month Guide*, by Valerie Ott (2006), are "Find Your Future," a program to share library resources on career choices, "Teens Teaching Teens," where group members share and learn each others' skills, and "Veg Out," a presentation on vegetarian eating that can also encompass general good nutrition (an important subject for both teen parents and their children).
- The Mid-Hudson Library System's "Youth Programs: Child to Teen" page (Mid-Hudson Library System n.d.) provides links to library programming ideas from sources across the Internet. Less common topics with teen parent appeal include community service and "fresh start cards" (fine reduction) programs and a bilingual Celebremos Mis Quince Años/Quinceañera Fair, along with links to craft, booktalking, and gaming programs.

Program Extras

Food

Never underestimate the power of food at your program or workshop. Adolescence is a time of great physical growth, requiring an increase of food intake. Offering a snack at some point, usually in the last part of your time together, gives everyone a chance to relax, revive, and mingle. It also helps the young parents to remain focused on the topic or activity. Simple, healthy snacks are optimal; your spread might comprise cheese, fruit, crackers or sliced French bread, nuts and raisins, and apple juice. Always make sure you check with the teen parents or partnering agency staff regarding allergies or dietetic needs.

A simple cooking activity (see chapter 6) can also be incorporated into your program, and the results will be the snack. This approach often garners an enthusiastic response from participants.

Gift Books

If funding is available, giving books to teen parents is a great addition to your program. It offers an incentive to participate in the program and helps parents build home libraries, creating a literacy-rich environment for the families. In addition to read-aloud books for their children (discussed at length in chapter 7), teen parents appreciate receiving parenting books and books just for their own reading enjoyment. Anyone who has been lost in the daily routine of child care or any other all-consuming task can appreciate the delight of stealing a few minutes here or there with a favorite book. Additionally, if the young parents are reading for their own pleasure, they serve as models to their children as lifelong readers and learners.

Informational Handouts

Librarians often have a natural inclination to provide handouts on any topic they present. We suggest trying to temper this impulse when you are working with teen parents. In general, they are not filers and keepers of pieces of paper, no matter how valuable the information may seem to the presenter. Teen parents tend to live very much in the present, and they won't routinely keep something for future use. In addition, as with any group, teen parents may not be visual learners; they may have difficulty following written directions, or they may not be interested in reading an informational article. Of course, their interest in written supplements depends largely on the specific nature of the group; you will have to informally assess the needs and interests of your particular audience as you get to know them. If you believe that a handout would absolutely heighten their learning experience, keep it concise and to the point; short bullet points that highlight the main ideas are usually the most effective way to present printed information to teen parents.

LIFE SKILLS

Teen-focused programs are an excellent opportunity to work with the young parents as they build the life skills that help them effectively deal with the demands and challenges they face every day. They may not have been taught how to meet their basic needs, problem solve, and comfortably live independently, or they may have underdeveloped skill sets in these areas. These tools can be conveyed overtly, such as by creating a monthly budget during a discussion on financial literacy. Or, the skills can be reinforced covertly through interactive activities and discussions. For example, when the teen parents are engaged in a library scavenger hunt in pairs, they are building their proficiency in teamwork and cooperation. The life skills gained during these programs will contribute to the teens' healthy growth and enable them to successfully care for their children.

Library Use

Central to the underlying principles of library outreach in any form is the belief that libraries, and the resources they offer, can improve the lives of the people they reach. Teen parents, who often face an uphill struggle to achieve what many young people their age take for granted, will renew any librarian's faith in the efficacy of the services offered. The challenges, of course, are to make teen parents aware of what the library has for them and get them to utilize the resources.

If the teen parents in your group had any exposure at all to the library when they were younger, it is very likely that it may have ended with overdue or lost materials, an angry parent, and no more library visits. Therefore, it is important to keep in mind that there may be fences to mend, and you may hope that their records have been purged from the patron database, so that they can get a fresh start. When introducing teen parents to the library, focus on these attributes of the library (which may vary, depending on the library):

- The library is a pleasant place to spend time, whether you are alone, with your child, or with friends.
- You are always welcome here.
- The library is open evenings and weekends.
- The library provides free programs for parents and children, assistance from library staff to find needed information, free computer literacy classes, and diverse resources through the library's website.
- Your free library card bestows many benefits, including free use of books, films, and music (as long as they are returned on time); free access to computer workstations for a few hours each day, including Internet use, word processing, and e-mail; and access to electronic databases and tutorials. Using library computer workstations enables anyone to accomplish important tasks like searching for jobs, completing online job applications, and uploading resumes.

Always stress the accessibility of library resources through the library's website and the availability of library computer workstations. Many teen parents do not have the luxury of computers or Internet access at home. You may discover that your teen parents are, in general, on the far side of the digital divide. Maybe they have cell phones but are not using the latest applications or staying in touch through social media. As the majority of our work and social culture moves online, teen parents need the computer access and training that libraries can offer.

Library Scavenger Hunts

Nothing introduces a teen, parent or not, to the school or public library environment quite like a scavenger hunt. Generating excitement in a group of teen parents can be tough, but mothers and fathers alike love the scavenger hunt challenge. For maximum impact, put together a custom list of questions specific to your library and your teen parent group. During open hours in a busy library, it is best to use a sheet of questions to be answered, rather than placing envelopes or items on shelves for participants to find. Keep your particular audience in mind, and tailor your hunt to their needs and interests. Think in terms of attention span, familiarity with the library, personal and cultural interests, academic level, and time allotted for the activity. When developing a library scavenger hunt, consider questions that:

- Point out artistic or architectural features of your library.
- Take teens into areas of the library that they would not normally visit.
- Require counting or locating basic facilities like drinking fountains, elevators, photocopiers, computer workstation printers, or restrooms.
- Tie in with current popular movies or television.
- Require them to find information about the library's program schedule, especially storytimes, teen events, and computer training classes.
- Identify the names of one or two key staff, such as the teen librarian and someone at a help desk.
- Highlight materials that they could use, such as picture and board books, children's music CDs, parenting books, test prep, and books on resume writing.

- Involve using the library's website and catalog, such as author, title, and subject searches, especially for topics popular with your group.
- Identify versions of the same item in different formats.
- Identify library hours, locations, circulation periods for different materials, and so forth.

A sample scavenger hunt from the Santa Clara City Library is appended to this chapter.

Give your group a brief tour of the library before the scavenger hunt in order to orient participants to locations of departments and features. Point out items that they will be asked to locate, such as the bathrooms or where to apply for a library card. Allow plenty of time, and, as much as possible, let participants work until they are finished. It is important to not have too many rules; let the group work together if they want. Help them find the answers, and be generous in your acceptance of quasi-correct answers. Make this about discovering the library, not about winning. If you decide to have small prizes, congratulate each person with a prize as they finish (and quietly give one to any non-finishers too). Most important, have fun! Remember to go over the answers with the entire group after everyone is done, letting the group give you the answers.

Adult Literacy

The demands of parenting often interfere with a teen parent's educational experience. Other factors within their life can also hinder the acquisition of strong reading and writing skills. Some young adults may have learning disabilities, they may have had to work since they were children to earn money for their family, or the traditional classroom environment may not cater to their specific learning styles. Whatever the reason may be, some teen parents in your program may have lower literacy levels than their peers. If you recognize that this is the case, it is important to be sensitive in how you respond and offer assistance, as young adults who have a low literacy skill set often hold feelings of shame and embarrassment. You can try normalizing the problem as a challenge that many people their age face. When sharing a resource in your community that can help individuals improve their basic reading and writing, offer it to the young parents as a resource "if any of your friends or family members might need it." Or, take them aside and individually talk to them about their literacy struggles and share any local resources that can help them.

Many public libraries have some type of free adult literacy program to help people improve their basic reading and writing skills. Most of these programs are learner-centered and goal oriented, helping adult students meet their specific needs in a flexible, safe learning environment. If they want to obtain their GED, get a high school diploma, pass the citizenship test, get a job, or learn how to read a book to their child, these library-based literacy programs can help teen parents reach these goals. Whether your teen-focused programs meet at the library or at the site of a partner agency, it is always important to promote the library-based services that can help the young families improve their quality of life. If your library does not have an adult literacy program, try contacting your local adult school or community college to see what kind of resources they can offer these young adult learners.

Information Literacy

In an era when job applications are submitted electronically, most people learn the news of the day (and even the hour) via television or the Internet, information is a world commodity, and many teens' social lives are as much digital as personal, the digital divide is rapidly becoming a crevasse. Recognizing that libraries, both school and public, can compensate for the disparity between the citizens who are wired up and those who are not, the United States government and public foundations have sought to create digital equality by supplying libraries with the means to offer free access to computers and the Internet to all. Despite the fact that the pace of technological change challenges public institutions to stay current, libraries still manage to significantly level the playing field. Teen parents, who generally reside on the far side of the digital divide, need to know of, and use, the technology that libraries offer.

Teen parents who manage to stay in school are usually receiving training in the basic computer skills that almost any employment beyond manual labor requires. However, they are not necessarily learning to be information-literate, which is necessary to avoid making unfortunate decisions based on inaccurate facts. Through the teachable moments that come when teens are engaged in an information search that is meaningful to them, youth librarians have the opportunity to help teen parents develop the critical thinking skills that are becoming a requirement of daily life.

Keep in mind that just as they do for most teens, web-based resources have many attractions for teen parents. With Internet access, information is available to teens anytime and anywhere. Websites are usually more current than books, and a well-conceived website makes it easier to find information than trying to locate it in a book. Websites' brief content entries suit teen parents' need for to-the-point and specific information.

Successful Digital/Information Literacy Instruction

Working with teen parents necessitates putting aside common assumptions about teens and their electronic expertise. Although every teen parent is different, many are not as computer savvy as the average teen. Plan your presentations accordingly:

1. Take your time when leading an Internet-based information session, as teen parents may not be quick studies at keyboarding and searching.
2. Let them work together. Internet presentations are often most successful when two teens are sharing one workstation, and the group is squeezed into a limited space. Spacious technology training rooms, with each person isolated in their own cubicle, do not encourage the interaction and mutual support that they may need.
3. Teach concepts, such as organization of information, search strategies, use of the library catalog and evaluation of websites, through a relevant, real-life topic. For example, demonstrate how to search the Internet when looking at a website dedicated to health or parenting.
4. If you have bilingual teens in your group, always be sure to highlight book and Internet resources in their other language. This simple act can impact entire families, as bilingual teens may have family members without an advanced understanding of English who would benefit from materials presented in their first language. In particular, there are more and more websites available in Spanish or that have a Spanish component.

While sophisticated teens (and teen librarians) are pushing the boundaries of digital innovation and use, you can measure success with teen parents in the digital arena if they can accomplish the basics (locating, evaluating, and integrating information). This especially includes information that they will need to survive in the world of technology.

Job Searching and Continuing Education

Teen parents will often have a different perspective on their futures than their nonparenting, college-bound peers. In many cases, earning money to support themselves and their families is their top priority. Unfortunately, the financial desperation they may feel can drive them to quit high school in order to acquire a job. While this may be a short-term solution, workplace advancement is almost impossible without at least a high school diploma, and often it demands further vocational training or a college degree. Child Trends.org, a nonprofit, nonpartisan research center, also reports that as more and more college graduates are available for employment, there are fewer positions for those individuals with solely a high school diploma, and even fewer for those with no credentials (Perper, Peterson, and Manlove 2010).

If teen parents are in a supportive program or school environment during their pregnancy and after their baby is born, they often recognize that education and job training are necessary to ensure the well-being of their child, as well as themselves. They therefore make a commitment to finish their education to the best of their abilities. Libraries can help young parents improve their chances for lifelong work success. Life skills that are needed to help teen parents overcome obstacles to education and training include learning how to access child care, transportation, and other support services needed for survival. Additionally, acquiring the knowledge of work opportunities and connections are critical skills for life success (Lankard 1994).

By connecting teen parents with local and national vocational, educational, and employment resources, in both book and digital formats, libraries can play an important role in this arena. Many library systems have created pages on their websites for job seekers and offer workshops and coaching to those looking for work. Librarians working with teen parents can collaborate with other library staff members to craft webpages or presentations targeted to their group's specific employment-related needs.

Career, Training, and Jobs Presentations

While some teen parents may be prepared to take the traditional four-year college route on their path to a career, the majority are interested in pursuing training that will prepare them for a job as quickly as possible. For them, the core components of career development are:

- Graduating from high school or passing the GED
- Using a self-assessment to recognize interests and abilities
- Choosing a career
- Determining the educational requirements necessary to obtain career goals
- Locating a school that offers a program in the chosen subject
- Finding affordable and convenient daycare
- Budgeting for expenses, and learning about and securing financial aid
- Finding a job (part-time while in school, and full-time after graduating)
- Succeeding on the job

This information is too much to cover during one program, and so it presents another opportunity to allow the group to set your course for you. A pre-planning discussion or questionnaire will indicate which topics are the group's top priorities.

There are a variety of resources that will offer background information and possible strategies for framing your presentation. *How to Get a Job If You're a Teenager*, by Cindy Pervola and Debby Hobgood (2000), *Teens' Guide to College and Career Planning*, from Peterson's (2008), and *What Color Is Your Parachute? For Teens*, by Carol Christen and Richard Bolles (2010), are excellent books that will provide you with a solid foundation on the topic. The most current and accessible information is available on the Internet, but you will soon discover that there are an overwhelming number of possibilities related to this topic. It is important to look for websites that are sponsored by reputable organizations, have content sections geared or accessible to teens, and are up-to-date. Additionally, look for the following components when evaluating the quality of websites:

- Aptitude and interest assessment questionnaires
- Descriptions of career fields, including salary and education requirements
- Listings of training programs, both public and private
- Information on securing financial aid
- Resume-writing instruction from self evaluation through formatting
- Job-interview preparation and behavioral advice
- Explanations of how to fill out job application forms
- Advice for succeeding on the job

State and Federal Resources

CareerOneStop.org, a website from the U.S. Department of Labor (2010), is a starting point for library staff seeking state and local career and training information, although its complexity may not make it best for use with teen parents. Sections targeted at students, and links to state workforce departments, make it useful for understanding the components of career exploration. Some state governments have put together tremendous web resources for youth employment. Many provide information similar to that of commercial websites but offer the authority of government sponsorship. Look for them under your state department of labor or workforce training. While some sections of these websites may be state specific, much of their information can benefit teen parents across the United States. Two exemplary examples are CareerZone.ny.gov from the state of New York, and its spin-off, California CareerZone.com.

Commercial Websites

Commercial job and career websites are very pervasive, and, not surprisingly, of varying quality. One website where the value of the information available far outweighs its for-profit aspects is MyPlan.com. With almost no advertising, and one page of career assessment tests for purchase, MyPlan.com offers video descriptions of careers; links to job boards, internships, and apprenticeships; and clear explanations of how to apply for financial aid and scholarships. Similarly, the "Job and Career Resources for Teenagers" page from Quintessential Careers.com posts articles on job seeking that are written specifically for teens, and it links to many other websites with job listings and career planning advice.

Graduating from High School and the GED

Teen parents who have quit high school can utilize GED test study resources, including books and online websites. Highlight in your presentation and discussion any databases available through the library's website that offer GED test practice, such as LearningExpress Library®, guiding the teen parents through the access process. Teen parents still in high school who live in one of the many states with a high school exit exam may be struggling to pass it. Departments of Education in many states, including California (California State Department of Education 2010), Massachusetts (Massachusetts Department of Elementary and Secondary Education n.d.), and New York (New York State Library 2010), post sample test questions and study guides on their websites. With some digging, it may be possible to find school districts that have also prepared study guides that have been uploaded to the Internet (e.g., Oswego City School District n.d.).

The federal Temporary Assistance for Needy Families (TANF) program, handled through state departments of human services, has provisions to help teen parents finish high school and receive vocational training that will make them more employable. Some states have created specific programs for teen parents under the TANF umbrella, such as Teen Parents Services in Illinois (Illinois Department of Human Services n.d.) and Cal-Learn in California (California Department of Social Services 2007). Contact local county welfare offices for information about TANF and other programs for teen parents. Teen parents who are enrolled in a high school continuation program, or are receiving other social services, may already be aware of these programs.

Finding a Career

Many teen parents will have had minimal exposure to the diverse array of possible career choices. Learning who you are, what your strengths are, and what you like are the first steps toward choosing the right career. Many career planning agencies use the Holland Code Assessment as a starting point. The basis of this assessment is the notion that what you do in life should be based on your interests and personality. The six personality types identified by the Holland Code are:

1. Realistic—practical, physical, hands-on, tool-oriented
2. Investigative—analytical, intellectual, scientific, explorative
3. Artistic—creative, original, independent, chaotic
4. Social—cooperative, supporting, helping, healing/nurturing

    5. Enterprising—competitive, leading, persuasive

    6. Conventional—detail-oriented, organizing, clerical

No one is considered to be just one type; rather, everyone is a blend of several types. Careers and vocations are identified by the predominant traits that they require. The results from a Holland assessment test are a letter code, which aligns with matching vocations.

Taking a Holland assessment test can be both fun and revealing. Many state career planning websites include free long and short versions of the Holland Code test. Find several online options at "Interest Inventories" on the Learn More Indiana website, a partnership of Indiana state agencies; and "Assess Yourself" on the California CareerZone.com website. "Discover Careers That Fit You," a reproducible Holland Code test form from Learn More Indiana is at the end of this chapter.

When evaluating assessment tools to use with teen parents, it is important to consider the test's level of sophistication. Some tests will use terminology and situations that are beyond the comprehension or interest levels of many teen parents. The Bureau of Labor Statistics Career Information Page starts with the question "What Do You Like?" and then offers both academic and personal interests such as "Nature," "Helping People," "Building and Fixing Things," "Science," and "Social Studies." Selecting an interest leads to a choice of several careers, with a variety of educational requirements, as well as to information about what you do at the job, how you get ready, what the job pays, and so on. The video presentation format of careers, like the over 400 offered on MyPlan.com, will appeal to teen parents.

Training and Education

Making teen parents aware of local education and training programs in your community is a significant component of your information package. Motivated teen parents will seek out what they need, once they know that it is realistic and doable. Include in any "Training and Education" program information about the following services: community and four-year colleges with training programs, vocational training institutes, federal government–sponsored programs (such as Job Corps and Americorps), and nonprofit youth development and training programs (such as the Youth Employment Institute in Portland, Oregon).

Familiarize yourself with the offerings of local institutions and showcase special programs. Be sure to clarify the difference between private for-profit vocational schools and public institutions, and always differentiate between the two when showing them to your audience. Teen parents need to be aware of the contractual and financial obligations that some for-profit vocational schools require. There are also national databases for vocational training. The ACCSC (Accrediting Commission of Career Schools and Colleges) website offers listings of accredited private vocational schools. It can be used both to locate schools by geographic area and to verify whether a school is accredited. The RWM Vocational Schools Database website is organized by state and training occupation. Included are private schools that offer certificates, diplomas, and associate's and bachelor's degrees in business and technical disciplines. Again, make sure that teen parents are aware of the potential costs of such programs.

Distance learning, which more and more institutions of higher education are offering, may prove challenging for teen parents. Many will not have reliable access to a computer or the family or institutional support to allow them the time to do their schoolwork. Also, because distance learning requires the student to work largely independently, it might not be a good choice for a teen with poor study skills and habits who needs a structured schedule and external accountability. However, for the motivated and self-disciplined teen parent, distance learning via an online program may be a viable option for obtaining a degree while raising a child.

Finding Child Care

Child care can be the biggest impediment to teen parents furthering their education. It is important to always look for the availability of subsidized or on-site child care for students. Community colleges and public universities frequently have on-site child care, and fees may be based on a sliding scale for low-income families. Even national training programs, such as

Job Corps and AmeriCorps, offer child-care assistance. JobCorps locations either have on-site child development centers or offer child-care placement and referral assistance. Some Ameri-Corps programs provide monthly child-care benefits.

In addition, as mentioned in the parenting section of this chapter, there may be sources of subsidized child care in the community available to teen parents, especially if they are being supported by state welfare programs. Look at listings on your county's website for child development services. Private technical and vocational schools are less likely to offer such services.

Financial Aid and Support

Many teen parents may not even be aware of the opportunities for financial aid that may be available to them. Schools where they enroll will assist eligible students through the process. The federal government provides most student aid through Pell grants, work-study, and low-interest loans. Some states also supply grants and fee waivers.

For a general understanding of how the system works in the United States, consult the Student Aid on the Web website from the U.S. Department of Education. Community colleges are strong supporters of financial aid services, and they offer clear explanations of the options and process on their websites. Consider doing a library program for teen parents on the FAFSA (Free Application for Federal Student Aid). Many financial aid packages and forms (including the FAFSA) require the applicant's parents' financial information. Unless the teen is over the age of 18, married, or emancipated, she will likely be considered a "dependent" of her parents even if she has a child and is living outside her parents' home.

Finding a Job

The resources for job searching include national websites that list job openings by state, and local websites just for your area. Check to make sure that the website is updated with current listings. Often these websites also include advice for job seekers. One website that is geared to the specific needs of teens is SnagAJob.com, which bills itself as the "nation's number one source for hourly employment." Additionally, look for local youth employment referral organizations, such as the Youth@Work.org (NOVA Youth Employment 2010) in Santa Clara County, California. Through its interactive database, teens can specify the type, hours, and location of employment they desire, and their information is matched to available positions. Don't forget to make teen parents aware of the employment possibilities at local libraries. Libraries that are open evenings and weekends may offer these teens the flexibility they need to fit work into their busy schedules.

On the Job

Teens who have limited work experience need to understand both their rights and their responsibilities at work. Understanding and carrying out standard workplace expectations is critical to success on the job. The Youth at Work website, from the U.S. Equal Employment Opportunity Commission, spells out what does and does not constitute workplace discrimination in simple language. The YouthRules! website, through the Department of Labor, provides information about employment laws for teens by state. SnagAJob.com also offers fun-to-read tips for new employees, including "Handling on the Job Screwups," "Ten Ways to Impress Your Boss," and "Fighting Sick Day Temptation: Should You Call In?"

Never underestimate the influence and inspiration that you model as a committed professional, and what it offers to teen parents. On more than one occasion, teen parents in the groups that Ellin Klor works with have commented, "You really like your job, don't you." Making the connection between work life and personal fulfillment, and seeing that jobs can offer something beyond a paycheck, is an important motivation to furthering one's education and training.

Financial Literacy

Becoming a new parent is expensive. If the mother or father is working, there will be a decrease in income caused by time off for the pregnancy, the birth, and taking care of the baby once he or she is born. There is a significant increase in expenses, including health-care costs (with or without insurance), baby equipment and supplies (diapers, formula, car seat, crib, clothes, etc.), and child care once the parent returns to work or school. Many teen parents experience unexpected pregnancies and therefore have not planned financially for these substantial expenses. Additionally, teen parents often have lower earning power, as they have minimal education and work experience. At a time when, developmentally, adolescents are trying to gain independence, teen parents often find themselves financially dependent on family or social agencies. This forced dependence can create tension and feelings of self-doubt.

Considering the many challenges that teen parents may face within their lives, including poverty, they may not have had the opportunity to learn even the very basics of money management. Your library teen-focused program, therefore, is an excellent venue for a discussion on financial literacy, and it can offer teen parents access to important information they may not gain elsewhere. Even if you are not a money expert, there are simple ways to help these young families gain an understanding of basic, yet important financial concepts, including paying bills on time, using a credit card and paying interest fees, budgeting, saving, balancing a checkbook, and accruing debt. A variety of resources exist to help reduce the intimidation that prevents many people from achieving their financial goals.

Money Matters

Parents as Teachers, Inc. is a national training and curriculum development organization that functions under the philosophy of providing parents with child development knowledge and parenting support. This organization has developed a relatively inexpensive workbook specifically designed for teen parents—*Money Matters: A Young Parent's Workbook for Finances—and the Future* (2007, available for purchase in English and in Spanish on their website). This user-friendly guide offers valuable information to teen parents, helping them navigate through the complexities of money management in a simple, clear way. The interactive exercises help teens discover where their money comes from, how much things actually cost, how to create a budget and actually stick to it, and how to save to realistically reach their financial goals. It also includes facts about various money traps, such as rent-to-own, check-cashing services, payday loans, and credit cards (traps that people with minimal money management experience often have a hard time avoiding). This workbook is a great way to start a dialogue with your teen parent group and get them thinking critically about money.

Project Money

Project Money.org (Project Read, San Francisco Public Library n.d.), created by a team of adult learners at Project Read at the San Francisco Public Library, is a website designed to help people feel more confident about handling their money. Breaking down complex financial jargon, the website, which offers a free workbook and workshop guides, lets people know that they are not alone in their confusion and worries about money management. This is a great resource to use when integrating financial literacy into your teen parent programs. The website has easy-to-read materials and worksheets on setting up a savings and spending plan (including a free downloadable workbook), bank accounts, credit cards, income taxes, and more. Project Money.org also provides two free 90-minute workshop guides about savings and credit that you can use with young families in your community.

The Real World

In the library services book *Teen Programs with Punch,* Valerie Ott (2006) describes an interactive program called "The Real World" that is designed to empower young adults with the capacity to make smart financial choices. To simulate the real world, teens are given at random a profession, family size, and income to work with and are placed in simulated situations that encourage them to think about the realities of possible financial ups and downs. The program offers the opportunity to partner with local businesses and organizations to get representatives from local agencies to participate. Invite the young mothers or fathers in your group to help plan this simulation, as they will know best what the rest of the group will be interested in learning.

Other Financial Literacy Resources

If you do not feel comfortable talking about financial literacy yourself, consider inviting a guest speaker to talk with your teen parent group about money management. The Jump$tart Coalition for Personal Financial Literacy is a nonprofit organization dedicated to promoting awareness of financial realities to students in pre-kindergarten through college. In addition to featuring a comprehensive resource list (including lesson plans), the website also links to partner state coalitions, many of which offer guest speakers. Alternatively, if your teens are computer savvy, guide them through the MoneySKILL.org free online curriculum. These lessons help young adults gain a basic understanding of money management in the areas of income, expenses, assets, liabilities, and risk management.

Health

Access to reliable health-related information for teen parents is extremely important for their own well-being and for a healthy start for their young, rapidly growing children. They may not feel comfortable discussing sensitive health topics with family members, may not have access to quality health care, or are not able to obtain accurate data from their peers. The Internet has evolved into a primary source for consumer health information, especially among young adults. In 2001, the Kaiser Family Foundation conducted a study that estimated 90 percent of teens had gone online. Out of this large group, approximately 75 percent had used the Internet to find health information. Four out of ten of these Internet users had changed their personal behavior as a result of the health information they read online, and seven out of ten had talked about the information they found with friends (Kaiser Family Foundation 2001). Just nine years later, when teens are now spending an average of 10 hours and 45 minutes per day using multiple media types at one time, there is little doubt that many teens turn to the Internet for the health information that they need in a timely manner (Kaiser Family Foundation 2010).

Research studies have also indicated that teen concerns about privacy and confidentiality lead them to favor the Internet for health information, although they also do have apprehension about the quality of online information (Vargas 2005). While Internet websites cannot and should not be a substitute for quality health care, they can educate teen parents and parents-to-be on how to make healthier choices for themselves and their children. Online resources can serve as a confidential source for sensitive topics and help the young parents understand subjects such as the physical changes of pregnancy and infant and toddler growth and development.

If you decide to create a workshop about how to access reliable information online, it is important not to overwhelm (or bore) the teen parents with too many websites; just choose three or four of the best. Keep your presentations brief and uncomplicated. If possible, post links to the websites on your library's website, so your teen parents can find them again. Also, consider making this presentation in installments, covering one aspect of the topic at a time. Some logical topic divisions are infant and toddler health, personal health, nutrition, and local resources. Teens who are pregnant will appreciate being shown pregnancy and childbirth information. As always, ask the young parents what health-related topics they are interested in learning.

Background Knowledge

Acquainting yourself with the topics and issues related to teen parent health issues does not have to be very time consuming. In addition to perusing the websites recommended for the teens themselves, consider consulting Advocates for Youth.org, Healthy Teen Network.org, and TeenHealthFX.com. By familiarizing yourself with some of these topics, you will gain an appreciation for the many fine organizations in the United States that are working at all levels of our communities and infrastructure to improve the lives of teen parents and their children. Having trouble locating website resources? CAPHIS, the Consumer and Patient Health Information Section, a section of the Medical Library Association, publishes an annually updated Top 100 List: Health Websites You Can Trust, with a section specific to "Parenting and Kids."

Explaining Website Evaluation

Teen parents want to know that the health information they access online is reliable and accurate. Yet, as with many other topics, simply lecturing the teen parents about how to evaluate websites may leave them tuning out and not retaining this important information. It is best to educate yourself on the most important concepts, and then use examples to demonstrate these ideas. Probably the most effective way to discuss website evaluation is by weaving it into your presentation of specific websites.

To help teen parents critically analyze medical information they find online, consider using these two sources: "MedlinePlus Guide to Healthy Web Surfing" (MedlinePlus n.d.), which is also available in Spanish, and "Evaluating Web-Based Health Resources" (National Center for Complementary and Alternative Medicine n.d.). Some general concepts to consider when evaluating health websites are:

1. **Responsibility:** Who is responsible for the website and its information? Is it a reputable group or organization? Is it government sponsored (like the National Institutes of Health)? Is it professionally sponsored (e.g., by a hospital or medical association)?

2. **Funding and purpose:** Who pays for the website? Does the website try to sell or promote certain products?

3. **Accuracy and validity:** Is the information current? Where is it coming from? Is it based on credible scientific research? Who evaluates the information?

4. **Aim and audience:** Who is the intended audience? What information does the website gather about users? What do they do with it? (MedlinePlus 2006 and National Center for Complementary and Alternative Medicine 2010).

Health Presentation Content

When considering what types of health websites to include in a presentation to teen parents, it can be extremely beneficial to include the following types.

1. **General family health websites:** Offer general websites to teen parents that cover both teen and children's health topics, such as KidsHealth.org from the Nemours Foundation, which divides its content into "Parents," "Kids," and "Teens" sections. This website enables you to demonstrate how your teen parents can use the resource as both parents and teens.

2. **Young men and women's health:** Provide examples of health information websites that are dedicated to young men and women's health. Suggestions include the Center for Young Women's Health.org from the Children's Hospital Boston and Go Ask Alice! from the Health Services at Columbia University, which allows for submission of questions. Teen Growth.com focuses on teen health issues and is written and overseen by health professionals and a teen advisory board. Young Men's Health.org, from Children's Hospital Boston, includes an excellent section on "Becoming a Father."

3. **Child health:** In addition to KidsHealth, offer examples of web information related to young children's health. The Bright Futures for Families website has a "Family Pocket Guide" PDF (Anderson, Cruz, and Popper 2000) that can be downloaded in sections, which makes it easy to focus on a specific topic such as "Before the Baby Is Born" or the "Child Care Checklist." Its assortment of helpful lists and forms for everything from "important phone numbers" to "making your home safe for your toddler," all in an appealing format, make the "Family Pocket Guide" an accessible resource. Family Doctor.org, the family-oriented website of the American Academy of Family Physicians, presents brief, straightforward explanations of medical conditions and advice for healthy living. Teen parents will be able to utilize many elements of the "Parents

and Kids" section of this website, which includes parenting advice on topics like toilet training and caring for infants, information concerning teen health, and a "Game Closet" (a collection of health-related quizzes and games for kids that many teens will enjoy playing too). Versions of many topics are also provided in Spanish.

4. **Local health resources:** Provide examples of local health resources, especially those offering access to health care and support in the community (including teen health clinics, pre- and post-natal services, low-cost health insurance, teen counseling services and hotlines, and teen parent services). Some states have website guides that allow searching by county to locate services, such as California's Californians for Patient Care.org, and First 5 California, which targets parents of children five years and younger. If your community is located near a large teaching or children's hospital, these community assets may be potential sources of information and referral. Other local resources include the health services sections of city and county government websites, and other community agencies serving teens and young families. "Teen Parent Services" is a useful search term to try when researching online.

When you are reviewing these websites with the teen parents, try highlighting where to find information about general topics of interest, including when to call a doctor, how to talk to your child's doctor, and how to prepare your child for visits to the doctor. As you are presenting the website information, remember to show the group your process of finding out the facts, and how to follow web links, especially on general websites like MedlinePlus. Navigating the Internet can be overwhelming, and some teen parents may not be savvy web users; going slowly and taking the time to go through every step is important to ensuring that everyone is on the same page.

Health websites provide a natural segue into the topics of sexual health and relationships. These topics are well covered on teen health–oriented websites, and it is probably not necessary to do more than point out what topics are covered, and then allow time (and privacy) for individuals to peruse them as they wish. Depending on your group, it may also be desirable to introduce some helpful websites for sensitive topics; it is a good idea to discuss this with the adult liaison at the partner agency. Many school-based teen parent classes work with outside groups, such as Planned Parenthood, to provide education and support for self-esteem and pregnancy prevention. Exemplary websites include It's Your (Sex) Life.com from MTV and the Henry J. Kaiser Family Foundation, Scarleteen.com, StayTeen.org from the National Campaign to Prevent Teen and Unplanned Pregnancy, and Teen Talk from Planned Parenthood. These websites are evenhanded in their handling of the facts about teen sexuality and pregnancy.

It is not surprising that teen pregnancy has become one of the battlegrounds for pro-life and pro-choice advocates. On the Internet, one can find a bewildering array of websites with every possible perspective on the subject. As library staff, we strive to remain impartial when providing information and resources to our patrons. We advise taking care in selecting the websites you present on these sensitive issues; make sure that you understand the website's purpose and philosophy.

Providing teen parents with access to and knowledge about health-related websites is one of the best opportunities library staff have to demonstrate the value and importance of libraries and information. It will also greatly benefit the healthy development of these families.

PARENTING

It is critical that young mothers and fathers be educated about parenting. Considering their age and maturity level, they may not be adequately prepared for the challenges of parenting, especially in the face of sleep deprivation and lack of personal time. They may have unrealistic expectations about their child's development, believing that their child thinks and understands on the same level as they themselves do, and subsequently they may overreact with extreme discipline techniques. Parents are made, not born. People tend to intuitively parent the way they were parented, which for many teen parents may have been dysfunctional.

Offering effective tools and strategies to help them meet the responsibilities associated with parenting will help strengthen the family, both now and in the future.

While library staff may not be parenting experts, this is an information need that is important to address in teen parent programs. Our talent for locating, understanding, and utilizing information makes us quick studies when it comes to learning new subjects, especially a topic like parenting, which is so closely aligned to the work we do with children and teens. Even if you are not a parent yourself, consider any parenting workshop you may offer as an arena for shared learning. You can provide the facts and best practices from research as suggestions of what to try with children, and the teens will share their experiences on what has worked or not worked with the rest of the group. This way, you are building on each teen's strengths as a parent, and looking at him or her as the expert on his or her own child. Try checking with the teachers or advisors at the partner agency you are collaborating with to see what type of parenting instruction, if any, is being offered. See what can be presented collaboratively with them, or to complement their established curriculum. Something as simple as a presentation on the materials and resources your school or public library can offer is a significant contribution.

Using Children's Books as Teaching Tools

The use of children's literature as a teaching tool is a powerful way to convey life lessons to both children and adults. Connecting with stories assists how we process experiences and their associated emotions. Research tells us that the human brain is designed to perceive and generate patterns and can therefore effectively connect the plot sequences of stories; the brain is a successful processor of both real and imaginary stories (Jalongo 2010). Picture books begin this process with images that guide the reader or listener through the experience. Within this framework, children can connect with, and relate to, characters and begin to understand complex concepts (e.g., divorce, loss of a loved one, sharing, going to school) and associated emotions in a developmentally appropriate context. They can learn positive behaviors, coping mechanisms, and values through stories, while building pre-literacy and listening skills.

Similarly, teen parents can understand concepts, explore emotions, and see the world through the eyes of their children when interacting with children's literature. When picking a theme or topic for a workshop, consider connecting it with a children's book to exemplify the ideas and increase understanding for the young parents. Discuss how they could use the book to teach a lesson to their own children in a positive way. Additionally, children and adults alike enjoy being read to, and it is possible that many of the teen parents rarely experienced this when they were growing up.

The use of children's books can be applied at any point during the workshop, but make sure you leave enough time for discussion, as the concepts in the books often stimulate questions and comments. When you try this, you will most likely hear comments like "My child does that all the time" and "I remember the time when that happened to my child and me" when reading relatable stories.

Children's literature has endless versatility as a tool for teaching. A picture book can be found for almost any topic that you or the teen parents you work with are interested in exploring. Perhaps the most comprehensive list of children's books by subject is *A to Zoo: Subject Access to Children's Picture Books*, by Carolyn W. Lima and Rebecca Thomas. The latest edition has 1,100 pages of nearly 13,000 titles and is organized for you to search by subject, author, title, or illustrator. This is an excellent resource for library staff and teachers. Additionally, King County Library System in Washington State has free printable resources that include lists of books appropriate to specific themes and coordinating activities. Visit the "Books to Grow On" page of their website for more information.

Adapting an Existing Curriculum

Whether you have worked with teen parents and their children at your library for years or this is your first time developing a program that works with this population, the existence of pre-established curriculums prompts the question "Why reinvent the wheel?" When experts in the field have researched best practices and created programming geared specifically toward young families, the finished product may be an excellent resource and guide for you to use at your library. Utilizing the information and background knowledge provided can assist in your own preparation, and the tools and techniques presented in a curriculum are often found to be most effective in the facilitation of learning for teen parents.

It is important to consider the diverse needs, strengths, and cultural influences of the teen parents in your own group if you choose to adapt an established curriculum to your library program. The structure of a lesson plan can be helpful to guide the workshop format, but if it does not meet the learning styles, personalities, and dynamics of your group, simply modify the activities while maintaining the information. Consider your own purpose and the needs of the young parents when you adapt how to convey the information, what materials to use, and which topics to present. Established curriculums are a rich source of information for program development and can be used as a moldable tool for libraries to adapt and adopt as necessary to maximize learning for teen parents.

Parents as Teachers—Issues in Working with Teen Parents

Parents as Teachers's curriculum, *Issues in Working with Teen Parents*, offers comprehensive insight, research, and strategies to utilize when working with this population. The background information on adolescent brain development, child development, and the parallel needs of both the teen parent and child helps the program facilitator gain a deep understanding of the young mothers or fathers they work with and how best to meet their needs. The curriculum presents strategies and activities that address the specific challenges faced by teen parents and their children, and it presents ways to organize personal visits and group meetings by topic. The lesson plans for group meetings are the most relevant and applicable for a library-based program.

The curriculum is divided into two sections: child-focused units and teen-focused units. In the child-focused units, topics include child care, discipline, emotions, health and safety, language and literacy, nutrition, sleep, and toilet training. The teen-focused units incorporate topics such as prenatal care, problem solving and goal setting, and relationships and support. Each unit includes an educator resource with background information on the subject, a personal visit plan, a group meeting plan, and reproducible parent handouts on CD. A sample of the curriculum and more information on the program can be found at the Parents as Teachers website.

Motheread, Inc.

Motheread, Inc. is another national training and curriculum development organization that has created research-based curricula that merge the teaching of adult literacy skills with child development and family empowerment issues. Through the medium of children's literature, parents and children learn to use the power of language to discover more about themselves, their families, and their communities.

The curriculum is divided into two sections, with the first part geared for use with parents and the second part for use with children. The first section helps parents learn how to be story readers, writers, and tellers. It promotes a sense of self-efficacy in the parents' abilities to read to their children. Each lesson is theme-based, covering such child and family development topics as expressing needs and feelings, establishing independence, understanding what families value, sharing and cooperating, and self-possibilities. The parents read a children's book together, practicing the art of story sharing, and read a related poem or short story and engage in a writing activity. The rich discussion that follows about how the theme presented in the children's book relates to their own experiences with their families is both self-reflective and informative. Teen parents can truly benefit from this unique way to connect with children's books.

The second section of the curriculum presents story sharing for children from birth through elementary school age. It offers structured activities for exploration, literacy, and learning. The same books used with the parents are used with the children, encouraging a shared experience that can be transferred to the home environment. The curriculum offers

29 lessons, and Motheread programs are typically 8 to 12 weeks long. Library staff interested in facilitating Motheread (or Fatheread) workshops for parents or story sharing groups for children must attend training at a fee of several hundred dollars per person. For more information, consult the Motheread.org website.

P.A.R.E.N.T.S—Parental Adults: Reading, Encouraging, Nurturing, Teaching, Supporting

Produced by the California State Library Foundation, *P.A.R.E.N.T.S. Program Guide* (Curtis 2005) is a curriculum designed to provide guidance in parenting skills to adults with lower literacy levels. This innovative curriculum uses quality children's books as instructional texts, and it functions under the family literacy philosophy that parents and caregivers are their children's first and most influential teacher. Within this context, P.A.R.E.N.T.S. supports parents in this role and shows them how to use these books as teaching tools with their children.

The curriculum has 15 one-hour lessons that are intended to be used with small groups or one-to-one tutoring. Topics covered include a discussion on what children need, how children learn, parents as teachers, parents as role models, and discipline models. It also includes handouts and detailed lesson plans. A core component of the program involves giving children's books to the parents to encourage reading in the home environment. The *P.A.R.E.N.T.S. Program Guide* is very user friendly and addresses many of the challenges faced by teen parents. It can be purchased at the California Library Literacy Services' website.

General Parenting Workshops

General parenting workshops, either a one-time offering or a short series of presentations, can be great ways to strengthen young parents' capabilities and increase their use of resources. As always, ask the teen parents what they are interested in learning more about and incorporate their suggestions into your workshops. Presenting a list of suggested topics to present to the group in advance may help facilitate idea sharing and additional suggestions from the group.

Parenting Materials for Teen Parents

Books. It will take only a little research to see clearly that most general parenting materials will be a tough sell to teen parents. Even books like the popular *What to Expect . . .* series (e.g., Murkoff and Mazel 2008), which have quite an accessible format, can seem overwhelming to a teen, mainly because the books are so thick and specific information is not easy to locate. In addition, many parenting magazines and commercial parenting websites seem to be aimed at a different demographic, usually older, educated professionals with disposable income.

When looking at parenting books, teens usually give a book a quick glance, and if something doesn't catch their attention, even if library staff point out its virtues, it goes back on the shelf. Look for materials with the following qualities.

- The visual format is easy to follow and includes a lot of cartoons or photos and a low per-page word count.
- Chapters are designed to make it easy to locate information.
- There is a detailed table of contents (forget about the index).

A title like *Baby 411*, by Denise Fields, is a good example of what will work, as are the series of books specifically geared to teen parents by Jeanne Warren Lindsay from Morning Glory Press. More recommended titles are listed in the "Recommended for Teen Parent Collections" list at the end of chapter 4.

Websites. Luckily, the websites of reputable parent and family related nonprofits and foundations have a lot of accessible information to offer teen parents. While there may be an overwhelming amount of information on these websites, their organization and search capabilities, once understood, make locating what you are looking for reasonably straightforward.

While teen parents may be less technology enmeshed than your other teens, they can also be quick studies once they have Internet access and given some guidance on where and how to look. This, of course, is where library staff can be extremely helpful.

While there is a plethora of websites on parenting (as with almost any topic), again it is best to follow basic website evaluation. Keep it simple, straightforward, and clear. While commercial websites may offer similar information, the overwhelming number of advertisements can make them challenging to use. Some recommended noncommercial websites for teen parents are FamilyTLC.net, KidsHealth.org from the Nemours Foundation, Parenting 24/7. org from University of Illinois Extension, and "Your Child 0 to 6" from FamilyEducation.com. Some recommended websites for library staff to use to develop program ideas are PBSKids. org from the Public Broadcasting Service and ZeroToThree.org from the National Center for Infants, Toddlers, and Families.

Many cooperative extension services from state land-grant universities across the country have developed extensive parenting information services. For example, "Parenting Newsletters" from the University of Wisconsin Extension and "Just in Time Parenting," sponsored by a national coalition of extension services, are excellent resources. While you may or may not decide to give these newsletters to your teen parents, they will provide you with easily digestible background information if you are new to the subject of parenting. "Teens as Parents of Babies and Toddlers," by Jennifer Birckmayer and colleagues (1997), is a "teens as parents" curriculum from Cornell University Cooperative Extension. It is available as a free PDF download and offers a variety of parenting topics and related hands-on activities. It will be a useful springboard for program ideas.

When selecting websites for teen parents, look for those that:

- Clearly feature information geared to their children's age groups (infants, toddlers, and preschoolers)
- Are unbiased in their opinions and perspectives and present commonly accepted practices
- Highlight local parenting education resources, classes, and opportunities
- Offer connections to local child care
- Focus on any concerns you are aware of in the group, such as premature infants

Other media. Short videos from vetted websites and selections from DVDs can serve as discussion starters on parenting topics, but they should not be used as a substitute for interactive activities and discussions that get the teens thinking and working together. Some examples are *Baby's First Year: Pregnancy and Preparing for Baby*, a DVD from Kids Healthworks, and *Fathering: What It Means to Be a Dad* and *How I Learn*, DVDs from Learning ZoneXpress.

Sample Parenting Programs and Topics

Early literacy and learning are major components of what libraries can offer young children and their families; these topics are discussed at length in chapters 7 and 8. In addition, there are many other important parenting topics that can be offered as library programs that would be valuable to teen parents. The following are a few examples of how to prepare for and implement these types of information-based programs.

"Young Children and Media." Most parents, not only teen parents, do not realize the impact of overexposure to media on young children, or how much exposure is too much. Discussion of this issue will provide teen parents with a basis for making choices about the amount of screen time they allow, as well as make them aware that media habits, which can last a lifetime, are formed early.

Background Research

- Committee on Public Education. American Academy of Pediatrics. "Policy Statement: Children, Adolescents, and Television." *Pediatrics* 107, no. 2 (2001): 423–426.
- Commonsense Media.org. "TV, Computers, and Movies: What's Really Okay for Young Children." (2010)

- Commonsense Media.org. "Common Sense on Baby Media." (2010)
- Kaiser Family Foundation. "The Media Family: Electronic Media in the Lives of Infants, Toddlers, Preschoolers and Their Parents." (2006)
- Nemours Foundation. "How TV Affects Your Child." (2008). Kids Health.org.
- Zero to Three: National Center for Infants, Toddlers, and Families. "Television and the Under Three Crowd." (2009). ZerotoThree.org.

Concepts to Share

- Children learn from interactions with parents and caregivers, not from watching television.
- Children should not have a television (or computer) in their bedroom.
- It is not recommended to have the television on during meals or when no one is specifically watching it.
- Children should not watch television at daycare.
- Parents should monitor and limit their children's screen time (TV, DVDs, computers, and even phone applications).
- The American Academy of Pediatrics recommends that children younger than two years have no screen time at all. Children over age two should be limited to two hours a day.
- There are web resources to help parents evaluate media.

Resources to Highlight

- Commonsense Media.org—A nonprofit, nonpartisan organization that evaluates everything media, from television and video games to mobile apps, and makes age-appropriate recommendations to help parents manage their children's electronic lives.
- Zero to Three.org—The premier website for parents, caregivers, and professionals working with children ages three and under.
- Parents Choice.org "Media Management Tips"—Presents concrete strategies that will work.

Method

Distribute a media survey for each parent to complete. A reproducible Family Media Questionnaire is in the appendix at the end of this chapter. Review the questionnaire by reading it aloud, compiling the answers, and discussing the results. Briefly present information found on the Commonsense Media.org website and other resources. Show evaluations of current films and television programs, including some media geared toward teens and some geared toward young children. Encourage discussion on the topic, and emphasize that the teens are not bad parents if they have not previously followed these guidelines.

"Family Traditions and Rituals." Traditions and rituals make memories and strengthen family bonds. Being aware of the traditions in their families encourages teen parents to carry them on and create new ones with their own children. Traditions can be big or small. Examples to mention to the teen parents include pancakes for breakfast on weekends, an annual visit to the local Christmas Tree Lane, taking walks at a local nature preserve, doughnuts at the doughnut shop after storytime at the library, and reading together every night before bedtime.

Background Research

- *The Book of New Family Traditions: How to Create Great Rituals for Holidays and Everyday* by Meg Cox.

- *How to Bury a Goldfish: And Other Ceremonies and Celebrations for Everyday Life* by Virginia Lang and Louise Nayer.
- *A Lithgow Palooza! 101 Ways to Entertain and Inspire Your Kids* by John Lithgow.
- "Creating Memories: Connecting the Generations" (2008) edited by Debbie McClellan. Parenting 24/7. University of Illinois Extension.

Concepts to Share

- Traditions bind families together.
- Children remember their family's traditions throughout their lives.
- Traditions can be for special occasions and holidays, or just to make daily life a little special.
- Traditions or celebrations don't have to be costly.

Method

The winter holiday season is a great time to highlight family traditions. Start with an interactive activity, such as making several quick and easy holiday crafts (see chapter 6) or decorating cookies. Then, you can read a holiday book that the parents will enjoy, such as *Christmas Cookies: Bite-Size Holiday Lessons*, by Amy Rosenthal, or *The Polar Express* by Chris Van Allsburg. Encourage the teen parents to share their own holiday traditions. For a warm-up, share a few of your own favorite family traditions, and ask the group leaders from the partner agency to do the same. Distribute identical index cards or paper slips and pencils. Ask each teen parent to write a favorite family or holiday tradition on the paper. Fold them up and collect them in a basket. Pass the basket and ask each parent to pull one and read it aloud. The anonymity of reading someone else's response reduces the anxiety of exposure while encouraging more personal expression.

"Toys." Help teen parents learn how to select age-appropriate toys for their children, and deepen their understanding of how intellectual and physical developmental levels determine what a young child can do.

Background Research

- Babyzone.com. "Amazing Toys." (2009)
- Dr. Toy.com (2010)
- Oppenheim Toy Portfolio.com (2010)
- Parents Choice.org "Best 25 Toys of 25 Years." (2010)
- Roufberg, Ruth. "Classic Toys." (n.d.) Parents Choice.org

Concepts to Share

- Good toys encourage the child's curiosity, desire to explore, and creativity.
- Toys should be easy to use and versatile enough to be played with in different ways.
- Toys need to be age appropriate, or else the child won't be interested.
- Safe household equipment and recyclables like boxes can be just as much fun as manufactured toys.
- There are inexpensive sources for toys such as garage sales, flea markets, and Goodwill (but you must make sure the toys are safe).

Resources to Highlight

- Oppenheim Toy Portfolio.com—This website has recommendations for children's toys, books, video, and music, from a mother-daughter pair of child development experts, Joanne and Stephanie Oppenheim.

- Parents Choice.org—Parents' Choice reviews books, toys, music, television, software, video games, websites, and magazines for children and families. The site recommends products that help kids grow and are fun and safe.

Method

Use the guidelines suggested in web articles to gather a randomly arranged display of recommended toys for infants through toddlers (or preschoolers, depending on the ages of the teen parents' children in your program). You can gather toys from the library's children's services department, friends, coworkers, or possibly the child-care center at your community site. Have two or three toys for each age group, and give them name labels. Ask teens to identify which they think would be best for their children and to guess which toys would be best for a specific age group. Provide a tally sheet divided by age ranges, and have them list the name of each toy under what they think is the appropriate age. Ask parents of children in each age group to share with the group toys their children like and why they think that is the case. Talk about the value of play and how the same toys can be used differently by children of different ages.

CONCLUSION

Providing information and recreational programs for this high-need population helps them to grow and develop as teens, as parents, and as members of the community. By integrating life and parenting skills as a core service for teen parent programs, the library is contributing to their future success and the healthy development of their children. Presenting the information in a way that builds on the teen parents' experiences and knowledge will help to strengthen their capabilities and sense of self-efficacy. Teen-focused programs, without children present, allow library staff to engage in rich, meaningful discussion and to see the strengths and resiliency of these young parents.

REFERENCES

Icebreakers

Bordessa, Kris. *Team Challenges: 170+ Group Activities to Build Cooperation, Communication, and Creativity.* Chicago: Zephyr Press, 2006.
West, Edie. *201 Icebreakers: Group Mixers, Warm-Ups, Energizers, and Playful Activities.* New York: McGraw Hill, 1997.

Teen Programming

Edwards, Kirsten. *Teen Library Events: A Month-by-Month Guide.* Westport, CT: Greenwood Press, 2002.
eHow.com. (2010) http://www.ehow.com/.
   Learn how to do almost anything from this website, including how to be a teen father or a single parent.
Honnold, Rosemary. *More Teen Programs That Work.* New York: Neal-Schuman, 2005.
Infopeople. "Workshop: Beyond the Bookshelf: Teen Programming" (2007), http://infopeople.org/training/past/2007/teen-programming/.
Instructables.com. (n.d.) http://www.instructables.com/.
   At the Instructables website, people share projects and how they do them. Main categories include Living, Outside, Play, Technology, and Workshop. The website is good for both projects and life skills. It grew out of the MIT Media Lab.
Mid-Hudson Library System. "Youth Programs: Child to Teen." (n.d.). http://www.midhudson.org/program/ideas/youth_programs.htm.
   Links to a broad range of programs from booktalking to community service and beyond.
Ott, Valerie. *Teen Programs with Punch: A Month-by-Month Guide.* Westport, CT: Libraries Unlimited, 2006.

Jobs and Continuing Education

ACCSC (Accrediting Commission of Career Schools and Colleges). http://www.accsc.org/index.asp.

Americorps. http://www.americorps.gov/Default.asp.

Bureau of Labor Statistics. BLS Career Information (2010), http://www.bls.gov/k12/.

California Career Resource Network. California CareerZone. http://www.cacareerzone.com/index.html.

California Department of Education. "Program Resources: Supplemental Information for the California High School Exit Examination (CAHSEE)" (2010), http://www.cde.ca.gov/ta/tg/hs/resources.asp.

California Department of Social Services. Cal Learn (2007), http://www.cdss.ca.gov/cdssweb/PG84.htm.

Christen, Carol, and Richard Bolles. *What Color Is Your Parachute? For Teens.* Berkeley, CA: Ten Speed Press, 2010.

Domenico, Desirae, and Karen Jones. "Adolescent Pregnancy in America: Causes and Responses." *Journal for Vocational Special Needs Education* 30, no. 1 (Fall 2007): 4–12.

Illinois Department of Human Services. "Teen Parent Services." http://www.dhs.state.il.us/page.aspx?item=32189.

Job Corps. http://www.jobcorps.gov/home.aspx.

Lankard, Bettina. "Career Education for Teen Parents." *ERIC Digest No. 148.* Columbus, OH: ERIC Clearinghouse on Adult Career and Vocational Education, 1994.

Learn More Indiana. (formerly the Indiana Career and Postsecondary Advancement Center.) "Discover Careers That Fit You." http://www.learning4liferesources.com/hollandcodes/Discover_Careers_that_Fit_You.pdf.

Massachusetts Department of Elementary and Secondary Education. "Massachusetts Comprehensive Assessment System Test Questions." http://www.doe.mass.edu/mcas/testitems.html.

My Plan.com. http://www.myplan.com/.

New York State Department of Labor. CareerZone. https://www.careerzone.ny.gov/.

New York State Library. "New York State Regents Exams." New York State Library (2010), http://www.nysl.nysed.gov/regentsexams.htm.

NOVA Youth Employment. Youth@Work. http://www.youthatwork.org/.

Oswego City School District. Regents Exam Test Prep Center. http://regentsprep.org/.

Ott, Valerie. *Teen Programs with Punch: A Month-by-Month Guide.* Westport, CT: Libraries Unlimited, 2006.

Perper, Kate, Kristen Peterson, and Jennifer Manlove. "Diploma Attainment among Teen Mothers." *Child Trends* (January 2010), http://www.childtrends.org/Files//Child_Trends-2010_01_22_FS_DiplomaAttainment.pdf.

Pervola, Cindy, and Debby Hobgood. *How to Get a Job If You're a Teenager.* 2nd ed. Fort Atkinson, WI: Alleyside Press, 2000.

Quintessential Careers. "Job and Career Resources for Teenagers" (2010), http://www.quintcareers.com/teen_jobs.html.

RWM Vocational Schools Database (2010), http://www.rwm.org/rwm/.

SnagAJob.com (2010), http://www.snagajob.com/.

Teens' Guide to College and Career Planning: Your High School Road Map to College and Career Success. Lawrenceville, NJ: Peterson's, 2008.

U.S. Department of Education. "Student Aid on the Web" (2010), http://studentaid.ed.gov/PORTALSWebApp/students/english/index.jsp.

U.S. Department of Labor. Employment and Training Administration. CareerOneStop (2010), http://www.careeronestop.org/.

U.S. Department of Labor. Employment and Training Administration. Youth Rules. http://youthrules.dol.gov.

U.S. Equal Employment Opportunity Commission. Youth at Work. http://www.eeoc.gov/youth/.

Youth Employment Institute (2010), http://www.yei.org/index.htm.

Financial Literacy

Jump$tart Coalition for Personal Financial Literacy. http://www.jumpstart.org.

MoneySKILL. www.moneyskill.org.

Ott, Valerie. *Teen Programs with Punch: A Month-by-Month Guide.* Westport, CT: Libraries Unlimited, 2006.

Parents as Teachers National Center, Inc. *Money Matters: A Young Parent's Workbook for Finances—and the Future.* St. Louis, MO: Parents as Teachers National Center, Inc., 2007.

Project Read, San Francisco Public Library. Project Money. http://www.projectmoney.org/index.html.

Health

Advocates for Youth. http://www.advocatesforyouth.org/.

American Academy of Family Physicians. Family Doctor.org. http://familydoctor.org/online/famdocen/home.html.

Anderson, B., K. A. Cruz, and B. K. Popper. *Bright Futures Family Pocket Guide: Raising Healthy Infants, Children, and Adolescents.* Boston: Family Voices, 2000. http://www.brightfuturesforfamilies.org/pdf_toc.shtml.

Californians for Patient Care. http://www.calpatientcare.org/.

Children's Hospital Boston. Center for Young Women's Health: Health Information for Teen Girls around the World. http://youngwomenshealth.org/.

Children's Hospital Boston. Young Men's Health: Health Information for Young Men around the World. http://youngmenshealthsite.org/.

Columbia University Health Services. Go Ask Alice: Columbia University's Health QandA Internet Service. http://www.goaskalice.columbia.edu/.

First 5 California. http://www.ccfc.ca.gov/.

Healthy Teen Network. http://www.healthyteennetwork.org/.

Kaiser Family Foundation. "Generation Rx.com: How Young People Use the Internet for Health Information." (2001). http://www.kff.org/entmedia/loader.cfm?url=/commonspot/security/getfile.cfm&PageID=13719.

Kaiser Family Foundation. "Generation M2: Media in the Lives of 8- to 18-Year-Olds" (January 2010), http://www.kff.org/entmedia/8010.cfm.

Medical Library Association. Consumer and Patient Health Information Section (CAPHIS). "Top 100 List: Health Websites You Can Trust." http://caphis.mlanet.org/consumer/index.html.

MedlinePlus. "MedlinePlus Guide to Healthy Web Surfing." http://www.nlm.nih.gov/medlineplus/healthywebsurfing.html. Also in Spanish: "Guía de MedlinePlus para una búsqueda saludable en Internet." http://www.nlm.nih.gov/medlineplus/spanish/healthywebsurfing.html.

MTV and the Henry J. Kaiser Family Foundation. It's Your (Sex) Life. http://www.itsyoursexlife.com/.

National Campaign to Prevent Teen and Unplanned Pregnancy. Stay Teen.org. http://www.stayteen.org/default.aspx.
    A dynamite website with videos and writings contributed by teens and a sensible and accessible message.

National Center for Complementary and Alternative Medicine. National Institutes of Health. "Evaluating Web-Based Health Resources." http://nccam.nih.gov/health/webresources/.

Nemours Foundation. Kids Health. http://kidshealth.org/.

Planned Parenthood. Teen Talk. http://www.plannedparenthood.org/teen-talk/.

Scarleteen: Sex Ed for the Real World. http://www.scarleteen.com/.
    Frank answers to the questions everyone wants to ask but feels too embarrassed to mention.

Teen Growth.com. http://www.teengrowth.com/.

TeenHealthFX. http://www.teenhealthfx.com/index.php.

Vargas, Karen. "Teenagers, Health, and the Internet: How Information Professionals Can Reach Out to Teens and Their Health Information Needs," *Journal of Consumer Health on the Internet* 9, no. 3 (2005): 15–68.

Parenting

Babyzone. "Amazing Toys." Babyzone (2009), http://www.babyzone.com/shopping/toys_games/amazing-toy-awards.

Birckmayer, Jennifer, Katherine Mabb, Bonnie-Jo Westendorf, and Jerridith Wilson. "Teens as Parents of Babies and Toddlers." Ithaca, NY: Cornell Cooperative Extension, 1997. http://hdl.handle.net/1813/3811.

Blumenthal, Deborah. *The Chocolate-Covered-Cookie Tantrum.* New York: Clarion Books, 1996.

Committee on Public Education. American Academy of Pediatrics. "Policy Statement: Children, Adolescents, and Television." *Pediatrics* 107, no. 2 (2001): 423–426. http://aappolicy.aappublications. org/cgi/reprint/pediatrics;107/2/423.pdf.

Commonsense Media. "TV, Computers, and Movies: What's Really Okay for Young Children" (n.d.), http://www.commonsensemedia.org/sites/default/files/CSM_ECEbrochure.pdf.

Commonsense Media. "Common Sense on Baby Media" (n.d.), http://www.commonsensemedia.org/sites/default/files/pdf/Tip-Baby.pdf.

Cox, Meg. *The Book of New Family Traditions: How to Create Great Rituals for Holidays and Everyday.* Philadelphia: Running Press, 2003.

Curtis, Jane. *P.A.R.E.N.T.S. Parental Adults: Reading, Encouraging, Nurturing, Teaching, Supporting.* Sacramento, CA: California State Library Foundation, 2005. http://libraryliteracy.org/learners/parents_guide/.

Disney Family Fun. http://familyfun.go.com/.

Dr. Toy.com. http://www.drtoy.com/main/index.html.
> Dr. Toy, Stevanne Auerbach, PhD, trained in child psychology, education, special education, and child development, is one of the nation's leading experts on children's play and toys. Her toy recommendations are evaluated for their educational value, developmental suitability, and skill building.

Family Education. "Your Child 0 to 6." http://life.familyeducation.com/parenting-toddlers-babies/early-learning/42858.html.

Fathering: What It Means to Be a Dad, DVD (Owatonna, MN: Learning ZoneXpress, 2009).

FirstTeacherTLC.com. "Family TLC." http://familytlc.net/index.html.

Fleming, Denise. *The Everything Book.* New York: Henry Holt, 2000.

Gavin, Mary. "How TV Affects Your Child." KidsHealth (2008), http://kidshealth.org/parent/positive/family/tv_affects_child.html?tracking=P_RelatedArticle.

How I Learn, DVD (Owatonna, MN: Learning ZoneXpress, 2006).

Jalongo, Mary Renck. "Stories That Teach Life Lessons." *Scholastic Parent and Child.* (2010), http://www2.scholastic.com/browse/article.jsp?id=1495.

Just In Time Parenting. http://www.parentinginfo.org/.

Kaiser Family Foundation. "The Media Family: Electronic Media in the Lives of Infants, Toddlers, Preschoolers and Their Parents" (2006), http://www.kff.org/entmedia/7500.cfm.

Kids Healthworks. *Baby's First Year. Vol. 1, Pregnancy and Preparing for Baby,* DVD (United States: Information Television Network, 2007).

King County Library System. "Books to Grow On." King County Library System (2010), http://www.kcls.org/bookstogrowon/#menu.

Lang, Virginia, and Louise Nayer. *How to Bury a Goldfish: And Other Ceremonies and Celebrations for Everyday Life.* Boston: Skinner House Books, 2007.

Lima, Carolyn, and Rebecca Thomas. *A to Zoo: Subject Access to Children's Picture Books.* Santa Barbara, CA: Libraries Unlimited, 2010.

Lithgow, John. *A Lithgow Palooza! 101 Ways to Entertain and Inspire Your Kids.* New York: Simon and Schuster, 2004.

London, Jonathan. *Wiggle Waggle.* San Diego: Red Wagon Books, 2002.

McClellan, Debbie, ed. "Creating Memories: Connecting the Generations." Parenting 24/7. University of Illinois Extension (2008), http://parenting247.org/article.cfm?contentid=689&agegroup=3.

Motheread, Inc. "Literacy Changes Lives—Motheread® Changes Literacy" (2010), http://www.motheread.org/.

Murkoff, Heidi, and Sharon Mazel. *What to Expect When You're Expecting.* 4th ed. New York: Workman Publishers, 2008.

Nemours Foundation. KidsHealth. http://kidshealth.org/.
> This website presents information on physical, emotional, and behavioral issues that affect children and teens. Each of three audiences (parents, children, and teenagers) has its own area of the website, which is tailored to that group's age level and needs.

Oppenheim Toy Portfolio (2010), http://www.toyportfolio.com/.
> A consumer review of children's media, including books, toys, video, and audio, by mother-daughter child development experts Joanne and Stephanie Oppenheim. They write about the good, the bad, and the ugly in toyland.

Parents' Choice: Children's Media and Toy Reviews. http://www.parents-choice.org/.

Parents' Choice. "Best 25 Toys of 25 Years" (2010), http://www.parents-choice.org/article.cfm?art_id=347&the_page=editorials.

Parents' Choice. "Media Management Tips" (2010), http://www.parents-choice.org/article.cfm?art_id=255andthe_page=consider_this.

Public Broadcasting Service. PBS Kids (2010), http://www.pbs.org/parents/.

Rosenthal, Amy Krouse. *Christmas Cookies: Bite-Size Holiday Lessons*. New York: HarperCollins, 2008.

Roufberg, Ruth. "Classic Toys." Parents' Choice (n.d.), http://www.parents-choice.org/article.cfm?art_id=137andthe_page=editorials.

University of Illinois Extension. Parenting 24/7 (2008), http://parenting247.org.

University of Wisconsin-Extension. Parenting Newsletters. http://parenting.uwex.edu/.

Van Allsburg, Chris. *The Polar Express*. Boston: Houghton Mifflin, 1985.

Zero to Three: National Center for Infants, Toddlers, and Families. http://www.zerotothree.org/.

Zero to Three. "Television and the Under 3 Crowd" (2009), http://main.zerotothree.org/site/Doc Server/media_-_recommendations.pdf?docID=10321&AddInterest=1503.

RESOURCES

Teen Programming

Honnold, RoseMary. *101+ Teen Programs That Work*. New York: Neal-Schuman, 2003.

Lillian, Jenine, ed. *Cool Teen Programs for Under $100*. Chicago: American Library Association, 2009.

Financial Literacy

Idaho Department of Health and Welfare. "Baby Budget." Life in the Fast Lane. http://www.teenageparent.org/english/costofbaby2B.html.
    A quiz-format exposition of the costs parents incur during their baby's first year.

Pollock, S. *Will the Dollars Stretch? Teen Parents Living on Their Own*. Buena Park, CA: Morning Glory Press, 2001.

Health

Hoffman, Saul. "By the Numbers: the Public Costs of Teen Childbearing." Washington, DC: The National Campaign to Prevent Teen Pregnancy, 2006 http://www.thenationalcampaign.org/resources/pdf/pubs/BTN_Full.pdf.

Medical Library Association. "A User's Guide to Finding and Evaluating Health Information on the Web." http://www.mlanet.org/resources/userguide.html.

MedlinePlus. "Children's Health." http://www.nlm.nih.gov/medlineplus/childrenshealth.html.

Parenting

American Academy of Pediatrics. *Healthy Children*. http://www.healthychildren.org/.

De Atires, Julia Reguero. "Exploring Diversity through Family Traditions." *Scholastic Parent and Child* 9, no. 3 (November 2001): 44–50.

Appendix

Library Interest Survey   Date _____

1. Do you have a library card?   ☐ Yes ☐ No

2. Do you ever go the library in your free time?   ☐ Yes ☐ No

3. Do you have a computer that you can use at home whenever you need to?

☐ Yes   ☐ No

   Is it connected to the Internet?   ☐ Yes ☐ No

4. How old is your child?   ☐ 0-12 months   ☐ 12-18 months   ☐ 18-24 months

☐ 2-3 years   ☐ 3 years or older

5. Interest Topics about Children (Check as many as you want)

☐ Learning games to play with your child   ☐ How to discipline

☐ Being a better parent

☐ How to find good child care and preschools   ☐ How children learn

☐ How to read to your child   ☐ Toilet training

☐ Books that your child will like   ☐ Songs to sing to your child

☐ Healthy eating and foods for children

☐ Free or inexpensive fun places to go with your child

☐ Your suggestions _____

_____

6. Topics for You (Check as many as you want)

☐ Career advice- choosing a career, looking for jobs, writing a resume, or interviewing
   for a job

☐ Crafts- making things for you and your child

☐ Suggestions for books to read for fun

☐ Taking care of yourself- health and beauty

☐ Finding what you want on the Internet

☐ Finding what you want at the library- books, music, movies

☐ Your suggestions _____

_____

Reproducible Library Needs Survey. (Ellin Klor)

Library Scavenger Hunt

Rules

You can work together on this. Look for the answers as we tour the library. Complete both sides. Please be respectful of others in the library.

1. Throughout the building there are signs that say "free2 . . ." List what 3 of these signs say.

2. How many water fountains are there in the library? (Hint: keep track on the tour.)

3. Name the art pieces ON the walls on the "boulevard" on the first floor. (Hint: there are four.)

4. How many computers are there in the Technology Center?

5. What are the 2 ways that you can check out books?

6. True or False: You will find Fiction books shelved by their titles first.

7. Name 4 book characters displayed in the Children's area.

8. If you wanted to read a simple book about something, where would you find one?

9. Besides reading a children's book, list 3 other ways that you can experience it.

10. Name two book titles pictured on the quilt in the children's area.

11. Where do you find the cardboard books for young children?

12. What is written on the steps of the children's garden?

13. What is the name of the Teen Services Librarian?

14. Name the people featured in the "Read" posters in Teen Central.

15. Which of the following can you find in the teen area?
    a. Manga   b. Anime DVDs   c. Fashion Magazines   d. Books on CD

16. Who wrote the teen book "Twilight"?

17. Name 3 things that you can buy to drink in the library café.

18. How many total adult magazines start with the letter "B"? Name two of them:

19. Finish this quote that is located in the Adult New Reader collection.

    "Teach an adult to read. You'll _____

    _____."

20. Find the call number for one of these: _____ GED test exams

    _____ Cookbooks _____ Parenting books

21. What the newest volume of the Chilton Auto Repair Guides in the reference books? (Hint: the call # is Ref 629.2)

22. Name 3 items that the library has by or starring Beyonce. (Hint: try a keyword search.)

A sample library scavenger hunt from the Santa Clara City Library. Adapted with permission from the original written by SCCL Teen Librarian Nan Choi. (Nan Choi)

Discover Careers That Fit You

INFOSERIES
IS-50

A career is an enjoyable job that challenges you. To find careers that fit you, you need to know what you like to do, what you're good at and what you want to achieve. Once you know your interests, abilities and goals, you can match them with career possibilities.

IDENTIFY YOUR INTERESTS
Dr. John Holland created a system of placing people's interests into groups. He believed every person's interests fit into at least one group and most fit into two or three groups. Your personal combination of Holland groups is your Holland Code.

To begin discovering careers that match your interests, **find your Holland Code by completing the Career Interest Checklist on page 2.** More in-depth interest inventories are available on the ICPAC Web site at http://icpac.indiana.edu.

FIND CAREERS THAT MATCH
Using your Holland Code, you can explore a variety of work options. **Look on page 3 for lists of careers that match your Holland Code groups.** Circle careers that interest you, and write down any career ideas you have that are not listed.

To learn more about these jobs, **request free career profiles** from ICPAC at http://icpac.indiana.edu. Profiles include information on salary, work environment, skills needed and other aspects of careers.

KNOW YOUR ABILITIES
As you explore careers, consider your abilities as well as your interests. You want to choose a career you will enjoy *and* excel in.

You have already learned many skills, and you will learn more for your career:

* **self-management skills,** or personal qualities, such as getting along with others and managing your time.

* **transferable skills** that can be used in many different careers; for example, the ability to write well and speak clearly are required by most careers.

* **specialized skills** which are learned for specific careers; nurses, for example, learn how to give medications.

Assess the skills you have
Think about your hobbies, jobs and school activities. Identify the abilities you gained from these experiences by listing your activities on a sheet of paper. Next to each activity, write all of the skills you learned and used. The list on the right may help you.

Determine the skills you need
On another sheet of paper, list the skills you will need for each of the careers that interest you. Use career profiles to help you find this information. Consider self-management and transferable and specialized skills. Next to the skills required for each career:

* check the skills you already have.

* circle the skills you need to improve or learn.

* make a plan for developing the skills you will need.

*Skills you need
for careers*

Assess the skills you have – and determine the skills you need – to find careers that match your abilities. You may have already learned to:

* manage time

* evaluate information

* make good decisions

* be reliable

* communicate well

* be accurate

* be efficient

* understand quickly

* be organized

* be enthusiastic

* motivate people

* be flexible

* analyze data

* solve problems

* write clearly

icpac.

Indiana Career
and Postsecondary
Advancement Center

**Take charge
of your future.™**   Hotline: 800.992.2076 • Web site: http://icpac.indiana.edu

CAREER INTEREST CHECKLIST*

Check mark any of the activities that might be enjoyable or interesting to you. In general, marking more activities provides more useful results.

1. ❏ Typing reports or entering data
2. ❏ Leading group activities
3. ❏ Reading art and music magazines
4. ❏ Carpentry and other building projects
5. ❏ Using a chemistry set
6. ❏ Making new friends

1. ❏ Keeping detailed records
2. ❏ Working on a sales campaign
3. ❏ Designing clothes
4. ❏ Decorating rooms
5. ❏ Doing puzzles or playing word games
6. ❏ Going to church

1. ❏ Word processing
2. ❏ Talking to salespeople
3. ❏ Acting in or helping to put on a play
4. ❏ Working with animals
5. ❏ Advanced math
6. ❏ Helping the elderly

1. ❏ Working nine to five
2. ❏ Being elected class president
3. ❏ Learning foreign languages
4. ❏ Cooking
5. ❏ Physics
6. ❏ Attending sports events

1. ❏ Using a cash register
2. ❏ Talking to groups of people
3. ❏ Drawing or painting
4. ❏ Fixing cars
5. ❏ Astronomy
6. ❏ Belonging to a club

1. ❏ Using office equipment
2. ❏ Buying clothes for a store
3. ❏ Writing stories or poetry
4. ❏ Fixing electrical appliances or repairing household items
5. ❏ Flying airplanes or learning about aircraft
6. ❏ Teaching children

1. ❏ Filing letters and reports
2. ❏ Talking to people at a party
3. ❏ Going to concerts or listening to music
4. ❏ Wildlife biology
5. ❏ Creating a project for a science fair
6. ❏ Studying people in other lands

1. ❏ Working with a budget and preparing financial reports
2. ❏ Selling insurance
3. ❏ Playing music
4. ❏ Putting together model kits or craft projects
5. ❏ Working in a lab
6. ❏ Helping people solve personal problems

Add up your interests to find your Holland Code

Count all the number 1s you've checked; put that total on the line in the circle marked "1s=C". Repeat this for numbers 2 through 6. Notice, each number corresponds with a letter. Write the letters of your three highest numbers in the "Holland Code" box below.

1s = C ____   **2s = E** ____   **3s = A** ____   **4s = R** ____   **5s = I** ____   **6s = S** ____

THIS IS YOUR HOLLAND CODE

Learn about your Holland groups and careers that match

Match the letters in your Holland Code to the first letters in the Holland groups listed on the right. For example, SAR matches the Social, Artistic and Realistic groups. Now, turn to page 3 and use your code to find careers that match your interests.

Holland Code Groups

Conventional people like to work with data, have clerical or numerical ability and attend to detail. They usually enjoy following other people's instructions.

Investigative people like to observe, investigate, learn, analyze, evaluate or solve problems.

Artistic people have artistic, innovative or intuitive abilities. They usually like to work in an unstructured situation, using their imagination or creativity.

Social people like to work with people. They like to inform, enlighten, help, train, develop or cure people. They may also be skilled with using language and words.

Enterprising people also like to work with people, but they like to influence, persuade or perform. They like to lead or manage for organizational goals or economic gain.

Realistic people have athletic or mechanical ability. They prefer to work with objects, machines, tools, plants or animals. They usually like to work outdoors.

*Adapted from Knowing Your Holland Code, Utah State Occupational Information Coordinating Committee, Form #71994

Conventional
- Accountant/Auditor
- Bank Teller
- Bookkeeper
- Broadcast Tech.
- Computer Operator
- Court Reporter
- Credit/Loan Clerk
- Dispatcher
- Electronics Assembler
- Expeditor/Production Controller
- General Office Clerk
- Legal Assistant
- Library Assistant
- Medical Record Tech.
- Payroll Clerk
- Postal Clerk
- Proofreader
- Receptionist
- Secretary
- Tax Preparer
- Transcriptionist
- Underwriter
- Webmaster

Artistic
- Actor
- Advertising Agent
- Architect
- Archivist and Curator
- Artist
- Choreographer
- Commercial Artist
- Composer
- Director
- Fashion Designer
- Graphic Artist
- Industrial Designer
- Interior Designer
- Landscape Architect
- Musician

- Merchandise Displayer
- Photographer

Investigative
- Actuary
- Agricultural Scientist
- Anthropologist
- Biological Scientist
- Chemist
- Chiropractor
- Computer Programmer
- Dentist
- Drafter
- Economist
- Engineer
- Geologist
- Hazardous Materials Technician
- Market Research Analyst
- Meteorologist
- Nurse Practitioner
- Optometrist
- Pharmacist
- Physician
- Psychologist
- Speech Pathologist
- Statistician
- Surgical Technician
- Systems Analyst
- Veterinarian

Social
- Air Traffic Controller
- Athletic Trainer
- Clergy
- Cosmetologist
- Counselor
- Dental Hygienist
- Dietician
- Elementary/Middle/ High School Teacher

- Health Administrator
- Historian
- Home Health Aide
- Law Enforcement Officer
- Librarian
- Loan Officer
- Mail Carrier
- Medical Assistant
- Nurse
- Personnel Manager
- Physical Therapist
- Podiatrist
- Radio/TV Broadcaster
- Radiologic Technician
- Recreation Guide
- Respiratory Therapist
- Social Worker

Enterprising
- Auto Salesperson
- Brokerage Clerk
- Business Executive/ Manager
- Chef/Dinner Cook
- Compliance Officer
- Customer Service Rep.
- Database Administrator
- Detective/Investigator
- Emergency Med. Tech.
- Financial Manager
- Flight Attendant
- Funeral Director
- Hotel/Motel Manager
- Insurance Agent
- Interpreter/Translator
- Lawyer
- Legislator
- Marketing/Public Relations Manager
- Occupational Therapist

- Park Ranger
- Real Estate Agent
- Reporter
- Restaurant Manager
- Security Guard
- Travel Agent
- Urban Planner
- Writer or Editor

Realistic
- Aircraft Mechanic
- Appraiser
- Auto Mechanic
- Bricklayer
- Building Maintenance
- Carpenter
- Computer Repairer
- Construction Manager/ Laborer
- Dental Lab Technician
- Electrician
- Engineering Tech.
- Farmer or Rancher
- Firefighter
- Fish/Game Warden
- Floral Designer
- Groundskeeper
- Heating/Cooling Mech.
- Jeweler
- Machinist
- Mechanical Engineer
- Office Machine Repairer
- Optician
- Pilot/Flight Engineer
- Plumber/Pipefitter
- Robotics Technician
- Sound Engineer
- Truck Driver
- Welder
- Zookeeper

More career options

To find additional careers in your Holland Code groups, **use ICPAC's web site at http:// icpac.indiana.edu** or call ICPAC at 800-992-2076.

PRIORITIZE YOUR GOALS

To help you choose a career, **consider what you want from your work** as well as your interests and abilities. Do you want a career where you earn lots of money? Do you want to have many responsibilities? The exercise below will help you discover what is most important to you in a career.

Read the 10 items that follow. Write a 1 next to the career goal that is most important to you. Then use numbers 2 through 10 to rank the remaining goals.

___ **EARNINGS**
how much the career pays

___ **SERVICE**
how much you help others

___ **PRESTIGE**
how much people respect your work

___ **GEOGRAPHY**
how important it is to live in a particular place

___ **INDEPENDENCE**
how much you are your own boss

___ **SECURITY**
how much the career promises long-term, stable employment.

___ **RESPONSIBILITY**
how much people depend on you

___ **TEAMWORK**
how much you will work as a member of a group

___ **ENVIRONMENT**
where most of the job will take place (outdoors, indoors, or both)

___ **VARIETY**
how much the job will have you doing different kinds of tasks

After you prioritize your goals, ask yourself the following questions:

* Which goals are most important to you? Why?
* Which goals are not as important to you? Why?
* What additional goals do you have for your career?

Use career profiles you requested from ICPAC to see how well each career meets your goals. You may want to make a list of the careers you are considering and note how each career will meet your various goals.

LEARN MORE ON CAREERS

New careers are emerging all the time, so you will want to keep exploring your options. As you discover careers that fit your interests, abilities and goals, find out more about them:

* **ask your guidance counselor about resources, like books and computer programs,** to explore careers more in depth; your counselor can also help you plan your education to prepare for careers.

* **use reference materials at public libraries** such as the *Occupational Outlook Handbook* and the *Dictionary of Occupational Titles*, which include information on jobs for the future.

* **talk with your parents and friends' parents about their work experiences;** ask them what they do in their jobs and how they chose their careers.

* **visit workplaces and meet people in careers that interest you;** you can take a tour of a company, conduct an informational interview, volunteer or job shadow.

Additional resources

To learn more about your career options and the skills you need to succeed, **contact ICPAC at 800-992-2076 or http://icpac.indiana.edu.** Ask for free copies of:

* Core 40 Booklet

* IS-41: Is the Military an Option for You?

* IS-42: All About Apprenticeships

* IS-46: Job Outlook Information – Careers for the Future

* IS-65: Career Areas to Explore and Jobs in Them

* IS-74: Job Shadowing, Internships and More Ways to Experience Careers

* IS-82: Success on the Job – Skills Wanted by Employers

IS-50 • 01/25/00 • LSM

Family Media Questionnaire

Select the answer that you agree with:

1. Your child will learn the most by doing which of the following activities?

    a. watching educational TV for an hour

    b. reading a book and playing with you

    c. sleeping

2. At what age is it OK for your child to have a TV or computer in their room?

    a. 0-2 years

    b. 3-6 years

    c. 6-9 years

    d. 10 years or older

    e. never

3. Children do better in school if they . . .

    a. copy characters they see on TV.

    b. watch TV before they go to bed.

    c. play games with their families.

Circle yes or no:

1. Is it OK to have the TV on . . .

    a. while you are eating?   Y   N

    b. when no one is watching it?   Y   N

2. Is it OK for a child . . .

    a. to be frightened by a TV show?   Y   N

    b. to watch TV at daycare?   Y   N

    c. to want something that they see on TV?   Y   N

    d. to turn on the TV without asking you?   Y   N

3. Is it OK for you . . .

    a. to talk about what's going on in the TV show while you're watching it?   Y   N

    b. to set rules about how much TV your child can watch?   Y   N

Reproducible Family Media Questionnaire. (Ellin Klor)

6

THE POWER OF PLAY:
TEEN PARENTS AND
THE LIBRARY

We have shown that the library can be a great informational resource for teen parents. In chapter 5 we discussed how to design and lead programs that provide teen parents with knowledge and skills to help them grow as individuals and as parents. It is also critical to recognize the library as a recreational resource and understand how this role can both enhance the quality of life for teen parents and attract them to become library users. Research demonstrates the power of play and how it helps to shape the brain, balance emotions, and enhance competencies for both children and adults (Brown 2009). Play, though it may be defined differently for different people, is inherently pleasurable, brings joy, reduces stress, and inspires learning and productivity. For the teen parent who faces the daily challenges associated with being a young mother or father, a library recreational program may be the only time she or he enjoys a few moments of peace. Additionally, many young parents may not have experienced the delights of innocence and play as a child. From crafts to storytelling to readers' advisory, the library can provide opportunities for teen parents to stimulate their imagination, explore new activities, and find balance through play.

CRAFTS

Creating something unique and special with their own hands can give teens satisfaction, pride, confidence, and a sense of accomplishment. Teen parents, many of whom live stressful lives, can especially benefit from and enjoy the act of artistic expression. Crafting, which experienced a downturn in popularity in the 1980s and1990s, is experiencing a cyclical renaissance, as evidenced by the popularity of scrapbooking, knitting, and the DIY (do-it-yourself) culture. The act of creating a finished product together is a shared experience that helps library staff connect with teen parents and encourage creativity and fun for all participants.

Often teen parents have had minimal crafting experience. Some may be hesitant to try creating something, worrying that the results will not be perfect and that they may be embarrassed in front of their peers. Over time, as they try multiple craft activities, and enjoy the results, they will relax and take more risks with their projects. In particular, they will come to enjoy the opportunity to make something that is a unique expression of who they are—made in their favorite color, with a design of their own choosing, or personalized just for them. Self-realization and its expression are basics precepts of teen development.

Guidelines and Tips for Craft Projects

Even if you, as the group facilitator, have minimal craft experience, this type of programming can be a fun, safe way to learn something new together with your patrons. Here are a few guidelines to consider when preparing for a craft-based project.

Determining Skill and Interest Level

Many teen parents have had limited experience using fine motor skills and will find intricate cutting or crafting projects too challenging. Search elementary-school-level craft books and websites for ideas. Look for simple, but not "childish" crafts, like yarn pom-poms, those fluffy, wooly puff balls that make fun toys or that decorate accessories or hair ornaments. Gauge your group's abilities, especially the participants' capacity to focus, and plan accordingly. After one or two craft sessions you will also be able to gauge the level of assistance from staff that the teens seem to need. Keep that in mind when deciding on future projects. Some groups may do best with one-on-one or small-group instruction.

Being Creative

Try not to use pre-assembled kits, foam craft sheets, or lots of poorly made plastic elements. These types of projects and materials limit creativity and individuality, and the finished product is often of low quality. Using higher-quality materials makes for finished products that will last for years and become cherished treasures. *Quality* materials does not have to mean *expensive* materials. A wooden clothespin doll made with an acorn-cap hat, pipe-cleaner arms, and felt clothes costs less than one dollar, but each will be a unique expression of its maker.

Compiling Project Directions

Made much easier by the Internet, locating directions for a project from several sources will enable you to work out the best ideas to make the simplest and most attractive product. For example, the directions for how to make a fleece scarf (below) were merged from three sets of instructions to best meet the needs of a specific teen parent group and the participants' abilities. Comparing different versions of a project also can make it possible to utilize less expensive materials and simplify the process.

The "Family Crafts" section of About.com makes locating craft projects easier than you might expect (Osbourn 2010). It offers search capability by age, theme, or craft material (use the latter when you have an abundance of something, such as Popsicle sticks, leftover from a previous project). Other quick sources for ideas are the books from Klutz Press. They offer attractive but simple projects that tend to be a good match for a teen parent's skill level, while still offering the chance for creativity. The books include consumable supplies to get you started, which can easily be replenished from a local craft supply store or by ordering from the Klutz Press website. (It is easy to buy just one book, and augment the supplies for an entire group.) Suggested titles include:

- *Handmade Cards: Simple Designs for Beautiful Cards* (A. Johnson 2002)
- *Make Your Own Paper Flowers* (Editors of Chicken Socks 2007)
- *Natural Beauty Book: Create Your Own Natural Spa Experience* (Johnson 2009)
- *Painted Rocks* (Editors of Klutz 2000)
- *Pipe Cleaners Gone Crazy: A Complete Guide to Bending Fuzzy Sticks* (Torres and Sherman 1997)

Time Constraints

Make sure that the group can finish the project in the allotted time, especially with crafts that involve a multistep process. Teen parents may not be able to attend a program for a second day, leaving them with an unfinished project, if time constraints have not been considered. Decide how the craft project is to be integrated into the program session. Will it be the main activity that takes up the majority of the time? Or will it be one of a series of activities? For example, consider the following agenda for a main activity "Fleece Scarf Craft" Program (one and a half to two hours):

1. Welcome the group and include a brief presentation of upcoming library events of interest.
2. Introduce the craft activity, including an explanation of project steps and demonstration.
3. Work on the project.
4. Close the activity with a snack, a display of completed scarves, and a discussion of feedback on the project.

As an alternative, when planning a multiple-activity program, consider the following example agenda of a "Making Storytime Toys" Program (30 to 40 minutes):

1. Welcome the group and explain what will happen during the program: first, parents will create simple toys to use in a storytime, and then parents will engage in a storytime with their children using the new toys will follow.
2. Introduce and demonstrate the projects; go over directions on how to, for example, make string spiders and glitter pipe-cleaner stars. Connect the project with singing "The Itsy-Bitsy Spider" and "Twinkle, Twinkle, Little Star."
3. Hold a storytime with the children, incorporating the songs and use of the new toys.

Facility Logistics

It is important to take into consideration the materials that will be used during the project and how your facility impacts the project's implementation. Will activities like painting, vegetable stamping, and tie-dyeing lead to spilled materials on a new carpet? Should you bring a plastic sheet to put on the floor? Will there be enough workspace or tables? Where are the electrical outlets (if you are using a glue gun, you may need an extension cord so it will reach to the working space). Will you need, and do you have, a place to put projects to dry?

Material Costs

Assume that you will need to provide all necessary materials. For both logistical and financial reasons, it is not realistic to plan on teen parents bringing their own supplies (for example, a T-shirt or bag to decorate). Depending on your budget or ability to secure donations, some crafts that would be popular, such as jewelry-making or T-shirt decorating, may be prohibitively expensive when purchasing materials for a group of 10 to 20 participants. Try to use inexpensive household and recycled materials as much as possible. This sends the message to the teen parents that you do not have to spend a lot of money to do these projects, that repurposed materials can be made into something attractive, and that these types of crafts can be done at home.

Staff Preparation Time

It is important to get an idea of the total time required to allow for the group's participation in an activity. What amount of staff time will be needed to purchase and prepare materials? How long will it take to make a sample or experiment to make a project workable for your group? How much time should be allotted for setup and cleanup before and after the program? Lack of preparation can make an entire presentation frustrating for the staff member and for the participants, who may be asked to complete a task in an unrealistic time frame.

Making a Sample Project

Teens will gain a better understanding of what to do if they watch a demonstration; it is helpful to have examples in various stages of completion for a multistep craft project in order to effectively demonstrate expectations and directions. While providing a handout to reinforce learning from printed resources can be beneficial, many teen parents may struggle to follow written instructions. Giving them clear instructions and modeling how to do each step enables the teen parents to feel confident enough to be creative with their projects. Whether it's a craft, recipe, or book, making a sample beforehand also ensures that the instructions you are using are clear and accurate. Do this step early in your planning process to avoid a room full of frustrated and confused teens!

A Sampler of Craft Projects

Potpourri Sachets

Supplies:

- dried spices, herbs, or flowers
- cinnamon chips, cloves, dried orange peel, lavender, rose petals (These can be purchased at a bulk herb supply company, craft store, or restaurant supply. Or they can be ordered from the San Francisco Herb Company website or via phone at 1-800-227-4530.)
- cotton fabric remnants at least 8 inches square
- narrow (⅛-inch to ¼-inch) satin ribbon (about 12 inches for each sachet)

Tools:

- pinking shears or pairs of fabric scissors
- measuring spoons
- scissors to cut ribbon
- 8-inch paper plates to use as cutting templates
- pencils or chalk to trace circles on fabric
- small bowls for mixing herbs, spices, etc.
- large bowls to hold herbs and spices before mixing together (optional)

Instructions:

1. In a small bowl, combine a mixture of the herbs, spices, and flowers to make a pleasing aromatic combination.
2. With a pencil, narrow marker, or chalk, trace the outline of the paper plate on the fabric.
3. Cut out the circle using pinking shears or a pair of fabric scissors. Put the fabric on the table with the wrong side of the fabric facing up.
4. Put about two to three tablespoons of your potpourri mixture in the center of your fabric circle.
5. Gather the edges of the fabric together to form a ball around the potpourri, and wrap and tie them tightly with a piece of ribbon.
6. Use sachets to scent clothing drawers, purse, car, or diaper bag. Babies can sniff them, but do not let them play with a sachet or put it in their mouth.

Yarn Pom-poms

(Note: This can be a time-consuming project if you are making a pom-pom three inches or larger. Allow one to one and a half hours.)

Supplies:

- inexpensive wool or acrylic medium-weight yarn in several fun colors (Ask your teen parent group what colors they like.)

- rigid cardboard (heavier than poster board, but not impossible to cut with a pair of scissors—cereal-box cardboard will work); bring enough to cut two 3-inch circles per person

Tools:

- several pairs of scissors heavy enough to cut cardboard and yarn (less than one per person is okay; people can share)
- pencils or pens for tracing on cardboard
- 2-½-inch to 3-inch diameter circle pattern (to trace onto cardboard)
- ½-inch diameter circle pattern to trace onto cardboard (Note: Plastic pom-pom patterns can be purchased at knitting and craft stores. One could be purchased as a template for making your own cardboard patterns.)

Instructions:

1. Trace two of the large circles (2-½-inch to 3-inch) onto the rigid cardboard for each person. Cut them out (this can also be done in advance, if desired).
2. Trace and cut the smaller circle out of the exact center of each large circle, so they look like doughnuts (this can be done in advance, if desired).
3. Cut several long lengths (two to three yards each) of yarn; they can be all the same or multiple colors.
4. Sandwich the two doughnut circles together. Hold one end of the yarn flat facing the outside edge of the cardboard circle, and start wrapping the yarn around the doughnut shape going through the hole in the middle. Continue wrapping lengths of yarn all around the doughnut *until the center hole is completely filled*, always starting with the ends facing the outside edge.
5. Turn the wrapped circle on edge, and use a pair of scissors to start clipping the yarn in line with the edge of the cardboard circle. Eventually you will cut down far enough to be able to clip between the two circles. Leave the cardboard doughnuts in place as you clip all the way around.
6. Cut the length of yarn for a tie (three feet to four feet). With the ends even, pass and wrap the tie between the two cardboard doughnuts, at the center of the yarn bundle. Tie the long piece of yarn tightly (without breaking) around the yarn bundle with a double knot. Pull away the cardboard circles, and fluff out your pom-pom.

Wrap yarn around the pom-pom template. Always start with yarns ends facing the outside edge. (Hal Jerman)

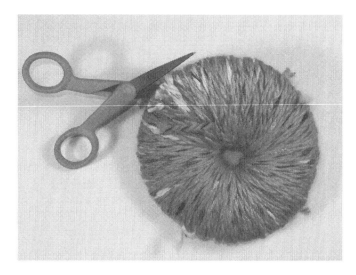

Clip the yarn along the edge of the template. (Hal Jerman)

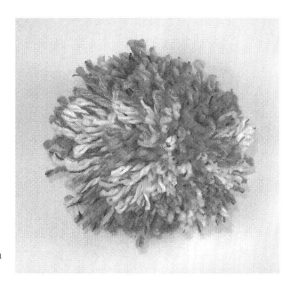

The finished pom-pom. Attach a length of yarn to make a toy. (Hal Jerman)

Fleece Scarves

The lengths of poly fleece are cut in advance, and the parents can fringe and decorate the scarves for themselves and their children. Be sure to inquire about their favorite colors before purchasing the fleece. Plan your program for early winter, when fleece fabric is on sale and the teen parents are able to use their scarves right away.

Supplies:

- 54-to-60-inch wide fleece yardage (Plan on a 9-by-54-to-60-inch-wide scarf for each teen, and a 5-by-36-inch scarf for each child. Buy ¼-yard extra fleece to give yourself some wiggle room. Purchase multiple colors so that the teen parents have choices).
- coordinating yarn colors for fringe and sewing on decorations and buttons
- scraps of fleece for decorating (remnants or ¼-yard cuts of coordinating colors)
- pearl cotton embroidery floss, with several coordinating and contrasting colors
- large, colorful buttons (flat, not shank; about 3 to 4 per scarf) (optional)

Tools:

- rotary cutter and large mat for cutting fleece lengths
- quilter's ruler

- fabric and pinking shears (one pair for every two or three participants)
- rulers (can also share)
- fabric glue (should be the washable type)
- large-eye needles to sew with pearl cotton and yarn
- masking tape (any width)

Instructions:

Preparation

1. Use the rotary cutter, mat, and ruler to cut 9-inch-wide lengths running the entire width (54-inch or 60-inch) of the fleece. Trim both ends about ½ inch to remove the selvage. Fleece is challenging to cut, but a rotary cutter gives the cleanest edge. A pair of scissors does not cut fleece well and will leave the edges uneven.
2. Cut some 5-by-36-inch child-size scarves.
3. Make a sample scarf.
4. Write a step-by-step list of instructions. This can be either a large version (recommended) to post on a wall, or a small handout.

Process—Adding Yarn Fringe

1. Measure and place a length of tape ¾ inch from each short end of the scarf.
2. Starting and ending ½ inch from the long edges, cut small holes ½ inch apart along the tape. Remove the tape.
3. Cut the yarn into 12-inch lengths, making two strands for each hole.
4. With the ends even, hold two strands together and fold in half lengthwise.
5. Push the folded end of the yarn through the hole, and down a couple of inches to make a loop.
6. Pull the loose ends of the yarn through the loop and pull tight.
7. Continue to make looped fringe through every hole along both edges of the scarf.

Process—Self Fringe

1. Lay a piece of masking tape across each short end of the scarf five inches from the edge.
2. Starting ½ inch from the long edge, make cuts ½ inch apart from the bottom edge of the fleece to the tape.
3. If desired, make a knot close to the top of each fringe.

Process—Decorating the Scarf

1. Cut simple shapes, such as flowers, or circles, with pinking shears or a pair of fabric scissors.
2. Either use fabric glue or sew them on with yarn or pearl cotton. A simple method is sewing a big X through the shape and tying the ends on top. Flat buttons can also be applied in the same manner.

Woven Paper Hearts

These hearts are ideal for writing messages of affection to friends and family. Parents can write secret messages to their children for Valentine's Day, or any other time. They are a little more difficult than they may appear, but they are inexpensive and look great when completed.

Supplies:

- photocopy-weight paper in white, red, and pink
- 3-by-3-inch squares of paper for messages

Modeling a finished scarf. (Vickie Shelton)

- woven heart pattern (many are available on the Internet; search for "woven paper heart")
- glue sticks (optional)
- yarn (optional)

Tools:

- pairs of paper scissors (teens can share)
- pens to write messages
- pencils
- rulers

Instructions:

1. Trace or photocopy the woven heart pattern on the red, white, and pink paper. Two pattern pieces are needed for each heart. Mixing paper colors is encouraged.
2. Select two colored sheets to use. Cut out each woven heart pattern around the outside edge. Fold the pattern piece in half, and cut the weaving lines. Leave the pattern pieces folded.
3. Interweave the two pattern pieces, with alternating colors on the outside in alternating rows, as illustrated in the photo. Be sure to make a sample, as the first two rows can be challenging until you understand the process.
4. Write a message to the recipient of the heart on a slip of paper and tuck it inside.
5. Add a paper or yarn loop for hanging through the top edge of the heart (optional).

Note: Instructions and patterns can also be found in *Paper-Folding Fun! 50 Awesome Crafts to Weave, Twist and Curl* (G. Johnson 2002). Look for the "Swedish Heart Basket" project.

Winter Holiday Crafts

Making simple holiday decorations and gifts lends a festive tone to winter meetings, and it dovetails nicely with a family traditions program. Suggested ideas include:

- Make the "Popsicle Stick Snowman" from Crafter's Touch.com. Be sure to use a wide (¾–1 inch) Popsicle stick; to simplify the project, skip painting the stick white, use 4-inch velour ribbon for the snowman's hat and scarf, and draw his face with a fine-tip permanent marker.
- "Candy Cane Reindeer" ornaments are a delightful craft for anyone age five and up. Just for fun, try adding a small jingle bell to the reindeer's neck ribbon. Find this craft at AmazingMoms.com (and many other websites).
- The "Gifts in a Jar," no-cook jars of ingredients to give as gifts (like a hot-chocolate mix and layered soup mixes) from the All Free Crafts website are fun to make. It is efficient to set up stations around the room and make a different mix at each station.

Woven paper hearts. (Hal Jerman)

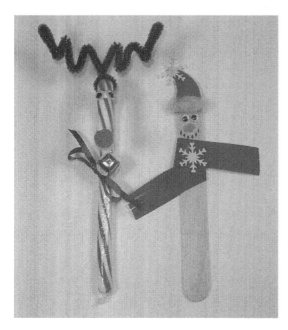

Easy-to-make candy-cane reindeer and Popsicle-stick snowman. (Hal Jerman)

Resources for Craft Projects

These resources have been selected as programs that may be successful when used with teen parents and, in particular, teen mothers.

Books

Cool Teen Programs for Under $100, by Jenine Lillian (2009), includes several programs that teen parents will like. "Bangles, Baubles, and Beads: Jewelry Making for Teens" will need both consumables and basic jewelry-making tools like wire cutters and pliers. You will find the basic bead jewelry instructions on the Beadage: All About Beading website very helpful. The required skill level for this program is medium, and the estimated time needed is two hours. An additional suggested program found in this resource is "Sensational Smoothies." Smoothie making can easily segue into a discussion about healthy teen (and child) snack options. This project will need two to three blenders or food processors, is easy for everyone to do, and will take about an hour. Ms. Lillian's "Día de los Muertos" is a multifaceted celebration, of which individual aspects can be utilized. This presents an ideal opportunity to include teen parent participation for planning, and for Hispanic parents to share their traditions with their children. Expect the event to last one and a half hours, but including teen parent planning and preparation involvement will add perhaps another hour in advance of the event.

Dangles and Bangles: Twenty-five Funky Accessories to Make and Wear, by Sherri Haab and Michelle Haab (2005), offers several accessories that are easy to make and have good-looking results. You can make a quick felt-flower pin or barrette by cutting and hand-stitching colorful felt. It's easy to do and will take about 30 to 60 minutes. Decorate your toes with "Beaded Toe Rings" made with elastic jewelry cord and beads. Plan on using about 30 minutes for this straightforward project.

101+ Teen Programs That Work, by RoseMary Honnold (2003), could be a teen librarian's programming bible because it's so full of popular ideas. Many teen parents will enjoy "Sand Art and Sand Painting" because this project is easy and will suit a wide range of levels of creativity, from reproduced designs to original artwork. Expect it to take 30 to 40 minutes. "Soaps and Lotions/Aromatherapy" is another fun option found in this resource. If you don't have access to a microwave to make soaps, you may want to focus on lotions and bath salts. You can keep your costs modest by using recycled containers. Plan on at least 30 to 60 minutes for this project. The "Fun Party Food Ideas" are no-cook food activities like a "Make Your Own Sundae Bar," "Tacos in a Bag," and "Scavenger Snack Mix," which combines a library scavenger hunt with making snack mix. Plan on 30 minutes, including eating time.

From *Teen Programs with Punch*, by Valerie Ott (2006), try the "Day of the Dead" project, making a memorial pocket shrine to a relative, friend, or favorite celebrity in a small tin. In the "Duct Tape Wallets" project, the teen parents can make wallets and more out of nothing but duct tape, which is now available in a rainbow of colors and patterns. For multiple duct-tape project ideas, consult *Ductigami: The Art of the Tape*, by Joe Wilson (1999), and *Got Tape? Roll Out the Fun with Duct Tape!* by Ellie Schiedermayer (2002). Both of these activities are of medium difficulty and require about 45 to 60 minutes.

Twenty-Five Latino Craft Projects, by Ana-Elba Pavon and Diana Borrego (2003), has some fun crafts, which will be especially meaningful to Hispanic parents. Try "Corn Husk Dolls," purchasing the corn husks, used for making tamales, from a Latino grocer or from the Latino section of a large supermarket. This activity will be most successful if everyone proceeds step-by-step together as the leader demonstrates. This is an easy project and will take about 30 to 40 minutes. Cutting and hanging "papel picados," colorful cut-tissue-paper banners, brings a touch of celebration to any program. For additional ideas, also consult Carmen Lomas Garza's beautiful book *Making Magic Windows: Creating Papel Picado/Cut-Paper Art with Carmen Lomas Garza* (1999). These are easy to do and will take about 45 minutes. Also make "paper flowers" along with your papel picados.

Websites

Andrea Graham's blog, **4YA** (n.d.), features the latest in cool teen crafts. Her instructions are clear, easy to follow, and illustrated with helpful photos. Simple projects like Thai string

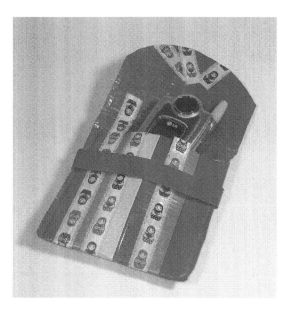

Duct-tape cell-phone case. (Hal Jerman)

dolls and fabric-wrapped bangles will appeal to teen parents. Her list of "15 Must Have Art Supplies" serves as a guide to stocking the craft supply closet. Ms. Graham also offers links to other relevant websites and topics, such as the Instructables.com (2010) annual DIY holiday guide, which has inexpensive ideas for gifts and decorations.

Disney Family Fun. Disney offers a home-style version of its stellar creativity on its Family Fun website. Teen parents will enjoy "Bleach Pen Drawing," using grocery-store bleach pens to make simple designs on colored T-shirts for both themselves and their children. Ask the teen parents for T-shirt sizes and color preferences in advance, and make sure that they understand the washing instructions that the shirts require. This is an easy activity that should take about one hour.

Kaboose.com. Kaboose (n.d.), an affiliate of Disney Family Fun, has a long list of projects on its "Teen Crafts" page. Many are quite simple and use inexpensive or recycled materials such as paper napkins and old wallpaper sample books. Winning ideas include "Handmade Paper Bead Necklaces," the "Decoupage Collage Box," and "Bath Salts."

The Mid-Hudson Library System's (n.d.) **"Youth Programs: Child to Teen"** section discussed in chapter 5 includes links to craft websites. Search both the children's and teen-oriented websites to find projects suitable for the wide spectrum of interests and abilities of your teen parent group.

Martha Stewart.com. Look to Martha Stewart.com for a broad spectrum of stylish projects, many of which are remarkably simple. From the home page, go to "Crafts," and explore the "Holiday and Seasonal Crafts," "Crafts by Technique," and "Crafts by Material." The "Kids' Crafts" pages will also have some easy projects that can be adapted to teens' tastes.

A typical project from Martha Stewart that will work with teen parents is the "Baby Photo Album Ring," made from baseball-card protectors and a plastic shower-curtain ring. This is an easy photo album that is safe for babies and toddlers to play with, and it will take about 30 to 45 minutes to make. The "Paper Picture Frame" is a piece of card stock embellished with scraps of decorative paper, ribbon, glitter, beads, and so on. A strip of adhesive magnet is attached to the back so it can easily hang on the refrigerator. This is another easy project that will take about 15 to 20 minutes. Also quick and easy are the "Recycled Ornaments," garlands and globes made from old greeting and holiday cards.

SIMPLE COOKING ACTIVITIES

Because they are growing, good nutrition is especially important for adolescents' health. Providing a nutritious snack at programs helps to ensure that the teens are not hungry and increases their attention span. Incorporating the preparation of the snack into the group's activity plan offers an opportunity for the young parents to learn healthy cooking skills that they can use at home with their families. Recipes that use seasonal fresh fruits, lower-fat dairy products, and whole-grain cereals and breads demonstrate that healthy eating can also taste good. Cookie and cupcake decorating can occasionally be incorporated into programs for a special treat!

When the program includes both the teen parents and the children, offering simple cooking activities for them to do together can be a shared learning experience. Cookbooks geared toward cooking with preschoolers, such as Mollie Katzen and Ann Henderson's *Pretend Soup* (1994), provide ideas for simple snack/cooking projects that can be coordinated for teen parents to do with their children. Be sure to think through and plan the process so that the parent-child component is feasible. Use recipes that have tasks that everyone can do together, such as stirring ingredients or assembling the final product.

Helpful Tips

When looking for program ideas, it is helpful to consider cooking activities as edible craft projects. Plan to do most of the peeling, slicing, grating, and so forth in advance in order to save time, limit the need for multiple cutting boards and knives, and avoid injuries. No-cook recipes work best for several reasons: everyone can make an individual snack at the same time with minimal wait time; there is less preparation (no dragging a microwave downstairs from the staff room); and many library and community agency facilities do not have functional kitchens with stoves or ovens.

The best ideas and recipes are found in children's cookbooks. These recipes tend to be uncomplicated and require few utensils. Offer choices that allow for individual taste and creativity, including several flavors of herbs for a dip, or a variety of vegetables to decorate a cream-cheese bagel face. As always, thoroughly think through the logistics, supplies, and tools that will be needed for successful implementation. It is important to try to foresee any potential bottlenecks in the process, such as participants having to wait in line to use one cutting board. When setting up, consider having two "serving" lines, with doubles of everything to speed up the process. An attractive, inexpensive tablecloth on your serving table adds a touch of festiveness to your event and can be used again and again.

Suggested Recipes

Apple Peeling

This fun activity is quick and easy when using an old-fashioned mechanical apple peeler. Available online from a variety of outlets for less than $25.00 (search "mechanical apple peeler" or by brand name, "Back to Basics Apple and Potato Peeler"), these magic machines simultaneously peel, core, and spiral cut an apple. Everyone—teen, adult, or child—is fascinated by watching this little machine go through its paces. All you need is one apple per person and the peeler. Clamp it to a tabletop, and everyone takes turns cranking the machine to peel their own apple. The only caveat is to be sure to use a firm apple like a Granny Smith; softer apples will disintegrate. For some reason, apples peeled this way taste better than usual.

Yogurt Granola Parfait

This nutritious recipe contains breakfast staples, including yogurt, fruit, and granola. Staff can prepare the fruit prior to the start of the program or solicit help from teen parents when they first arrive.

Supplies:

- 1 quart vanilla low-fat yogurt (one per eight teens)
- ½ cup granola per teen
- 3 to 4 types of sliced fresh fruit: bananas, strawberries, grapes, melon, pineapple (prepared ahead)

- 9-ounce clear plastic cups
- plastic spoons
- napkins

Tools:

- knives to cut fruit
- cutting board
- trays for fruit
- bowl for granola
- spoons for fruit, yogurt, and granola

Instructions:

1. Alternate layers of yogurt, granola, and fruit in a clear 9-ounce cup, repeating layers until the cup is full. (Be sure to show parents a premade sample, to illustrate.)
2. Eat and enjoy!

Fresh Fruit or Vegetable Kebabs

This recipe is a creative way to serve and eat fresh fruits and vegetables. Every participant skewers his or her own kebabs, selecting their favorite fruits.

Supplies:

For the fruit kebabs, select three to four fruit choices and four to six of each item per person.

- melon cubes
- grapes
- strawberries
- orange sections
- pineapple chunks

Note: bananas, apples, and pears have been omitted due to their tendency to turn brown after cutting.

For the vegetable kebabs, select four to six vegetable choices plus bread and cheese cubes; have on hand four to six of each item per person.

- giant olives
- cherry tomatoes
- pickle slices
- carrot rounds (thinly sliced)
- zucchini rounds
- bell pepper squares
- cucumber rounds
- cheese cubes
- French bread cubes

Give the teen parents the option of making their own salad dressings in small, individual cups. Supply a sour cream and yogurt base to which they can add herbs and spices. Mix together one cup of low-fat sour cream and one cup of low-fat yogurt. For the fruit-kebab dressing, offer honey, cinnamon, vanilla, ginger, and nutmeg. For the vegetable-kebab dressing, provide a variety of ingredients to choose from, including salt, pepper, oregano, garlic salt, basil, thyme, cumin, chili powder, soy sauce, lemon juice, and dry mustard. Any type of vinaigrette or Italian salad dressing, bottled or homemade, is also a good choice to serve with the vegetable kebabs.

Consumables:

- 6-inch wooden skewers (two to three per person for each type of kebab)
- paper plates
- napkins
- plastic spoons (optional for dressings)
- small paper cups (optional for dressings)

Tools:

- platters for fruits or vegetables
- paring knives for slicing fruits and vegetables
- cutting boards
- bowls for dressing base (optional)
- spoons for dressing base (optional)

Preparation and Setup:

1. Wash and cut up selected fruits, vegetables, cheeses, and bread.
2. Arrange the materials on platters, either several platters with a variety of items on each or an assembly-line style on separate plates.
3. Lay out skewers and plates at the beginning of the serving line.
4. Make sample skewers, alternating different fruits or vegetables. Hint: grapes or bread cubes make good "stoppers" to keep fruits or vegetables from falling off the end of the skewer.
5. Optional: Mix yogurt and sour cream dressing base, and put out flavorings with spoons, if needed. For sanitation reasons, set up flavorings in shaker bottles or bottles that do not require spoons.

Instructions:

1. Show everyone the sample skewers. Be sure to mention that it's not necessary to use fruits or vegetables that you do not like.
2. Optional dressing: Demonstrate mixing a sweet or savory dressing. Put a small amount of the sour cream base in a cup, and add flavorings. When explaining about adding flavoring, encourage using restraint and tasting to determine whether more seasoning is necessary.
3. Let everyone thread their skewers as they pass down the line, doing one skewer of each to start, and coming back for a second or third if time permits.
4. Mix dressings as desired.
5. Eat and enjoy!

Just for Fun Food Crafts

Take a look at Clare Crespo's *The Secret Life of Food* (2002), to see just how much fun can be had when you play with your food. Here are some successful playful food projects for use with teen parents:

- "Marshmallow Snowmen," from About.com: Simplify this project by using tinned chocolate icing to join the marshmallows, and pretzel sticks for arms. Other alternatives from the website directions include using shredded coconut for hair, and mini M&M's™ for buttons and eyes. Bring along some toothpicks in case a "spine" is needed to stop the snowmen from keeling over.
- "Edible Valentines," from About.com. Teens "glue" candy message hearts to graham crackers with icing.
- "S'More Eyeballs," from About.com. These are perfect for Halloween—marshmallow eyeballs with chocolate-chip pupils stuck to graham crackers with icing.

Marshmallow snowpeople and S'More eyeballs. (Hal Jerman)

Resources for Cooking Activities

Recipes in *Big Snacks, Little Meals: After School, Dinnertime, Anytime*, by Rose Dunnington (2006), direct cooks to customize individual batches of popcorn with a choice of flavorings or make personalized trail mix using raisins, nuts, banana chips, coconut, miniature pretzels, and chocolate chips. The "Fruity-Tooty Salad" recipe combines seasonal fruits with dressings made with honey, vanilla, or maple syrup.

No-cook recipe ideas in *FamilyFun Super Snacks*, by Deanna Cook (2004), include "Spiral Sandwiches," flour tortillas spread with fillings, rolled up, and sliced into spirals; and "Cookie Puppets," round cookies baked on sticks, with faces made from icing and candies.

Mollie Katzen and Ann L. Henderson's whimsical recipes in *Pretend Soup and Other Real Recipes: A Cookbook for Preschoolers and Up* (1994) are too fun to leave just to the younger kids. Healthy and tasty options include "Bagel Faces," made with vegetables and sunflower seeds on a bagel spread with cream cheese, and fruity "Pretend Soup," a mix of juice and yogurt with bananas and berries. Making "Homemade Lemon-Lime Soda Pop" demonstrates that a homemade drink can taste better and costs less than a commercial serving of soda. (You might even want to calculate the cost difference.)

SELF-CARE

With the daily demands of learning how to parent effectively and how to transition into adulthood, it is extremely common for teen parents (and many other busy individuals!) to forget to take care of themselves. The importance of self-care as a means of stress management should never be underestimated. Chronic stress damages a person's physical and emotional health and makes it difficult to care for others. While juggling school, work, a new baby, adolescent pressures, and family dynamics, teen parents may not understand the significant worth of making time for themselves. It can be extremely beneficial to discuss with teen parents how exercising, eating healthy foods, getting enough sleep, abstaining from substance use, and pursuing creative endeavors can help them be more productive in other areas of life. Stressing how self-care can help them be better caretakers for their children can reinforce the connection between their health and the health of their family. A one-time program or a series of group discussions and classes can be both fun and educational.

Exercise

The benefits of being physically active are many; it does far more than just burn calories. While new mothers may feel better about their appearance if they lose some baby weight, exercise can also help reduce stress and fatigue, increase overall self-confidence, and decrease the risk of heart disease. Even if you are not a fitness expert, planning some type of exercise program for the teen parents can be fun for everyone involved.

Collection Connection

If space and equipment permit, bring an exercise video from your library's collection to go through together. Bring other videos from the collection as samples of what the teen parents can check out themselves and try at home. Prior to the program, let the parents know to wear comfortable clothing and tennis shoes and to bring towels to wipe off the sweat. Providing water is important to demonstrate the importance of staying hydrated. Having a quick snack before starting the video will let them know that working out on an empty stomach is not healthy. If you feel comfortable, join the young mothers or fathers during the workout video to model that even if you feel silly or don't know all the moves, the important things are to try, to keep moving, and to have a good time.

Walking

Taking a power walk with the teen parent group is a great way to get outside, demonstrate a simple exercise that they can do on their own, and provide an opportunity for chatting and relaxing. Again, let the young parents know that walking will be a part of the program so that they can dress appropriately. Things to consider when planning a walk include:

1. Child care—is there someone to watch the children, and are parents allowed to leave the premises while their children are being cared for?
2. Safety—is it safe to walk through the neighborhood? Will the parents feel comfortable walking around in a group?
3. Physical ability—will anyone have trouble keeping up due to a physical condition?

Remember to stretch together before and after the power walk. Talk to the teen parents about how stretching can prevent injuries and about the importance of a warm-up and a cooldown.

Exercise at Home

Many teen parents will not know how to make time to incorporate exercise into their routines at home. Deborah Reber, in her book *Chill: Stress-Reducing Techniques for a More Balanced, Peaceful You* (2008), goes through different activities that can be accomplished in a limited time period. For example, if there is no time to work out during the day, she suggests walking up stairs instead of taking an escalator or an elevator. If the teen parent has 10 minutes to spare, Reber proposes going for a quick walk around the block or dancing in the living room. Mary Beth Sammons and Samantha Moss, in their book *InSPAration: A Teen's Guide to Healthy Living Inspired by Today's Top Spas* (2005), suggest some simple exercises using soup cans as weights to tone arms. Review these ideas with the teen parents in your group and ask them for more home-exercise ideas that have worked for them in the past.

Mental Health

Stress for teen parents can come from a variety of places. Internally, they may be struggling with forming their own identity, deciding what they want to do with their lives and wondering whether they are good enough parents to their children. Externally, they may worry about paying the bills, pleasing their own parents, or finding a stable place to live with their children. Creating programs that give teen parents a little bit of time to relax and reflect can be just as important as helping them find a job.

Journaling

The act of regularly writing down thoughts, ideas, and experiences in a journal can be ideal for reducing stress. Providing the opportunity for teen parents to express their feelings through words has the potential to be a powerful exercise. Journaling can be its own hour-long activity, where parents "free write" for 20 minutes and share with the group when they are finished, or you can incorporate 10 minutes of journaling into any other program. Some teen parents may be resistant to journaling because of limited writing skills. Tell them that the most important part of the activity is for them to get their thoughts down on paper. Encourage a free flow of ideas, and remind the participants that grammar and spelling do not matter for this activity. Journal writing does not have to be in complete sentences; lists, diagrams, drawings, or any other way the teen parent feels comfortable expressing thoughts on paper can be used. Sometimes, writers may need a prompt, or a question or phrase that stimulates the writing process. Suggest, for example, that the teen parents write about a frustrating part of their week. Other sample writing prompts are "What is your favorite time of the day?" and "What is your favorite song and why?"

Yoga

Yoga is a type of exercise that helps to make both the body and the mind stronger. In addition to the physical benefits of yoga, including an increase in flexibility and muscle strength, yoga is also an excellent form of meditation. Yoga emphasizes breathing exercises, which can reduce stress and anxiety. It can calm the body and the mind. If you are planning a yoga program with a teen parent group, ask local yoga studios if any of their instructors would be willing to teach a yoga class to the teen parents at the library. Or, find a yoga video or book that describes various poses to review with the teen parents. *Breathe: Yoga for Teens* (Chryssicas 2007) is an excellent book that walks you through various poses and practices to build strength, self-confidence, and inner peace. It also comes with a helpful DVD.

Self-Pampering

A facial or massage is a great way to de-stress. Unfortunately, spa treatments are usually expensive and time consuming. Do-it-yourself pampering can be a fun program for teen parents to relax and enjoy. *InSPAration: A Teen's Guide to Healthy Living Inspired by Today's Top Spas*, by Mary Beth Sammons and Samantha Moss, has directions for face masks and facials. A "Dazzling-Duo Organic Facial" is made from teabags, plain yogurt, honey, lemon juice, and oatmeal and is designed to make the skin feel fresh, radiant, and relaxed. The "Mega-Veda Mask" uses ingredients from the grocery store to make a variety of face masks that can help oily or dry skin and keep your spirit calm and peaceful. Both are easy to do and will take about 40 to 50 minutes.

LEISURE READING

Teen parents may not have much time to fit reading for pleasure into their daily schedules, which makes connecting them with a book that much more meaningful. Youth librarians know very well the pleasure, solace, and emotional support that books can offer teens, and teen parents are no exception. Additionally, when these young parents are taking the time to read for pleasure, they are modeling reading and lifelong learning to their children and encouraging their children become readers themselves.

Readers' Advisory

Youth librarians' standard readers' advisory practices, using their familiarity with teen literature to feel out a teen's reading interests, works for teen parents. Establishing a trusting and respectful relationship with them, as a group and as individuals, facilitates readers' advisory success. Be sure to be careful when gauging reading level; some teen parents may be reading at a middle school level or below. As with all teen readers' advisory, keep in mind the following guidelines to best connect the teen parents with potential reading material.

- Practice active and empathetic listening.
- Stay attentive and interested in what the teen is saying.
- Ask open-ended and specific questions as appropriate.

- Respect teens' likes and dislikes.
- Keep it conversational (Booth 2007).

Connecting with Reluctant Teen Readers (Jones, Hartman, and Taylor 2006) also suggests the following guidelines.

- Ask the teen to tell you about a book that he or she enjoyed reading. Listen for the qualities that made the book appealing so you can recommend another book with similar attributes.
- Ask about the teen's preferences in music, movies, and television, then relate those preferences to book suggestions.
- Make sure that the teen is aware of all the book formats that the library offers, including graphic novels, comics, and audio books.
- Allow time during library visits for teens to browse and recommend books to one other.

Teen parents will like the same books favored by comparable teens in your community but also may be less familiar with the array of genres available. Some fiction suggestions are pop, chick-lit, urban literature, mysteries, horror, romance, and books based on movies. Short-story collections on themes of interest to them are also a good choice to fit into teen parents' limited leisure time. Easy-to-digest humor, like Jim Benton's "It's Happy Bunny" series, may be popular too.

General nonfiction interests can include health and beauty care, relationships, child care, and popular culture (especially celebrities and music). They may enjoy books that depict an individual's triumph over challenging circumstances, such as Francisco Jimenez's collection of stories about his life as a migrant child, *The Circuit* (1997), or the inspirational *Chicken Soup for the Teenage Soul* collections (Canfield 1997). Themed lists can be combed for titles with appeal for teen parents. The following books are great resources for reading lists.

From *Best Books for Young Adults* (Koelling 2007):

- Fiction: "Family in Crisis," "Family Redefined," "Friendship," "Love and Romance," and "Short Stories"
- Nonfiction: "Exceptional Women" and "Fascinating True Stories"

The Big Book of Teen Reading Lists, by Nancy Keane, offers the option of reproducible booklists and bookmarks. Some genre topics with teen parent appeal that Keane (2006) includes are:

- "Narrative Nonfiction for Young Adults"
- "Short and Sweet"
- "Tearjerkers"
- "Chick Lit with Minority Characters"
- "Kindness of Strangers"
- "Meaning of Life"
- "Reluctant Girl Readers"
- "Romance for Boy Readers"

In *Teen Genreflecting 3: A Guide to Reading Interests*, by Diana Tixier Herald (2010), look for these genres and themes:

- Contemporary—"Ethnic and Racial," "Coming-of-Age," and "Relationships"
- Issues—"Outsiders," "Abuse," "Homelessness and Runaways," "Addiction and Substance Abuse," and "Family Situations"
- Paranormal and Horror—"Occult," "Vampires," and "Unexplained Phenomena"
- Mystery and Suspense—"Contemporary Mysteries" and "Suspense"
- Romance—"Chick Lit" and "Soap Opera"
- Multicultural—"Closer to Home: Native American, African American, and Latino"

Though it is current only through 2006, *Connecting with Reluctant Teen Readers* (Jones, Hartman, and Taylor 2006) has a list of 57 "turnaround" titles, which are great books that youth librarians have seen turn teens on to reading.

Internet Sources

The Young Adult Library Services Association's (YALSA) "Popular Paperbacks for Young Adults" and "Quick Picks for Reluctant Young Adult Readers" booklists, selected by youth librarians and found on the YALSA website, are reliable sources. Selections from the 1998 to 2008 versions of both lists have been compiled into a single volume under the title *Quick and Popular Reads for Teens* (Holley 2009). Topical booklists, based on requests sent to YALSA's book discussion listserv, YALSA-BK, have also been compiled and published as *Annotated Booklists for Every Teen Reader* (Bartel and Holley 2010). While not specifically targeted for teen parents, the websites Teen Reads.com (by the Book Report) and Reading Rants.org (by Jennifer Hubert Swan) are go-to sources for the latest in teen reading.

Pregnant and Parenting Teens in Fiction (and Fact)

There is an entire subgenre of fiction about pregnant and parenting teens. For example, Angela Johnson's powerful *First Part Last* (2003) is a Michael L. Printz Award winner for excellence in young adult literature. While these books might seem obvious choices to recommend for teen parents, this genre should be approached with sensitivity. Some teen parents may connect with these books instantly. For others, when the teen's personal experiences are potentially so closely aligned with those of the book's characters, a teen parent may have an adverse reaction to it. When recommending one of these titles, be sure to explain enough of the plot so that the teen reader won't have any surprises.

A number of these stories, such as Sarah Dessen's *Someone Like You* (1998), are a great read but also possess an element of the "cautionary tale" about the consequences of being sexually active, which teen parents and teen parents-to-be may not appreciate (Bittel 2009). Some books, like *Hanging On to Max* by Margaret Bechard (2002), *The First Part Last* by Angela Johnson, and *Slam* by Nick Hornby (2007), are narrated by a teen father, which could prove insightful for both teen moms and dads. Many teen parents may find these books helpful as they watch the characters resolve problems similar to their own. The pendulum of bliss and trauma, found in many books of this genre, may be satisfying to some readers and not to others. For a list of newer fiction titles published from 2002 to 2009, consult *Teen Genreflecting 3: A Guide to Reading Interests* (Herald 2010).

Nonfiction titles like *You Look Too Young to Be a Mom* by Deborah Davis (2004) or *Daycare and Diplomas: Teen Mothers Who Stayed in School* (Students at South Vista Educational Center 2000), collections of short essays by teen parents, might be a better suggestion, depending on the teen. Some teen moms will relate to the experiences and advice offered by American Idol winner Fantasia and reality TV star Toya Carter in their autobiographies *Life Is Not a Fairy Tale* (Fantasia 2005) and *Priceless Inspirations* (Carter 2011).

Storytelling and Reading Aloud to Teen Parents

Few librarians or teachers read aloud or tell stories to teens, but it is worth making time for these activities. Teen parents, perhaps because they have children, seem more receptive to storytelling and being read to than mainstream teens might be. Spending a few minutes sharing a story they will enjoy is another way to model family literacy for teen parents, and it introduces them to storytelling as a family tradition. Try the following strategies, which seem to work best.

1. Casually tell or read a story when there are a few extra minutes here or there, or while the teen parents are having a snack.
2. When telling the story or conducting a read-aloud, do it matter-of-factly, without overblown dramatics, as if you were telling an anecdote to a friend.
3. Don't expect a huge response, but try storytelling a couple of times to see if their interest grows (de Vos 2003).

Storytelling

While the interests of every teen parent audience are different, start by telling stories that they might want to share with their children. This includes stories that use simple supplies or props, such as draw-and-tell, cut-and-tell, and handkerchief-folding tales. Refer to the following resources for storytelling suggestions.

From *Paper Stories*, by Jean Stangl (1984):

- "Morris Mouse and His Christmas Trees" (But skip the cute animal names.)
- "The Little Orange House"—a gentle Halloween story
- "Six Little Girls and One Valentine"

From *Drawing Stories from Around the World*, by Anne Pellowski:

- "The Baby Surprise"—fold a handkerchief and see what you get.
- "The Smart Shopper"—wait until you see this thrifty gal!

Tell cut-and-tell, draw-and-tell, or paper-folding stories once through yourself, and then pass out paper, pairs of scissors, markers, or whatever the activity requires and tell the story again, having the parents follow along. Sending a handout home may help the teen parents more effectively repeat this activity with their children.

Teen parents may also enjoy stories that are humorous or have a surprise. Try "The Yellow Ribbon" from *Juba This and Juba That* (Tashjian 1995), which is a classic "he said, she said" crowd-pleaser with a silly ending. Stories that involve solving a riddle, that involve making a judgment, that appeal to ethical and moral qualities, that gently express a precept, or that explore family relationships will appeal to teen parents. Consider trying "Language Power" in *The Storytelling Handbook*, by Anne Pellowski (1995), a story that demonstrates that it pays to be bilingual. Below are more examples of similar stories.

From *Apples from Heaven*, by Naomi Baltuck (1995):

- "The Gossiping Clams"—ever wonder why clams are buried in the sand? Too much gossiping!
- "The Most Noble Story"—which son can do the noblest act and inherit his dying mother's estate?
- "The Sage's Gift"—men (and women) are made wise by stories.
- "Wisdom"—everything you need to know can be boiled down to 15 words.

From *The Cow of No Color*, by Nina Jaffe and Steve Zeitlin (1998):

- "The Jury"—does the defense attorney convince the jury?
- "The Magic Seed"—it's a seed that will grow only for someone who has never told a lie.
- "Sharing the Soup"—there is only one higher power who treats all people the same: death.
- "The Test"—make sure everyone has their story straight!
- "The Wise King"—even fairness is relative.

From *Drawing Stories from Around the World*, by Anne Pellowski:

- "The Peasant's Clever Daughter"—use handkerchiefs to solve a riddle that hails from ancient Greece.

Many of these stories are also suitable as read-alouds, but you will find that a told story is much more compelling. For more storytelling tips and suggested stories, consult *Storytelling for Young Adults: A Guide to Tales for Teens*, by Gail de Vos.

Reading Picture Books Aloud

When reading mature picture books aloud to teen parents, clearly acknowledge that what you are reading is formatted like books for younger children, but point out the sophisticated message or humor and the aesthetic qualities of the illustrations. Wait until you have established a good rapport with the group, and read picture books to them that resonate for you. Select books to read aloud with themes such as humor, emotions, ethics, historical morality tales, family, inspirational biography, and parodies of familiar fairy tales. While listeners are captured by the words of storytelling, the right picture book's blend of theme and illustrations can be equally as captivating. Try the following picture books.

- Robert Coles's *The Story of Ruby Bridges* (1995), the six-year-old who integrated the New Orleans schools in 1960
- Demi's *The Empty Pot* (1990) and *The Greatest Power* (2004)
- *How Are You Peeling?* by Saxton Freymann (1999)
- Kathleen Krull's biographies *Wilma Unlimited* (1996), about Wilma Rudolph, and *Harvesting Hope* (2003), about Cesar Chavez
- Todd Parr's wacky but sensitive books *It's Okay to Be Different* (2001), *Things That Make You Feel Good/Things That Make You Feel Bad* (1999), and *This Is My Hair* (1999)
- Patricia Polacco's *Thank You, Mr. Falker* (1998) (about reading disabilities), *The Butterfly* (2000) (about WWII Occupied France), *Pink and Say* (1997) (about the Civil War), or *Junkyard Wonders* (2010) (about learning disabilities)
- Jon Scieszka's *The Frog Prince, Continued* (1991), *The Stinky Cheese Man* (1992), and *Squids Will Be Squids* (1998)
- *Wangari's Trees of Peace*, by Jeanette Winter (2008), the story of the Nobel Prize–winning female African environmentalist
- The elegant *Seven Blind Mice*, from the book by Ed Young (1991)

Helping teen parents evolve as readers and experience the richness that literature can add to life benefits both the parents and their children. Modeling sends the most powerful message, and teen parents who enjoy reading are peerless examples for their children.

BOOKS AND TOYS: CREATING GIFTS FOR THEIR CHILDREN

Bookmaking

Teaching teen parents to make individualized books for their children can benefit the entire family. Parents gain insight into how books work and develop a deeper connection to books by making them personal. The children receive a special book created just for them by their parent(s), allowing the parent and child to share a literacy-rich experience. In order to have a successful bookmaking activity, it is important to remember that some teen parents may have never looked at a picture book from the perspective of understanding its layout and structure. They may not know how to proceed if the instructions are simply "Make a book!" Presenting ideas for thematic structures is a good place to begin. Showing the group published books as examples helps them to generate ideas and exposes them to more quality children's literature. It is important that the examples are simple and have an easily transferable concept. Books with a repetitive structure are the easiest to use. Consider sharing the following types of books as examples before the bookmaking activity.

1. Counting books—1 dog, 2 cats, 3 birds, and so on. Counting books are quick to make with stickers.
2. Shape books—use pre-cut paper shapes or stickers to make circles, squares, triangles, and so on. Shapes can also be combined to make recognizable objects, as seen in *Changes, Changes*, by Pat Hutchins (1971).
3. Color books—what better example could there be than *Brown Bear, Brown Bear, What Do You See?* by Bill Martin (1996)?

4. Nursery rhymes or songs for text—examples are *Big Fat Hen*, by Ken Baker (1994), Rosemary Wells's version of *Bingo!* (1999), and *1, 2, Buckle My Shoe* by Anna Gross-nickle Hines (2008).

5. Days of the week, months of the year, or hours of the day—*The Very Hungry Caterpillar*, by Eric Carle (1994), is a classic example.

6. A simplified alphabet book—make it easy by spelling out the letters of the child's name. Example: "A is for apple," "N is for nickel," "T is for toe," "H is for house," "O is for orange," "N is for nut,' "Y is for yogurt." "Put them all together and they spell "ANTHONY!"

7. Favorite things—include the child's favorite color, animal, food, place, toy, and people.

8. Repeated, patterned text—use a repeated phrase as demonstrated in perennial favorites like *I Went Walking*, by Sue Williams (1996), *This Is My Hair*, by Todd Parr, and *The Very Busy Spider*, by Eric Carle (1984).

9. Lift-the-flap books—use pre-cut pieces of felt slightly smaller than the book page size for flaps. They are attached with colored duct tape to the pages. This works well for repeated and patterned text, like variants on *Brown Bear, Brown Bear*, such as "(Child's name), what do you see?" or *Where's Spot?* (Hill 2000).

10. Texture books—these provide opportunities for the use of expressive language. Gather textured fabrics (velvet, burlap, corduroy, and fur), fuzzy yarns, cotton balls, shapes cut from wood and foam, foil, and cellophane.

Bookmaking Format and Materials

The bookmaking process involves multiple steps, including creating the physical book, writing the story, and executing artwork and text. It is therefore important to offer ideas that are simple and directions that are easy to follow. To avoid overwhelming participants, book length should be no more than 10 to 12 pages. The size of the actual book should be relatively petite, such as 5-½ inches by 8-½ inches, so that it is easier to complete and more manageable for handling by children. Introduce the process by using a picture book to explain the conventions of the book format, including the cover with author and illustrator's names, title page with copyright date, and dedication. Show examples of some of the different story formats discussed above. Always encourage creativity; if teen parents want to follow their own format, it is more than okay!

Making a Blank Book

There are a variety of ideas on how to make the physical book in very simple ways. An excellent web resource is Susan Kapuscinski Gaylord's website MakingBooks with Children.

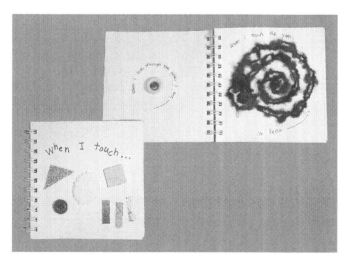

A handmade texture book. (Hal Jerman)

In the "Free Activities" pages, there are instructions for making nine different book formats using only computer printer paper and a few other supplies. For example, the "stick and elastic book" can be folded, punched, and secured in minutes. The MakingBooks with Children website links to another creative website, Art Junction: a Collaborative Art Space for Teachers and Students, which provides instructions for making a book from a paper grocery bag. Other bookmaking ideas:

- From *Creating Handmade Books* (Golden 1998)—"Simple Accordion" book, "Fan Book," and "Concertina with Tabs"
- From *The Kids' Guide to Making Scrapbooks and Photo Albums* (Check 2002)—"Hole Punch Design"
- From *Totally Cool Journals, Notebooks and Diaries* (Pensiero 2003)—"Basic Book #2," "Birthday Books," and "Cookie Cutter Books"
- From *Paper-Folding Fun! 50 Awesome Crafts to Weave, Twist and Curl* (Johnson, Ginger, 2002)—"Accordion-Fold Book with Pockets" and "Color Magic Flip-Flop"

Purchasing Blank Books

Short blank books are available to purchase on several websites. The greatest variety of choices is found on teacher resource websites. Look for books that have a minimal number of pages, preferably no more than 16. Prices range from $1 to $3, depending on size, paper quality, and length. Here are some examples of websites where you can purchase blank books:

- From the Teachers Paradise website: A 16-page 7-inch by 10-inch book.
- From the Rainbow Resource Center website: "Bright Ideas" blank storybooks, 6-inch by 9-inch books with 16 pages and heavy tag board covers. Smaller books, 4-¼ inches by 5-½ inches, are also available.
- From the BookBlanks website: "Chunky Board Books," available in different sizes and page counts, with hardcovers.
- The Klutz Press website sells "Klutz Build a Book" kits with 10-page wire-bound books in two sizes, 4 inches square and 7 inches square. The kits include foam shapes, wiggle eyes, and patterned papers.

Book-Illustrating Materials

Tools:

- colored markers
- crayons
- glue sticks
- paper scissors
- pencils
- rulers
- stencils (optional)
- white glue (for foam pieces or textured materials)

Decorating materials (No need to have everything; just provide a selection):

- colored papers
- gift wrap
- magazines with photographs of animals or everyday items
- movable eyes
- origami paper
- personal photographs of the child and family

- recycled greeting cards
- scrapbooking paper
- stickers
- textured materials (see texture books, above)
- tissue paper
- yarn and ribbon

Illustration and Layout Tips

1. Cut papers into smaller pieces to avoid waste (about the size of your book pages).
2. Ask that when cutting paper or fabric, participants cut shapes close to the edge, rather than cutting one shape out of the center and discarding the rest.
3. To prevent mistakes, suggest writing each page's text on a strip (or more) of paper that can be moved around on the page before being glued down for the best fit with the illustrations.
4. If there is any interest, use simple collages of colored shapes or examples from picture books to illustrate these basic visual principles: objects that are lower on the page appear larger; objects that are smaller appear farther away, especially when also placed higher on the page; overlapping objects creates depth; a light-colored object will appear bigger than a dark object of the same size.

Toys for Play and Storytime

It can be very empowering for a parent to create simple toys that his or her child will enjoy using. When the teen parents make toys related to a book, it not only makes the story come alive, but also promotes literacy and learning. Optimally, this type of program will include time for the parents to create the toys, followed by a special storytime that includes using the toy with a fingerplay or story. Having the toy to keep encourages the teen parents to repeat the activity at home, establishing more frequent play and learning routines. Making toys from inexpensive household materials demonstrates to teen parents that toys do not need to be costly or even store-bought. When creating homemade toys, be sure to follow the safety precautions outlined in chapter 8, especially those concerning choking and toxic products. Listed below are examples of homemade toy projects, some with corresponding stories, songs, or fingerplays.

A handmade lift-the-flap book. (Hal Jerman)

Homemade toys are just as fun! (Vickie Shelton)

Toy Projects

String Spiders

Supplies:

- medium-weight kitchen or packaging string (kite string is too thin)
- ¾-inch round colored office labels
- ¼-inch round colored office labels

Tools:

- pairs of scissors
- ruler or measuring stick

Process:

1. Cut one length of string about 24 inches long. This will be the spider's hanging thread.
2. To make the spider's body, hold together four fingers of one hand, and wrap another 18-inch piece of string around them twice (this will make eight legs).
3. Center and knot the 24-inch string at the center of the loops on your hand, slipping the loops off your hand as you do so. Knot the hanging thread together at the top.
4. Cut the loops in half to make legs.
5. Attach a large round label to each side of the spider's legs' knot to make the body. Put two ¼-inch labels on one side for eyes.
6. Sing and play "The Itsy Bitsy Spider!"

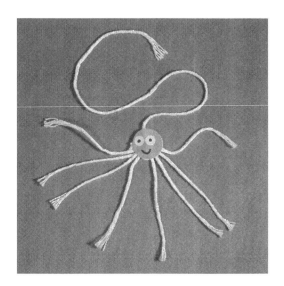

An eentsy-weentsy string spider. (Hal Jerman)

Egg Shakers

Supplies:

- plastic eggs that can be opened and filled (one per participant)
- uncooked rice (1 to 2 tablespoons per egg)
- white glue or narrow (¾-inch) colored plastic tape

Tools:

- 2 to 3 soup spoons (to share)
- 2 to 3 pairs of scissors

Process:

1. Measure 1 to 2 tablespoons of rice into each egg.
2. Seal the egg by running a line of glue around the outside edge of one half of the egg and pushing the two halves together. Allow it to dry. Or, close the egg and seal it shut with an overlapping length of heavy plastic tape wrapped around the seam.
3. Use for rhythm activities and singing.

Resources for Toy-Making Activities

Projects to make from *Baby Play: 100 Fun-filled Activities to Maximize Your Baby's Potential*, edited by Wendy Masi and Roni Cohen Leiderman (2001), include "Rippling Ribbons," dangling gift ribbons attached to a dowel or chopstick to wave for baby's delight. Two more sensory toys are the "Shake, Rattle, and Roll," a small plastic bottle filled with sand, dried beans, or pebbles and duct-taped shut, or the "Bottle Roll," a plastic baby bottle filled with a variety of dried beans to roll and shake. All are easy and quick to make, each taking about 20 minutes.

The Colossal Book of Crafts for Kids and Their Families, by Phyllis Fiarotta and Noel Fiarotta (1997), is filled with old-fashioned fun. Try "Spinning Star Wheels," a version of the traditional pinwheel that can be used with "Twinkle, Twinkle, Little Star" by independent preschoolers, or by parents with infants and toddlers. Dads (and moms and kids) will love flying "Gliding Paper Airplanes." Be sure to allow for plenty of flight time, especially for toddlers who may need some assistance to perfect their trajectory. The "Braided Yarn Octopus" and "Tie a Yarn Doll" are classic 1950s toys to braid from yarn, and they will appeal to older infants, toddlers, and preschoolers, with supervision. They may be slightly more challenging for teen parents to make and will take 45 to 60 minutes. Fold a "Paper Captain's Hat" from large sheets of newsprint or construction paper. This is easy to make in 15 minutes or less and fun to wear for toddlers and preschoolers, with supervision.

An offshoot of Disney's FamilyFun website, *Family Fun Crafts*, by Deanna Cook (1997), offers a number of projects that can be directly linked to fingerplays and stories. A "Felt Storytelling Board" can be made from a shoe box and scraps of felt are cut into shapes, numbers, people, flora, and fauna. Be sure to share some flannel board stories or rhymes (see chapter 7) as examples. This is for adult use with an older infant; toddlers and preschoolers can use it with help from an adult. This project will take 45 minutes or more. Assemble "Puppets-Thumbs Up," finger puppet lambs, pigs, cows, and so on from felt rectangles, adding bits of felt to make specific animals. Use them with nursery rhymes like "Baa, Baa, Black Sheep," "This Little Piggy," and "Hey, Diddle Diddle." Everyone has fun making "Watercolor Butterflies" from white coffee filters and watercolor paints or food coloring. Clip a clothespin in the middle and spread your butterfly's wings. Use with *The Very Hungry Caterpillar*.

There's an adorable "Eentsy, Weentsy Spider" with his own paper towel tube spout to make in *The Little Hands Nature Book* by Nancy Castaldo (1996).

Toddler Play: 100 Fun-filled Activities to Maximize Your Toddler's Potential by Wendy Masi (2001) has some terrific, easy toddler toys. Try "Paper-Bag Blocks" made from paper grocery bags; a "Paper Puzzle," a large, colorful photo glued to piece of heavy paper and cut into four large sections; and "Ribbon Rings," strips of fabric or fabric ribbon tied onto canning rings and used when dancing to music. Best of all is the "Rain-Stick," a cardboard poster tube filled with rice that makes a noise like rain, for a delightfully soothing sensory experience.

These simple projects from Martha Stewart.com do not disappoint. Try a "Sponge Ball" made from strips of colorful dry sponge tied together with string (can be played with wet or dry) and "Tinsel Stars," which can be simplified by using silver pipe cleaners. Perfect to use when singing "Twinkle, Twinkle . . ."

CONCLUSION

Incorporating hands-on activities and supporting teen parents' use of the library's recreational resources adds significantly to your program. These types of fun programs support teen parents' exploration of their own tastes, creativity, and identity and provide a respite from the pressures and stress of their daily lives. Additionally, activities that provide entertainment reinforce the concept of the power of play for themselves and as a method of early learning for their children. Finally, by offering recreational activities, librarians and staff have a powerful opportunity to establish deeper relationships with their group of teen parents, thereby enhancing the overall quality of services provided to this population.

Quick-to-make toys: a sponge ball and pipe-cleaner tinsel star. (Hal Jerman)

REFERENCES

General

Brown, Stuart and Christopher Vaughan. *Play: How it Shapes the Brain, Opens the Imagination, and Invigorates the Soul.* New York: Penguin Group, 2009.

Crafts

All Free Crafts.com. http://www.allfreecrafts.com/.
Amazing Moms.com: Keeping Life Fun and Festive. http://www.amazingmoms.com/.
Beadage: All About Beading! http://www.beadage.net/index.html.
    Basic instructions for making many types of bead jewelry, stylish project instructions, and listings of suppliers.
Editors of Chicken Socks. *Make Your Own Paper Flowers.* Palo Alto, CA: Klutz Press, 2007.
Editors of Klutz. *Painted Rocks.* Palo Alto, CA: Klutz Press, 2000.
Editors of Klutz. *Tissue Paper Flowers.* Palo Alto, CA: Klutz Press, 2000.
Family Fun.com. "Crafts." http://familyfun.go.com/crafts/.
Garza, Carmen Lomas. *Making Magic Windows: Creating Papel Picado/Cut-Paper Art with Carmen Lomas Garza.* San Francisco: Children's Book Press, 1999.
Graham, Andrea. 4YA: Inspiration for Youth Advocates. (n.d.). http://www.the4yablog.com/.
    Keep up on what's popular in the teen world with the 4YA blog. Lots of ideas for au courant programming.
Haab, Sherri, and Michelle Haab. *Dangles and Bangles: Twenty-five Funky Accessories to Make and Wear.* New York: Watson-Guptill, 2005.
    Quick and sassy projects, many of which make use of recycled and inexpensive materials. Only basic tools and skills required.
Honnold, RoseMary. *101+ Teen Programs That Work.* New York: Neal-Schuman, 2003.
Instructables.com. "Have a DIY Christmas!" (2010). http://www.instructables.com/id/DIY-Christmas/.
Johnson, Anne Akers. *Handmade Cards: Simple Designs for Beautiful Cards.* Palo Alto, CA: Klutz Press, 2002.
Johnson, Anne Akers. *Natural Beauty Book: Create Your Own Natural Spa Experience.* Palo Alto, CA: Klutz Press, 2009.
Johnson, Ginger. *Paper-Folding Fun! 50 Awesome Crafts to Weave, Twist and Curl.* Charlotte, VT: Williamson, 2002.
Kaboose.com. "Crafts for Teens and Tweens." (n.d.). http://crafts.kaboose.com/crafts-for-teens.html.
Klutz.com. http://www.klutz.com.
    Books from Klutz Press are not usually purchased by libraries because they contain consumable supplies and pages to be torn out or drawn on. That said, they are full of stylish, creative, user-friendly projects. Consider purchasing titles of interest for your professional/reference collection.
Lillian, Jenine, ed. *Cool Teen Programs for Under $100.* Chicago: American Library Association, 2009.
Mid-Hudson Library System. "Youth Programs: Child to Teen." (n.d.). http://www.midhudson.org/program/ideas/youth_programs.htm.
Osbourn, Sherri. "Family Crafts." About.com: Family Crafts. http://familycrafts.about.com/.
    Links to hundreds of crafts, which can be searched by holiday, material, or age (recommend searching elementary and tween, in addition to teen).
Ott, Valerie. *Teen Programs with Punch: A Month-by-Month Guide.* Westport, CT: Libraries Unlimited, 2006.
Pavon, Ana-Elba, and Diana Borrego. *Twenty-five Latino Craft Projects.* Chicago: American Library Association, 2003.
    Crafts are, for the most part, related to Hispanic holidays such as Cinco de Mayo and Hispanic Heritage Month (September 15–October 15).
San Francisco Herb Company. http://www.sfherb.com.
Schiedermayer, Ellie. *Got Tape? Roll Out the Fun with Duct Tape!* Iola, WI: Krause Publications, 2002.
Torres, Laura, and Michael Sherman. *Pipe Cleaners Gone Crazy: A Complete Guide to Bending Fuzzy Sticks.* Palo Alto, CA: Klutz Press, 1997.
Wilson, Joe. *Ductigami: The Art of the Tape.* Erin, ON: Boston Mills Press, 1999.

Cooking Activities

About.com: Candy. "Marshmallow Snowmen." http://candy.about.com/od/kidfriendlytreats/r/mmsnowmen.htm.
About.com: Teens. "Edible Valentines." http://parentingteens.about.com/od/recipesforkids/r/kids_recipes98.htm.

About.com: Teens. "S'More Eyeballs." http://parentingteens.about.com/od/recipesforkids/r/hallow een209.htm.

Cook, Deanna. *FamilyFun Super Snacks*. New York: Disney, 2004.

Crespo, Clare. *The Secret Life of Food*. New York: Hyperion Books, 2002.
    Adventures in trompe l'oeil food crafting.

Dunnington, Rose. *Big Snacks, Little Meals: After School, Dinnertime, Anytime*. New York: Lark Books, 2006.

Katzen, Mollie, and Ann Henderson. *Pretend Soup and Other Real Recipes: A Cookbook for Preschoolers and Up*. Berkeley, CA: Tricycle Press, 1994.

Self-Care

Chryssicas, Mary Kaye. *Breathe: Yoga for Teens*. New York: DK Publishing, 2007.

Reber, Deborah. *Chill: Stress-reducing Techniques for a More Balanced, Peaceful You*. New York: Simon Pulse, 2008.

Sammons, Mary Beth, and Samantha Moss. *InSPAration: A Teen's Guide to Healthy Living Inspired by Today's Top Spas*. New York: Watson-Guptill Publications, 2005.

Readers' Advisory

American Library Association. Young Adult Library Services Association. "Popular Paperbacks for Young Adults" (2010), http://www.ala.org/ala/mgrps/divs/yalsa/booklistsawards/popular paperback/popularpaperbacks.cfm.

American Library Association. Young Adult Library Services Association. "Quick Picks for Reluctant Young Adult Readers" (2010), http://www.ala.org/ala/mgrps/divs/yalsa/booklistsawards/ quickpicks/qphome.cfm.

Bartel, Julie, and Pam Spencer Holley, eds. *Annotated Booklists for Every Teen Reader*. New York: Neal-Schuman Publishers, 2010.

Bechard, Margaret. *Hanging On to Max*. Brookfield, CT: Roaring Brook Press, 2002.

Benton, Jim. *It's a Happy Bunny: Love Bites*. New York: Scholastic, 2005.

Bittel, Helen. "From Basketball to Barney: Teen Fatherhood, Didacticism, and the Literary in YA Fiction." *The ALAN Review* 36, no. 2 (2009): n.p.

Booth, Heather. *Serving Teens through Readers' Advisory*. Chicago: American Library Association, 2007.

Canfield, Jack, ed. *Chicken Soup for the Teenage Soul: 101 Stories of Life, Love, and Learning*. Deerfield Beach, FL: Health Communications, 1997.

Carter, Antonia "Toya." *Priceless Inspirations*. Las Vegas, NV: Farrah Gray Publishing, 2011.

Davis, Deborah. *You Look Too Young to Be a Mom: Teen Mothers Speak Out on Love, Learning, and Success*. New York: Perigee, 2004.

Dessen, Sarah. *Someone Like You*. New York: Viking, 1998.

Fantasia. *Life Is Not a Fairy Tale*. New York: Fireside Books, 2005.

Herald, Diana Tixier. *Teen Genreflecting 3: A Guide to Reading Interests*. Westport, CT: Libraries Unlimited, 2010.

Holley, Pam Spencer, ed. *Quick and Popular Reads for Teens*. Chicago: American Library Association, 2009.

Hornby, Nick. *Slam*. New York: G.P. Putnam's Sons, 2007.

Jiménez, Francisco. *The Circuit: Stories from the Life of a Migrant Child*. Albuquerque: University of New Mexico Press, 1997.

Johnson, Angela. *The First Part Last*. New York: Simon & Schuster, 2003.

Jones, Patrick, Maureen L. Hartman, and Patricia Taylor. *Connecting with Reluctant Teen Readers: Tips, Titles, and Tools*. New York: Neal-Schuman Publishers, 2006.

Keane, Nancy. *The Big Book of Teen Reading Lists: 100 Great, Ready-to-Use Book Lists for Educators, Librarians, Parents, and Teens*. Westport, CT: Libraries Unlimited, 2006.

Koelling, Holly. *Best Books for Young Adults*. 3rd ed. Chicago: American Library Association, 2007.

Students at South Vista Educational Center. *Daycare and Diplomas: Teen Mothers Who Stayed in School*. Minneapolis, MN: Fairview Press, 2000.

Swan, Jen Hubert. Reading Rants.org. http://www.readingrants.org/.

The Book Report, Inc. Teen Reads.com. http://www.teenreads.com/index.asp.

Storytelling and Reading Aloud

Baltuck, Naomi. *Apples from Heaven: Multicultural Folk Tales about Stories and Storytellers*. North Haven, CT: Linnet Books, 1995.

Coles, Robert. *The Story of Ruby Bridges*. New York: Scholastic, 1995.

de Vos, Gail. *Storytelling for Young Adults: A Guide to Tales for Teens*, 2nd ed. Westport, CT: Libraries Unlimited, 2003.

Demi. *The Empty Pot*. New York: H. Holt, 1990.

Demi. *The Greatest Power*. New York: Margaret K. McElderry Books, 2004.

Freymann, Saxton. *How Are You Peeling?* New York: Arthur A. Levine Books, 1999.

Jaffe, Nina, and Steve Zeitlin. *The Cow of No Color: Riddle Stories and Justice Tales from Around the World*. New York: Henry Holt, 1998.

Krull, Kathleen. *Harvesting Hope: The Story of Cesar Chavez*. San Diego: Harcourt Brace, 2003.

Krull, Kathleen. *Wilma Unlimited: How Wilma Rudolph Became the World's Fastest Woman*. San Diego: Harcourt Brace, 1996.

Parr, Todd. *It's Okay to Be Different*. Boston: Little, Brown, 2001.

Parr, Todd. *Things That Make You Feel Good/Things That Make You Feel Bad*. Boston: Little, Brown, 1999.

Parr, Todd. *This Is My Hair*. Boston: Little, Brown and Co., 1999.

Pellowski, Anne. *Drawing Stories from Around the World and a Sampling of European Handkerchief Stories*. Westport, CT: Libraries Unlimited, 2005.

Pellowski, Anne. *The Storytelling Handbook: A Young People's Collection of Unusual Tales and Helpful Hints on How to Tell Them*. New York: Simon & Schuster, 1995.

Polacco, Patricia. *The Butterfly*. New York: Philomel Books, 2000.

Polacco, Patricia. *Junkyard Wonders*. New York: Philomel Books, 2010.

Polacco, Patricia. *Pink and Say*. New York: Philomel Books, 1994. Also in Spanish: *Pink y Say*. New York: Lectorum, 1997.

Polacco, Patricia. *Thank You, Mr. Falker*. New York: Philomel Books, 1998. Also in Spanish: *Gracias, Señor Falker*. New York: Lectorum, 2006.

Scieszka, Jon. *The Frog Prince, Continued*. New York: Viking, 1991.

Scieszka, Jon. *Squids Will Be Squids: Fresh Morals, Beastly Fables*. New York: Viking, 1998.

Scieszka, Jon. *The Stinky Cheese Man: And Other Fairly Stupid Tales*. New York: Viking, 1992.

Stangl, Jean. *Paper Stories*. Belmont, CA: Fearon Teacher Aids, 1984.

Tashjian, Virginia. *Juba This and Juba That*. 2nd ed. Boston: Little, Brown, 1995.

Winter, Jeanette. *Wangari's Trees of Peace: A True Story from Africa*. Orlando, FL: Harcourt, 2008.

Young, Ed. *Seven Blind Mice*. New York: Philomel Books, 1991.

Bookmaking

Art Junction: A Collaborative Art Space for Teachers and Students. http://www.artjunction.org/.

Baker, Keith. *Big Fat Hen*. New York: Harcourt Brace, 1994.

Book Blanks.com. http://www.bookblanks.com/: Inexpensive ready-made blank books for bookmaking.

Carle, Eric. *The Very Busy Spider*. New York: Penguin, 1984.

Carle, Eric. *The Very Hungry Caterpillar*. New York: Philomel, 1994.

Check, Laura. *The Kids' Guide to Making Scrapbooks and Photo Albums! How to Collect, Design, Assemble, Decorate*. Charlotte, VT: Williamson Publishing, 2002.

Gaylord, Susan Kapuscinski. MakingBooks with Children. http://makingbooks.com/.
    Includes quick, inexpensive books to make from household materials and suggestions for book subjects, supplies and materials, and techniques.

Golden, Alisa. *Creating Handmade Books*. New York: Sterling Publishing, 1998.

Hill, Eric. *Where's Spot?* New York: G. P. Putnam's Sons, 2000.

Hines, Anna Grossnickle. *1, 2, Buckle My Shoe*. Orlando, FL: Harcourt, 2008.

Hutchins, Pat. *Changes, Changes*. New York: Macmillan, 1971.

Johnson, Ginger. *Paper-Folding Fun! 50 Awesome Crafts to Weave, Twist and Curl*. Charlotte, VT: Williamson Publishing, 2002.

Martin, Bill. *Brown Bear, Brown Bear, What Do You See?* New York: H. Holt, 1996.

Parr, Todd. *This Is My Hair*. New York: Little, Brown, 1999.

Pensiero, Janet. *Totally Cool Journals, Notebooks and Diaries*. New York: Sterling Publishing, 2003.

Rainbow Resource Center: Learning Tools for Home and School. http://www.rainbowresource.com/index.php: Source for blank books.

Teachers Paradise.com. http://www.teachersparadise.com/: Order blank books for bookmaking.

Wells, Rosemary. *Bingo*. New York: Scholastic Press, 1999.

Williams, Sue. *I Went Walking*. San Diego: Harcourt Brace, 1996.

Toy Projects

Castaldo, Nancy Fusco. *The Little Hands Nature Book*. Charlotte, VT: Williamson Publishing, 1996.

Cook, Deanna. *FamilyFun Crafts*. New York: Disney, 1997.

Fiarotta, Phyllis, and Noel Fiarotta. *The Colossal Book of Crafts for Kids and Their Families*. New York: Black Dog and Leventhal. 1997.

Martha Stewart.com. http://www.marthastewart.com/.

> Martha has an endless number of stylish, and often inexpensive, craft ideas. The website is particularly strong on holiday ideas.

Masi, Wendy, ed. *Toddler Play: 100 Fun-filled Activities to Maximize Your Toddler's Potential*. San Francisco: Creative Publishing International, 2001.

Masi, Wendy, and Roni Cohen Leiderman, eds. *Baby Play: 100 Fun-filled Activities to Maximize Your Baby's Potential*. San Francisco: Creative Publishing International, 2001.

RESOURCES

DickBlick.com. http://www.dickblick.com/.

> An onlinesource for art supplies offered at reasonable prices.

Honnold, RoseMary. *See YA Around: Library Programming for Teens*. http://www.cplrmh.com/.

> RoseMary Honnold, author of several compilations of teen programs, also maintains this website with ideas for programming, Teen Read Week, and Summer Reading programs.

Honnold, RoseMary. *The Teen Reader's Advisor*. New York: Neal-Schuman Publishers, 2006.

Kaboose. "Crafts for Teens and Tweens." http://crafts.kaboose.com/crafts-for-teens.html.

Kan, Katherine. *Sizzling Summer Reading Programs for Young Adults*. Chicago: American Library Association, 2006.

> Ideas that would be popular with teen parents include "butt pillows," "make your own sundaes," "pasta salad in a baggie," and a chocolate tasting.

MacDonald, Margaret Read. *Peace Tales: World Folktales to Talk About*. Hamden, CT: Linnet Books, 1992.

MacDonald, Margaret Read. *The Storyteller's Sourcebook: A Subject, Title, and Motif Index to Folklore Collections for Children, 1983–1999*. Detroit, MI: Gale Group, 2001.

MacDonald, Margaret Read. *Three-Minute Tales: Stories from Around the World to Tell or Read When Time Is Short*. Little Rock, AR: August House Publishers, 2004.

Nichols, Kristen. "Facts and Fictions: Teen Pregnancy in Young Adult Literature." *The ALAN Review* 34, no. 3 (2007): 30–38.

Pellowski, Anne. *The Family Storytelling Handbook: How to Use Stories, Anecdotes, Rhymes, Handkerchiefs, Paper, and Other Objects to Enrich Your Family Traditions*. New York: Macmillan, 1987.

Pellowski, Anne. *The Story Vine: A Sourcebook of Unusual and Easy-to-tell Stories from Around the World*. New York: Macmillan, 1984.

Rogge, Hannah. *Hardwear: Jewelry from a Toolbox*. New York: Stewart, Tabori and Chang, 2006.

Spa Index: Spa at Home Tips, Recipes and More. http://www.spaindex.com/HomeSpa/HomeSpa.htm.

Wallace, Mary, and Jessica Wallace. *The Girls' Spa Book: 20 Dreamy Ways to Relax and Feel Great*. Toronto, ON: Maple Tree Press, 2004.

Witmer, Denise. "Bath Salts Recipes." About.com.Teens. http://parentingteens.about.com/cs/bathcrafts/a/blbath.htm.

Witmer, Denise. "TeenCrafts." About.com: Teens. http://parentingteens.about.com/od/crafts/Crafts_Craft_Project_Ideas.htm.

> A wide-ranging resource for craft project ideas from friendship to jeans to journaling crafts.

Zarate, Christina. "Día de Los Muertos: A User's Guide." Program of Latino History and Culture, Smithsonian National Museum of American History. http://latino.si.edu/DayoftheDead/DODManual.pdf.

> Background information and instructions for related craft projects such as paper marigolds, papel picados and sugar skulls.

7

PARENT-CHILD
INTERACTIVE
LITERACY PROGRAMS

Shared time between teen parents and their children has the potential to strengthen the parent-child bond, enhance the children's language and literacy development, and stimulate growth for the family. Library programs that offer shared activities facilitate meaningful parent-child interactions and demonstrate the efficacy of early learning to the young parents. Through observation of the child's responsiveness and pleasure while singing, reading, and playing, the young parent is encouraged to continue these activities beyond the library program. Understanding the importance of these interactive activities and the parents' own role in their children's development is critical for a healthy start.

Throughout this chapter, the watchwords are simplicity and experiential learning (for both the parent and the child). Many teen parents may struggle with their own reading skills and are hesitant to try reading with their child. These shared activities should encourage young parents to think, "I can do that!" and "This is fun!" while creating a basis for the discussion of the connection between experiences and learning. Use a subtle approach when imparting early learning concepts. Try to slip them naturally into the discussion through an occasional one-sentence observation about a concept. Teen parents want to know, but not be told. Learning happens as a component of the total experience.

EARLY BRAIN DEVELOPMENT

Neuroscience research reveals that for adequate development, a young child's brain needs a variety of interesting daily life experiences and positive stimulation from caregivers (Brotherson 2005). For a young child, an interesting daily life experience is not an earth-shattering event, nor is positive stimulation a challenging pursuit. They are just the simple ways that parents generally engage their children, including talking, singing, reading, and playing.

At birth, a baby's brain has almost all the brain cells (neurons) that it will ever possess. But, only about 25 percent of the wiring that allows neurons to pass impulses along is in place. At that point, the brain is directing basic life functions such as breathing and digestion. The development of the complex web of connections that results from brain activity and stimulation is still yet to come. As neurons mature and receive data from the senses, they try to connect to other cells by sending out two types of branches: axons, which transmit information out of the cell, and dendrites, which bring information in. Cells link their dendrites and axons

Reading together. (Vickie Shelton)

to each other to form connections, called synapses, which allow the flow of neurotransmitters (chemicals that carry the messages) from cell to cell. This process allows the brain to manage all its functions, from simple to complex. During infancy and childhood, synapses continue to be made: at birth each neuron has about 2,500 synapses, but by age three the number has peaked at 15,000, which is many more than in the adult brain. This makes a preschool child's brain more active, connected, and flexible than an adult's brain (Gopnik, Meltzoff, and Kuhl 1999).

It is this series of chemical connections from cell to cell that build our thoughts, habits, and memories. Through our five senses, the outside world shapes the brain's development (Brotherson 2005). Differences in early experiences can cause the brain to develop in different ways. It is even thought that living in a chaotic or stressful environment in early childhood can adversely affect brain development (Hawley 2000).

Therein lies the limiting factor, which is the amount of sensory stimulation that a child receives. The brain does not get wired up without experiences, and only pathways that are repeatedly stimulated permanently connect. Throughout most of childhood, the brain connects and disconnects neural pathways based on use. Over-pruning of the pathways, which can lead to brain deficits, takes place if a young child does not receive a normal level of positive experiences. Problems arise when children are rarely spoken to and have few opportunities to explore and play (Hawley 2000).

In addition, there are some functions that must develop during a specific time frame in a child's early years or be forever compromised. For vision and hearing, the time period is from birth to six months of age; for language acquisition, from birth to two years; for emotional attachment, from birth to 18 months; and gross motor skills development extends from birth to age four (Cobb 2007). While a child must be severely neglected to be drastically compromised in these areas, there is little doubt that any child's potential intellectual abilities develop in relation to the level of secure and positive stimulation he or she receives (Hawley 2000).

Young parents, due to immaturity and lack of personal experience and education, may not realize the importance of engaging in the talking and playing that young children need, or they may not feel comfortable interacting with their child in this capacity. Through modeling and by coaching teen parents, library staff can have an important role in bettering their children's chances for success. An uncomplicated explanation of their impact on brain development can help teen parents understand the critical role that they play. The following ideas should be included in a discussion about the young child's brain development.

- No one's intelligence is decided only by genetics. It is the combination of nature (what you are born with) and nurture (what you gain from your environment) that determines a child's future intellectual ability.
- At birth, unlike other body organs, the brain has not finished developing. It still needs to be wired up. You see the results of brain development as the child masters behaviors like smiling, talking, and coordinating her movements to grasp objects and to crawl.
- The wiring takes place when the child feels safe, secure, and loved and is played with and talked to by the grown-ups in her life.
- Listening to adults talk to each other, or to people talking on the television, does not work. The communication needs to be directly between the adult and the child (Hawley 2000).

Use "Help Your Child's Brain Develop through Love and Play," an attractive and accessibly written list, from the Oregon's Child: Everyone's Business website, to talk about brain development. It simply expresses the important concepts that teens need to know. Viewing with the teen parents the DVD *The First Years Last Forever*, part of the *I Am Your Child* series from Parents Action for Children, would be another good starting point for discussion.

GOALS OF TEEN PARENT–CHILD INTERACTIVE LITERACY PROGRAMS

Parent-child programs have multiple impacts. They can:

1. Demonstrate early learning practices through storytimes, books, and reading.
2. Enhance children's language and literacy development.
3. Show the pleasure and importance of experiences for young children.
4. Provide opportunities for positive parent-child interaction through activities.
5. Guide parents to understand that they are their child's first and most influential teacher.

For clarity, a distinction must be made between the terms "early literacy" and "early learning." Early literacy, or language and pre-literate development, is one component of early learning, which encompasses the spectrum of thinking skills that the young child works so diligently to acquire. Early literacy is the natural province of library services to young children and is covered extensively in this chapter, which presents methods of sharing early literacy techniques, including interactive reading, songs, and rhymes, to use with teen parents. Chapter 8 focuses on hands-on activities and play, which address the larger early learning needs of the children of teen parents.

Practices that Promote Early Learning

Early cognitive and language development are both well served by the basic triad of early literacy: talking, reading, and singing. The importance of these activities is not necessarily intuitive. Often teen parents have not seen or experienced meaningful parent interaction with very young children. They may believe, as many people do, that babies do not understand what is being said to them. Unfortunately, it is necessary to make a habit of interacting with what seems to be an inert little being over a period of time before parents tend to see a response. Showing teen parents what is effective and connecting these activities to their children's immediate responses is the best strategy. Don't try to bombard parents with the facts of early learning all at once; present them in a conversational context over time. Important messages to convey to the young parents include the following concepts.

Talking

1. Children learn how to talk because adults talk to them.
2. Speak slowly and clearly to young children in order to train their brains to identify individual sounds.

3. When your baby babbles, respond to what your baby says to you. For example, if she says "ma-ma," answer with "Yes, mama is here."

4. Speak face-to-face with your baby because infants watch your mouth to match the shapes it makes with the sounds they hear.

5. It doesn't matter what language you speak to children in; it's the stimulation that is important.

Reading

1. Read to your child from an early age—even in the first days.

2. Reading offers children rich language experiences that they don't get in day-to-day conversation.

3. Pick a time to read when you and your child are in a good mood. When you find a good time of day, try to make a habit of regularly reading at that time.

4. Share books every day; even just a few minutes every day is important. You both will cherish this special time together.

5. At first your baby may not seem like she is paying attention, but she is still hearing your voice. The sooner you start reading, and the more you do it, the more your baby will pay attention.

6. Keep reading a short and fun experience; it's okay to change the words or skip a few!

7. Show your child the book, point to objects in the pictures, and name them.

8. Even with babies, but especially with toddlers, ask questions about the story—"Where's the cat?" or "What sound does a cat make?" Pause after asking, and then answer the question. This helps the child learn new words and also learn that conversation is about taking turns. If your child talks, repeat and affirm your child's answer.

9. Children love to hear favorite stories again and again.

10. Have board books that your child can play with. Show her how to hold a book and turn the pages. If your child wants to hold the book and won't let you read, let her hold another book while you read to her. It's a good thing when a child gets attached to books.

11. Carry a favorite book in your diaper bag; pull it out to read together whenever you have time.

12. Show your child that words are everywhere. Read the *environmental print*, the words on signs and packaging, that you see every day.

Singing

1. Songs and fingerplays offer repetition and the awareness of sequences and patterns, both of which help young children learn. Repetition also improves their memory (Zero to Three 2002). Examples are "Ring around the Rosie" and "Row, Row, Row Your Boat."

2. Music introduces children to the sound and meaning of words, and it helps them hear the smaller parts of word sounds, which they need to learn to talk and, later, to read. Examples are "Apples and Bananas" and "The Eentsy-Weetsy Spider."

3. Children can learn many things from singing and rhymes, including how to follow directions, basic ideas like beginning and end, cause and effect, and important concepts like counting, colors, and facts about the natural world (Rosenkoetter and Knapp-Philo 2006). Examples are "The Wheels on the Bus," "Head, Shoulders, Knees, and Toes," and "Where Is Thumbkin."

4. Physically moving to songs helps children improve their motor skills and coordination. Different tempos let the child move in a variety of ways: fast or slow, quietly or noisily. Examples are "Motor Boat, Motor Boat" and "The Bubble Song."

A lap is always big enough for two! (Vickie Shelton)

5. Clapping to music helps children learn about rhythm.

6. Singing can be soothing and comforting. It shows your child that you care about her, even if she can't understand the words yet. An example is a folk song like "Kumbaya."

7. It doesn't matter if you are a good singer or not; your child will love to hear your voice.

8. Don't sing too fast; children need a slow pace and clear speech to be able to hear the words.

MAKING READING A PART OF EVERY CHILD'S LIFE

Literacy development is a continuous process. Therefore, conveying to teen parents the importance of creating a literacy-rich home environment will help them integrate early learning activities that you model into their children's daily lives.

Books in the Home

In order to successfully bring reading into the home, families must have access to age-appropriate, quality books. To accomplish this, options for book sources include the following ideas.

- Funding for gift books to build home libraries
- Gently used library discards or donations
- Circulating collections that may be checked out but do not incur fines or charges for lost books
- Regular checkout of library materials

Most funders and grants in the literacy field understand the importance of gift books as a part of the project package. Library and school foundations are often amenable to funding books for teen families. It is a relatively small investment that can have a significant long-term payoff.

Sturdy board books are recommended to allow for frequent handling by children themselves. Keep in mind that teen parents are not always clear about the young child's developmental learning curve and may assume that their children are capable of understanding and remembering concepts like "being careful" far beyond their actual ability. Concern about torn pages and rough handling can lead to books becoming an issue instead of the pleasure they should be.

Selecting Giveaway Books

Try to pick books that have the literary and visual quality and child appeal that will stimulate repeated readings. Age appropriateness is very important, particularly because teen parents, who may be doubtful about the usefulness of reading aloud to begin with, will be further discouraged if their child will not sit still for a book. When choosing books to give away, select books with the following characteristics.

- Brief stories that the child can relate to, such as *Goodnight Moon*, by Margaret Wise Brown (1991), or *Counting Kisses*, by Karen Katz (2001).
- Text that is short and concrete (like *Where's Spot*, by Eric Hill), has repetition of phrases (like *I Went Walking*, by Sue Williams), includes patterned text (like *Quick as a Cricket*, by Audrey Wood), or incorporates rhyming phrases (like *Tomie's Little Mother Goose*, by Tomie DePaola).
- Be cautious when selecting books that have single-word or no text. Some teen parents may not have the skill to invent or extend a story by interpreting the illustrations.
- Illustrations that are clear and simple with bright, distinct colors and black outlines. Avoid soft pastel pictures because they are hard to decipher.

Remember, these are general guidelines. Most important, select books that are meaningful and relevant to your specific group of families. Also, these rules are often meant to be broken. Don't reject busy little board books with lots to look at, like Jerry Smith's pudgy board book version of *Wheels on the Bus* (1991), just because the illustrations are not clear and simple. During group storytimes, hand out copies of small books to parents and ask them to read along with you. They may not actually read the words, which is fine, but they will turn pages and show the pictures to their children as you read.

Toddlers and older children can be fascinated by photographs of other children in books (such as *Mrs. Mustard's Baby Faces*, by Jane Wattenberg). But the detailed nature of a photograph can be visually confusing. When selecting books illustrated with photographs, look for pictures with plain backgrounds and that have a clear subject. Margaret Miller and Tana Hoban are two children's book photographers who successfully accomplish this.

Introducing Teen Parents to Children's Books

Helping teen parents enjoy children's books as much as their children do can be a great challenge. When introducing these young parents to the books, try making your presentation into an interactive game. Start with a pile of great infant and toddler books (both board and traditional format) from our booklists. Be sure to include some books with colors, numbers, or animals to identify and some that have song lyrics or rhymes for text. Also select a group of picture books geared toward older preschoolers, like Dr. Seuss's longer books, Laura Numeroff's *If You Give a . . .* series, or Jonathan London's *Froggy* books. Plan on bringing two to three books per parent. Gather your group around a table, or sit in a circle on the floor. Form small groups of parents whose children are similar in age—under one year, one to two years, two to three years, and possibly three to four years. Distribute a selection of books to each group, and ask them to take about 5 to 10 minutes to look through them and think about whether their children might like them. Let them share and chat informally with each other while they peruse their books. Read one of your personal favorites to them, and add an anecdote about the book, if you have one. For instance, for *The Very Hungry Caterpillar* (Carle 1994), you could say "I think that I must have read this book 200 times over the years, but I never get tired of it." Now start the game, in which you describe a type of book and ask the teens to hold up a book from their stack that matches your description. If the teens want, let them talk about the book, or you can make a comment about one or two. The following is a suggested format for the game.

Round 1

1. Say to the teen parents, "Hold up a book that has simple pictures that will be easy for a young child to figure out."
2. Then say, "Hold up a book that has pictures with lots of little details. Would a two-year-old be interested in this book?"
3. Mention that books with simple, clear illustrations that are easy to interpret are best for little children.
4. Help the teen parents understand that it takes repeated exposure for children to understand that pictures represent things in the real world.

Round 2

1. Say to the teen parents, "Hold up a book that has a short, uncomplicated story about a topic your children know."
2. Then say, "Hold up a book that has a story that has a pattern; it repeats the same basic sentences with a different twist or end to it each time."
3. Next say, "Hold up a book that has a story that is too long or strange for a two-year-old."
4. Mention that repetition helps children learn and understand the book, and little children like books about their world.

Round 3

1. Say to the teen parents, "Hold up a book that is written in rhyme." Explain that rhyming is when one word sounds like another word.
2. Then say, "Hold up a book that is a collection of rhymes."
3. Ask, "What else do we do with children that have rhyming words?" (answer: sing).
4. Show them a book that has text that is the lyric of a song.
5. Explain that rhyming helps children hear the sounds that make up words, which is how they learn to talk and, later, to read.

Round 4

1. Say to the teen parents, "Hold up a book that has things in it that make noises."
2. Then say, "Hold up a book that would help children learn their colors, their numbers, or the names of things."
3. Mention that children learn best from the interactions between themselves and a grown-up with a book you're reading together. You can point things out in the pictures, talk about the words and story, and, of course, make all the noises, silly or otherwise, that you can manage!

Round 5

1. Choose a book that can be read expressively and that invites parent-child interaction. Say to the teen parents, "Now I want to read a book to you."
2. Read the first part of the book in a monotone voice, and then switch to a lively and expressive way, asking questions and making comments.
3. Ask, "What did you think of my reading? Which way would be more entertaining for your child?"

Round 6: True or False?

1. "You should make a child sit and listen to a book, even if you have to sit on them." (False: Reading should be fun for both of you, and if your child won't sit still, she will still hear the words. Sometimes, if your child wanders off and you keep reading out loud, something you say will intrigue your child and she will come back to listen.)

2. "Only read books that *you* like, and only read them once." (True and False: If you don't read books you like, you won't want to read. But you will have to read them over and over again, because little children both learn from and love repetition.)

3. "You should never read to your child more than once a week." (False: Read together as often as possible, and try to do it every day.)

4. "The only time to read a book to your child is before bedtime." (False: You can read anytime when you and your child are in the mood; the more often the better. Try to find regular times every day that work.)

5. "Babies as young as six months will listen to a book." (True: The more often you read to them, the more they will listen. Reading can be a special time to spend with your child.)

6. "When a mother talks to her child a lot, starting at birth, the child will know 300 more words by age two than a child whose mother doesn't talk to her much." (True: the more you talk to your child, the more she learns.)

Round 7: Closure

1. Ask the audience for one last book request for you to read aloud to the group. If no title is suggested, have your own selection ready to go.

2. Read the book aloud, commenting on techniques to use when reading to make the experience interactive between the parent and child.

3. Give everyone, including yourself, praise for a job well done!

Modeling Read-Aloud Methods

Always model reading for your group. This can be part of a storytime program, part of one-on-one reading with parent and child, or during a demonstration with just the parents. It may be desirable to use a doll to demonstrate how to hold a child and a book in tandem while reading. Modeling should encompass the following concepts.

1. Read with expression, because an interesting voice (especially a parent's voice) will draw the child into the story.

2. Notice and focus on what interests the child. It isn't always necessary to read all (or any) of the words. You can narrate the pictures and tell your own story.

3. Find opportunities for participation from the child, such as making sounds or movement, counting the numbers of objects on pages, and identifying or looking for things in the pictures. Imitate what happens in the story with hand gestures (Rosenkoetter and Knapp-Philo 2006). At first the adult will do it alone, but with repetition the child will begin to participate. An excellent example is *Here Are My Hands*, by Bill Martin (1998). As each body part is mentioned, the reader can point to the "hands for touching and holding" in the illustration, and then touch the child's hands. After repeated readings, the child can be asked, "Where's your hand? Touch your hand. Where are the child's hands in the picture?"

4. Connect the book to the child's life. When using a board book version of *The Wheels on the Bus*, say, "Look at all the people getting on the bus in the picture. We take the bus to get to school, don't we?"

5. Talk about concepts found in the book. For example, if you read *Big Fat Hen*, by Keith Baker (1994), say, "That's the mother hen. She's big, isn't she? Those are her baby chicks. They are small. Just like I'm your mommy, and I'm big; and you're my baby and you're small."

Communicating Early Learning Concepts

Read-aloud sessions present a concrete context where communicating early learning concepts to young parents can occur naturally. As you plan your program, think about the concepts related to your program's elements. Considering these concepts in advance will enable you to (sparingly) point them out during the program. It is important to not lecture, but instead casually make reference to how these activities benefit the child as they occur in your program. Here is a list of some learning concepts that can be highlighted.

- Sounds (words) and symbols (pictures, for example in books) have meaning and represent things (Rosenkoetter and Knapp-Philo 2006). Pointing this out to children will help them make the connection.
- Children learn through repetition. Use as an example any fingerplay or book with a repetitive text, like "Where is Thumbkin?" or *Peek-a-Moo*, by Marie Cimarusti (1998).
- Children begin to understand object permanency, the concept that objects exist even when not seen. Use as examples fingerplays and books where objects appear and disappear, such as "Two Little Blackbirds," lift-the-flap books like *Dear Zoo*, by Rod Campbell (2007), and the game of peekaboo.
- Children learn basic concepts such as size, counting, and colors. As an example use "Great Big Ball," and *Brown Bear, Brown Bear, What Do You See?* by Bill Martin (1996).
- Children learn about the world around them. Use as examples "The Eentsy-Weentsy Spider," "Apple Tree," and *The Very Hungry Caterpillar* and *From Head to Toe* by Eric Carle. *From Head to Toe* is especially powerful because it makes connections between how the child's body works and what animals do.
- Children learn about themselves. Use as an example "Head and Shoulders, Baby" or *Clap Hands*, by Helen Oxenbury (2009).

Incentives

Reading logs or calendars for tracking daily reading can be used as a basis for offering monthly incentive prizes. Begin by having the teens make a "reading calendar" for their child. Use a 12-inch by 18-inch piece of colorful construction paper or poster board for the back. Duplicate a blank 8-½-inch by 11-inch calendar sheet for the current or next month. Turning the construction paper with the long side vertical, attach the calendar sheet to the bottom half of the larger paper with tape. Offer stickers and markers to decorate the top half of the calendar with the child and parent's names. Send stickers home so that parent and child can mark each day that they read together. Reading logs can be modeled after your children's services summer reading program's reading log. Encourage families to bring their completed calendars or reading logs to your visits. Reward completed calendars with small prizes, such as extra books or small, safe toys.

PRACTICING ONE-ON-ONE READING

If time allows, and your group is amenable, working with small groups of parents and children to practice reading aloud and fingerplays can be very rewarding. It provides a focused setting for parents to observe the techniques you want them to learn, and it gives you a chance to bond more closely with the young families. In a more intimate group, the teen parents may be most receptive to hearing the connections between early learning concepts and the activities you are doing. When forming a small group, consider the following guidelines.

- Work with no more than three families at once.
- Group them by the age of their child.
- Plan to work with each group for about 10 to 15 minutes.
- Negotiate a quiet space away from the rest of the group, such as outside on a patch of grass or in a spare room.
- Bring a blanket to spread out that is big enough for you and the parents to sit on with their children. Infants can lie on their backs, facing their parent.
- Bring multiple copies of the same book so that you and every parent have a copy; also provide a printed list of a few favorite fingerplays and songs, one for each parent.
- If available, also bring wrist bells and puppets to use with songs and fingerplays,

A one-on-one reading and singing session. (Vickie Shelton)

- Let each parent choose a song or fingerplay that they would like to learn from the handout. Explain the order of the program so everyone knows what to expect from the activity.

If there is a pregnant teen in your parent group, encourage her to partner with a friend and his or her child to participate in the parent-child literacy and learning activities. Often, there are parents with more than one child; if both parties feel comfortable, have the pregnant teen engage in the activity with the second child. This way she can feel involved and have gained some knowledge and experiences for when she has her own baby.

Once everyone in your group is comfortable, you can begin the program, which can include the following components.

1. To begin, the storyteller sings a favorite song.
2. The storyteller reads the book and models conversation to help the child connect with the book.
3. The storyteller leads one of the chosen fingerplays.
4. Parents hold their children in a comfortable position and read the book aloud to them.
5. Close with another selected song or fingerplay.

One-on-one-reading practice sessions also present an opportunity to demonstrate the ways in which small children might respond to books. Even an infant may try to grab the book and help turn the pages, while a toddler will pick up a book and try to read it on her own. Be sure the teen parents appreciate that this is how it starts—a first indicator of their children's lifelong friendship with books. Take a minute or two to survey the group for comments or questions. Offer positive, specific remarks about the session. These sessions are particularly valuable for parents with infants. Their children's smiles and happy reactions are conducive to reinforcing the idea that children are never too young to engage in talking, reading, and singing activities.

GROUP STORYTIMES

Storytime experiences have many benefits for all children, but for teen parents and their families, they are both a special treat and a gateway to literacy. Many of the basic skills needed in preschool and beyond are gently introduced during storytime, such as being part of a group, listening, and following directions.

Expect and accept some level of chaos and wandering during most of your program. Remember that young children listen and learn even when they are not sitting quietly with rapt attention. Don't expect your young parents to stay totally engrossed, either. Some may be concerned with controlling their child's actions, dealing with a runny nose, or a variety of things. The pregnant teen moms in the group can have the hardest time relating to what is going on during the storytime. Be aware that this is not an environment in which to try to be instructive about storytime etiquette. Creating and maintaining goodwill with your audience is the top priority.

In some groups, social dynamics can contribute to a reluctance to participate. Teens can abhor looking dumb in front of their cohorts. Where an older parent may join in without a bit of self-consciousness, a teen who has, relatively speaking, barely left childhood behind can feel very uncomfortable acting childish. As the group gets to know you, and feels more comfortable, there may be more willingness to participate. Most often, though, it is their children's enthusiastic responses to the storytime that draws the parents in to the activity.

Often, the age range of children in teen parent groups is three years and younger. Generally, due to limited early learning experiences, older preschool children will happily participate in what would be considered infant/young toddler programs. Therefore, programs for this age group should be geared to what would be exciting and engaging for toddlers. This section presents detailed information on techniques that will make your programs a success for everyone involved, including participants who are new to storytime.

What Teen Parents Need to Know about Storytime

When introducing the concept of storytime to teen mothers and fathers, mentioning these suggestions will benefit both the parents and their children.

- Your child may want to just observe, and that is fine.
- Parents can model good listening and participation.
- If your child is crying and screaming, take him or her outside to calm down.
- A young child often can't do the movement activities alone, so you should work with your child and do the movements for your child.
- Repeating any of these activities regularly at home is a great thing to do for your child.
- Storytimes are a regular event at the public library. They are free, and all families are welcome to attend.

Having teen parents watch a library storytime during a library visit without their children can also be a useful exercise. Armed with a "Storytime Observation" checklist (find a sample at the end of this chapter) to help them scrutinize the storytime parents' behavior, they will observe the following components.

- The storytime's general structure and program, allowing them to know what to expect so that they will feel comfortable when they bring their own child
- Good and poor examples of parents modeling listening and participation
- The pleasure that children (and parents) derive from the program

Who, Me—Do a Storytime?

If you are a children's librarian, teen librarian, school librarian, teacher, or literacy specialist, it won't be difficult to add storyteller to your list of roles. If this is all new, start by attending and observing storytimes at your public library. Throw yourself on the mercy of the librarians responsible for the infant and toddler storytimes. There are many, many talented storytellers out there, and some, undoubtedly, work at your local library. In general, librarians love to share their knowledge and pass on the tricks of the trade.

Look at lots of picture books from infant and toddler booklists. Choose the book that speaks to you. Dredge up from your memory those nursery rhymes and songs that you loved when you were five. Children still love them today. Practice on any young children that cross your path. Put together a program, or use one listed in this book. Find your performance persona. Borrow a flannelboard and some stories. Practice doing a storytime on your own. Think about how important it is to show young parents that learning can be a joyful bonding experience for them with their children. Don't worry if everything isn't perfect, but reflect on what needs tweaking to work better. Remember to be patient with yourself; becoming a storyteller is a learning process. Most important, have fun!

Storytime Program Development and Presentation

Programs for teen parents and their children (ages three and under) work best if they are tightly structured and planned. This is not an audience to try "winging it" with; the presenter must move smoothly from one activity to the next to keep the audience's attention. For better or worse, their reaction hinges on your performance. The presenter's energy, enthusiasm, and responsiveness to the group are critical.

Having a well-planned program actually opens the door to unexpected opportunities for group participation, such as when a child spontaneously helps you with Old MacDonald's puppets, or runs and brings you book versions of "Twinkle, Twinkle" and "The Eentsy-Weentsy Spider" as you are singing them. Happy interruptions will not make you lose your way if you have your program list in hand. Welcome the chance to let children initiate involvement; it creates bonds between you and them. All parents love to see their children perform and will be drawn in themselves. This will result in positive associations for everyone with books, reading, the library, and you. Don't be surprised if there are instances when the program may have to be cut short. If you are losing your audience, try to end the story or activity as quickly as possible. Then gauge whether it makes sense to continue with the rest of your program, or just move to your closing song or fingerplay.

Program Template

A program template can be used to plan your storytime. Add notes about comments that you wish to make concerning connections to early learning concepts and modeling techniques. Another method is to use index cards to organize your program: on each card write a single song, fingerplay, book title, or activity. Shuffle and organize the cards in the order you wish to use them, and keep them next to you for reference during the program. However, do not hold them up and read directly from your cards during the program. It is necessary to know the rhymes well enough to maintain eye contact with your group as you perform them. Otherwise, you will lose the audience, and the storytime spell may be broken. The delight must come from your heart, via your voice, facial expressions, and body language.

For infants and children who are not accustomed to listening to stories, plan to do sets of two to three fingerplays and songs between no more than two or three books or flannelboard rhymes and stories. When planning programs, put together a mix of movement activities without repeating too many of the same type one after another. As babies get heavier but are not yet mobile, it's a workout to lift a 20-pound infant over your head multiple times in a row! The object is to make the first fingerplay in your set the most active, and gradually tone them down to prepare everyone for the next listening activity. Ending a set of fingerplays with a relaxing song, like "Twinkle, Twinkle, Little Star," can have an especially calming effect. It is also possible to use your voice to indicate closure by deepening it and slowing the final line of the last rhyme.

Making the decision to repeat a movement activity or book during the storytime is situational. The first time a young child is exposed to a new book, game, or other activity, he or she struggles just to comprehend it. If the audience responds positively the first time around, and you repeat, there is often an almost audible sigh of relief as they sit back, relax, and just enjoy. For example, a reading of the pop-up book *Peekaboo!* by Mathew Price and Jean Claverie (1985), almost always bears repeating. Children delight in the pop-up surprise element of this short book and rarely turn down a second reading. When it's obvious that an activity

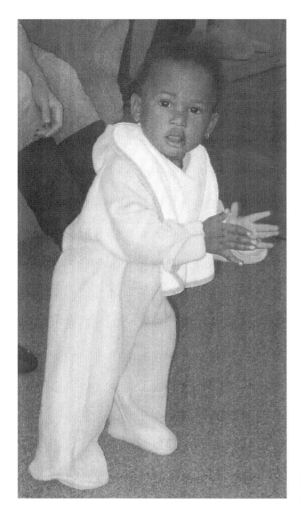

Clapping along to "If You're Happy and You Know It." (Vickie Shelton)

is unfamiliar, everyone will retain more if it is done again. However, rigidly repeating everything will lose you your audience, especially the toddlers. Here is an example of a basic template for storytime.

1. Welcome song
2. Two to three songs or fingerplays
3. Book or story (usually the gift book, if you have one)
4. Three songs or fingerplays
5. Book or flannelboard story
6. Two to three songs or fingerplays
7. Closing song

Review the following outline as an example to guide your own storytime program development.

1. Welcome song: "If You're Happy and You Know It" (Mention the importance of learning to follow directions.)
2. Fingerplays: "Jack Be Nimble" and "Two Little Blackbirds" (Mention the concept of object permanence.)
3. Book: *The Everything Book*, by Denise Fleming (Gift book—model reading and talking about the book.)
4. Action songs: "The Eentsy-Weetsy Spider," "Pop Goes the Weasel" (use pop-up toy), and "Row, Row, Row Your Boat"

5. Flannelboard song: "I Don't Want to Wear My Coat" (Song and pattern pieces are in the appendix to this chapter.)
6. Fingerplays: "Hickory Dickory Dock," "Pat-a-Cake, Pat-a-Cake," and "Beehive."
7. Book: *I Kissed the Baby*, by Mary Murphy (2003) (Let parents and children use puppets.)
8. Song: "Where Is Thumbkin?"
9. Closing song: "The Wheels on the Bus" (Mention learning through repetition.)

(Several more program outlines are listed in the appendix to this chapter.)

Naturally, this format is not cast in concrete. Bubble blowing, dancing to recorded music, and so on can be added or substituted. Overall, strive for a program that fits both infants and toddlers and maintains the interest of the teen parents. Many of the children will potentially have had little exposure to books and other storytime elements, so it is better to err toward the younger side, but without making everything too babyish. The audience's attention will be at its peak at the beginning of the program, and then gradually wane. Start with a song to draw them in, then do the stories that require the most focus at the beginning, and move to more active components (like dancing, using bells, etc.) at the end. Also, ending on an active note spares you the frustrating challenge of trying to settle everyone down again for a quiet activity.

Bilingual Programs

If parents in your group have a first language other than English, they will enjoy having some components of the program in their native language. More important, bilingual programs will affirm for the parents that children can learn in either language, a significant motivator for parents to read and speak to their children in their first language. If you are not bilingual, try asking the teen parents to assist you; there is no better way to engage them to participate. If no one is willing, perhaps a staff person or community volunteer can be recruited to help. The following options can help you implement a bilingual storytime.

- Readers use their own copy of the book (either a bilingual version or one in each language) and read each page or section of the book in English, and then in the second language (Peck 2009).
- Select repeated words or phrases in a book to say in both languages. Read the text in English, and either alternate with the other language or say the phrase every time in both languages. Encourage the group to repeat the phrases with you.
- Invite the bilingual speakers to lead some songs or fingerplays in the other language during the program.

Only a little preplanning is necessary to implement a bilingual program. Determine which book(s) will be read bilingually, which fingerplays or songs will be used, and the order of activities during the program. Collections of rhymes and songs by Ada Flor Ana and Jose-Luis Orozco are useful resources when Spanish is the native language of your group participants. If time is available, a brief run-through of your joint reading will put both parties at ease. Even if your presentation is a little rough around the edges, the group's pleasure in hearing their first language will far outweigh a less than perfect performance. For planning assistance, consult the training materials from these sources.

- Ana-Elba Pavon's workshop on the Infopeople website, "Planning, Doing, and Sustaining a Successful Bilingual Storytime." Included are a planning sheet, bibliographies of Spanish-English bilingual books, translations, books in English with some Spanish, and programming resources such as a fingerplay list, storytime checklist, and bilingual evaluation and survey forms.
- The "Storytimes in Languages Other than English" presentation by Marcela Sánchez from Hennepin County (Minnesota) Library, which provides the rationale and planning and presentation information for this type of programming.

- "Bilingual Storytimes: Building Early Literacy and Community," by Laura Tarango and Valerie Wonder, on the WebJunction website, highlights programs at the San Francisco and Seattle Public Libraries.

Setting the Scene

Ideally, the young parent–child storytime takes place in a cozy room that is just big enough for everyone to feel comfortable, yet small enough to minimize running around. In this room, there are only enough chairs for parents-to-be (and maybe the storyteller), so that everyone else sits on the floor together in a semicircle on a storytime rug or carpet squares. Your flannelboards, books, and props are organized at your fingertips and are out of the reach of small children. Infants have blankets to lie on, and soft, melodic music plays as the group enters.

In reality, parent-child storytimes usually take place in a busy child-care room, scattered with cribs, toys, tables, and big and small chairs. Or, the program occurs in a corner of a classroom, cleared for the moment, with desks pushed back around the room. Wherever you are, these tips will help ensure a successful storytime in a variety of environments.

1. Bring all supplies (including a lap/twin-size blanket) in a large tote bag.
2. Pick or push a small table or shelf against a wall where you can set up your flannelboard (make sure that it's stable and high enough so that everyone is able to see it).
3. Select a low chair or seat for yourself so that you look accessible and are not towering over your group (Nichols 2007).
4. Try to display your books within your arm's reach on a shelf, windowsill, or blackboard.
5. Tuck the flannelboard pieces (in order) behind the flannelboard.
6. Position your notes in a place where it is easy to glance at them.
7. Hide anything you do not want touched in advance (puppets, toys, etc.) inside the tote bag, and put it behind you.
8. Set up a few chairs or cushions in a rough semicircle facing your flannelboard, to create a visually contained space for your audience (but don't expect the entire group to sit there). Or, use the lap/twin-bed-size blanket to define your space.
9. Turn around and face the audience with a large, enthusiastic smile.

Reading Aloud

During the book-sharing part of the storytime, utilize the basic guidelines for group read-alouds.

1. Hold the book up high and open it wide so that your audience can see the pictures.
2. Know the text well enough so that you do not have to look at the page to read every word.
3. Move the book from side to side at a comfortable pace as you read so that everyone can see the pages. Our brains move faster than our mouths, so it is possible to read ahead and finish the text as you move the book. Reading the words and then moving the book will stall the program.
4. Make eye contact with the audience as you are moving the book (Peck 2009).

When reading, try to create as many opportunities for participation as possible. You can use animal noises, hand gestures, sound effects, and group recitation of repeated phrases. Reading at a variety of speeds, pitches, and volumes (depending on the text) can help keep your audience with you and will model for the parents how to read aloud effectively. After using these techniques to read a story, casually point out what you did. For example, sharing the comment "It's always fun to say 'Shhh'" at the end of each page in *The Napping House*, by Audrey Wood (1984) is sufficient.

If you are giving every family the same book as a gift, or have multiple copies to borrow from your library, try having everyone read along with you. This may produce mixed results. One benefit of handing out a copy to everyone is that you can model book handling and reading techniques and give parents and children an opportunity to practice. Individual books can also solve the problem of how to use a worthwhile title whose illustrations are too small for sharing in a group setting. On the other hand, books in everyone's hands can become a distraction and can prevent your audience from giving you their full attention. Reading a book, and then repeating it in a more exciting format (such as with a flannelboard or with puppets), can be beneficial. The repetition seems to "imprint" the story better in everyone's mind.

Making the Storytime Come Alive

Children's librarians often rely on themes as the basis of their storytime planning. This may not be necessary for young family audiences. Ensuring that your materials are age appropriate, engaging, and fun are of greater importance. Keep in mind that children's worlds slowly grow as they do, beginning with the intimate circle of a newborn's life, and then expanding to include family, neighborhood, friends, and community as they get older. Use this concept to gauge the materials you choose.

Many of these children will have had limited life experiences and will connect best with stories and activities that relate to their world and what they know. Stories that involve creatures engaging in activities that children do (such as Eric Hill's *Spot*) allow this connection to occur. There is no reason to exclude traditional childhood topics such as animals or food, because they need to stretch their range of experience, but proceed with care when it comes to topics outside of their range of experience or intellectual development like monsters, holidays, spelling songs (e.g., B-I-N-G-O), or abstract concepts.

Choosing Appropriate Storytime Books

When choosing picture books for use in storytime, all the criteria for selecting the gift books should also apply. Books with a single coherent illustration per page, with a single line of text, will make more sense to both you and your audience when read aloud. Again, choose the following types of books.

- Books with brief stories that the child can relate to
- Text that is short and concrete
- Books that have repetition of phrases, or a patterned text or rhyming
- Books that have clear and simple illustrations with bright, distinct colors and black outlines Soft pastel pictures are difficult to read in a group setting
- Books that you like and can "sell" to the group

Songs, Fingerplays, and Movement Activities

Songs, fingerplays, and movement activities are a storyteller's best friends because they increase interaction and the energy level of the group. They model simple but potent early learning activities, bring you and the group together, let everyone enjoy some shared fun, and give active children a chance to let loose within the framework of the program. Do not underestimate the power of the fingerplay as a learning tool. By melding language and rhyme with movement and sound, these rhymes address multiple learning styles (auditory, physical, and verbal) and create a satisfying simultaneous physical/intellectual experience. The rich rhyming language of the fingerplay or song is an ideal early learning tool for the parent or caregiver to use at home.

What Teen Parents Need to Know about Songs and Fingerplays

Many parents, not just teens, do not feel comfortable babbling and talking to a young, unresponsive baby. Songs and fingerplays provide a ready-made vehicle for language enrichment. Active children may not be willing to sit still for even the shortest book but will gladly join in a rhyme or song. It's a great way to feed them language enrichment on the run. Additionally, songs and fingerplays have the following perks:

- They are easy to teach and learn.
- They require no "equipment," and can be done anytime and anywhere.
- They develop both large and fine motor skills.
- They provoke an enthusiastic response from children, which encourages young parents to do them again.

Opening and Closing Your Program with Songs and Fingerplays

Try to use consistent opening and closing songs; they make mental bookends for your audience, drawing the group in at the start and creating closure at the finish. Use songs that feel comfortable and genuine to you. Following are some suggested opening and closing songs, from familiar storytime resources.

From *Crash Course in Storytime Fundamentals*, **by Penny Peck (2009):**

- Opening: "Hello Everybody, Yes Indeed"
- Closing: "The More We Get Together" or "Wave High, Wave Low"

From *I'm a Little Teapot*, **by Jane Cobb (1996):**

- Opening: "Let's Clap Our Hands Together," "Hello Everybody" (different version from Penny Peck's), "You'll Sing a Song and I'll Sing a Song" by Ella Jenkins
- Closing: "So Long," "Now It's Time to Say Goodbye"

Storytime Magic, by Kathy MacMillan and Christine Kirker (2009), and *Early Literacy Storytimes @Your Library*, by Saroj Nadkarni Ghoting and Pamela Martin-Diaz (2006), also have examples of hello, good-bye, and transition songs. If your visit takes place at a child-care center, and the center's staff have a special welcome song that they routinely sing, ask a staff member to sing it with you to draw the children into the program.

Teaching Fingerplays

Consistent with a young child's intellectual and physical development, fingerplays and motion activities move from bounces and tickles performed by the caregiver to movements done by the child him- or herself. Happily, given the mix of infants, toddlers, and preschoolers that you may encounter in a teen parent-child group, most fingerplays can be adjusted to fit any child's developmental level. An example is the perennial favorite "The Wheels on the Bus."

"The Wheels on the Bus"

The wheels on the bus go round and round,
Round and round, round and round.
The wheels on the bus go round and round
All through the town.
The people on the bus go up and down,
up and down, up and down.
The people on the bus go up and down
All through the town.

A very young infant can lie on his or her back on a blanket, and the parent can cycle the child's legs round and round for the wheels, move them from side to side for the wipers, lift the child for "up and down," and gently tap the chest with a fist for the horn's "beep-beep-beep," and so on. An older infant can sit in his or her parent's lap, and the parent can still cycle the child's arms or legs, lift the child up in the air for "up and down," and so on. For a toddler, the parent might still do some of the action, while helping the child do other

Use a doll to teach fingerplay movements to parents. (Hal Jerman)

movements independently. If a preschooler already knows the rhyme, the parent's job is to model and participate; if he or she does not know it, the parent can help the child learn the movements. Program planning will include deciphering for yourself how each age group would perform the movement activities and songs you will use. Linda Ernst provides suggestions for infants and young toddlers in her book *Baby Rhyming Time* (2008), as do Jane Marino and Dorothy Houlihan in *Mother Goose Time* (1992).

When first working with a group of young parents and children, the librarian or storyteller needs to specifically explain how each age group can participate. Try to be as brief as possible, or the audience's attention will wander. Usually just demonstrating a couple of the motions is enough to give them the idea. Unless someone will loan you a baby (which does happen on occasion), using a soft doll with flexible limbs is the best way demonstrate what to do.

Teens can be especially sensitive about wanting to do everything right and may have unrealistic expectations for what their children are able to do. It can be useful to casually remind them that everyone is learning and that the important thing is to try the activities and to have fun. If a parent is trying to coax a child to participate and the child is not responding, mention that some children like to observe activities before doing them and that the parent's participation encourages his or her child's involvement.

Writing the words of single fingerplays and songs in large print on single sheets of a flip chart or pieces of poster board and displaying them as you do the activities can help parents participate. One consideration with this technique is whether you, the storyteller, can manage to juggle one more thing during your program! Distributing a handout with the words for use during the program is not recommended. It takes the parents' attention away from you, and it often ends up being more of a distraction than a help.

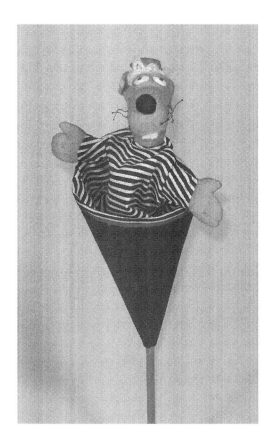

A pop-up puppet. (Hal Jerman)

While fingerplays and their variants number in the hundreds, simplicity is key with young families. Keeping in mind that the goal is to encourage the teens to continue to do these activities on their own, it is most effective to stick to the basics (traditional folk and nursery rhymes). Rotating through and repeating a small core collection of fingerplays in a consistent program format is also the best way to help everyone feel comfortable joining in and to help the young families learn. Unless your programs are scheduled weekly, there is little chance of boredom setting in. Often librarians put unnecessary pressure on themselves to try new things. In the context of the teen parent-child program, that impulse is best served by trying new storytelling techniques and props that will appeal to your group.

Many bilingual teen parents will have favorite songs and rhymes that they sing to their children in their other language. Don't be surprised if they are reluctant to share them with the whole parent group. When working one-on-one, or in a small group, they may be willing to teach them to you, and then you can share. One inadvertent result of making a hash of performing it yourself may be that the parents will take over from you!

Reproducible lists of recommended fingerplays are in the appendix of this chapter. They can be duplicated on 2-inch by 4-inch labels and attached to index cards for individual use by the storyteller or can be photocopied for use as traditional handouts. If you would like a visual presentation of how to do an effective fingerplay, the King County Library System's "Tell Me a Story" wiki has links to YouTube videos of children's librarians demonstrating them.

Puppets, Flannelboards, and Other Special Effects for Group Storytimes

It is important to accept the fact that reading books, even with extensive attempts at making them participatory, won't always keep your audience captivated. In addition to songs and fingerplays, adding other presentation techniques to the docket will help. Nothing has to be too elaborate, as it does not take a lot to fascinate a two-year-old.

Puppets

With a slim grasp on the line between fantasy and reality, young children don't always seem to know whether puppets are inanimate or not, and they are delighted in any case. There will be huge smiles all around as soon as a puppet appears. Here are some tips to help you manipulate puppets.

1. Direct your puppet's eyes to the audience when speaking to them (Axtell 2002).
2. Open and close the puppet's mouth in time with its speech, opening it with each major syllable (Arts in Education n.d.).
3. Keep the puppet's mouth closed when it isn't talking.
4. If the puppet doesn't have a mouth to open and close, move its head or body in rhythm with its speech.
5. Make the puppet express emotions through body language, such as jumping up and down in excitement, looking around at the audience in wonder, or slumping over in sadness.
6. When using a puppet with arms but not a movable mouth, keep the puppet's arms and hands together or at its sides, not sticking straight out, when it isn't gesturing.

When to Use Puppets:

1. Use a puppet when performing a song or fingerplay, such as a spider for "The Eentsy-Weentsy Spider," a mouse for "Hickory Dickory Dock," or a turtle for Vachel Lindsay's "There Was a Little Turtle."
2. Puppets can be used as characters in a book, such as the animals in *I Went Walking*, by Sue Williams (1996), *I Kissed the Baby*, by Mary Murphy (2003), or *The Very Busy Spider*, by Eric Carle (1984); the mother hen and chicks (even just one) in Keith Baker's *Big Fat Hen* (1994); or the caterpillar, transforming before your very eyes into a butterfly, in *The Very Hungry Caterpillar* (Carle 1994).
3. Use a puppet to sing a song, like the farm animals for "Old MacDonald;" farmer, wife, child, nurse, (or just the animals) for "The Farmer in the Dell;" or a fuzzy bear for "The Bear Went Over the Mountain."
4. Pass out multiple puppets to willing parents, and have them participate with you. Instruct the teen parents in how to manipulate their puppets. Mention that they should be gentle when introducing the puppet to their children and to give their children time to explore the puppet to avoid frightening them. Having parents be your puppeteers forces participation, much to their children's delight!

Finger and glove puppets are another option when working with a small group. These can be easily made using inexpensive work gloves from the hardware store. Attach Velcro to the glove's fingertips and to the backs of small felt flannelboard-type pieces. Finger and glove puppets are especially effective to use for counting-down rhymes like "Five Little Speckled Frogs" or for a closed-hand/open-hand rhyme like "Here Is the Beehive." Expect puppets to give and receive snuggles and kisses; don't bring a puppet that is too fragile to withstand a series of enormous, bone- (and hand-) crushing hugs.

Toys

Toys that have an element of surprise, such as pop-up clowns or nesting dolls, fascinate little children. A pop-up can accentuate the punch line of a song like "Pop Goes the Weasel." A nesting doll can simply be opened before the audience with a short narrative, counting the numbers of things or describing them. (Be sure to start by shaking it, so children know there is something inside). Using a nesting fruit set, try showing the toy and say, "Here's the apple. Let's open it up and see what's inside." (Open and lift out the pear.) "Look! It's a pear." (Shake again.) "What do you think is inside the pear?" (Open and lift out the orange.) "It's an orange! What's inside the orange?" (Open orange and lift out the strawberry.) "Look, it's a teeny-tiny

A nesting fruit set. (Hal Jerman)

Inexpensive nesting gift boxes from IKEA bring an element of surprise to storytime play. (Hal Jerman)

strawberry! Now, let's put them back together. Let's start with the strawberry." (Reassemble the toy, counting and naming fruits as you do.)

Sets of nesting gift boxes are easy to find, especially around holiday time. Hide a little toy inside the smallest box, and you are set. After showing your boxes to the children, it's worth mentioning to your teen parents that boxes like these make an inexpensive toy that teaches object permanence and the concept of size.

Bubbles also bring a touch of excitement to your program. The best strategies when incorporating bubbles into the storytime are to pass the bubble wand and bottle of bubble mix around and have parents take turns using it, or to have a set for every parent. This will encourage participation and parent-child interactions.

Flannelboard Stories

A flannelboard story is a story told using felt or marker-colored Pellon® interfacing figures and objects on a felt- or flannel-covered board. This method of storytelling has a magical appeal for young children. The simple placement and removal of the colorful story pieces from the board gives children a visual support to help them comprehend the story, and it creates enough movement and action to bring the story to life. Best choices for flannelboard storytelling are similar to those for reading aloud, with the following caveats.

- Stories should have a patterned, repetitive structure like *It Looked Like Spilt Milk*, by Charles Shaw (1993). A more abstract or complex story will lose your audience.
- Many nursery rhymes and songs make ideal flannelboards.
- Pieces need to be easy to read from a distance—simple, bold, and large enough.

The number of pieces should be manageable. That does not necessarily mean limited in number. A song like John Langstaff's version of "Oh, A-Hunting We Will Go" has more than 20 pieces, but they are deployed in a simple, logical manner that makes using them a breeze.

Making a Flannelboard and Story Pieces

Crafty librarians will enjoy making their own flannelboard and story pieces. If "crafty" isn't among your list of attributes, seek out another staff person or volunteer to help. A simple, durable flannelboard, which will provide years of service, can be easily made from a paperboard artist's portfolio with ties. This type of flannelboard is easy to take on outreach visits, with your story pieces tucked inside.

Making Your Flannelboard

Supplies:

- a rigid paperboard artist's portfolio, about 20 inches by 26 inches. (Available at art supply stores or online from the Dick Blick website—search for "Cachet Deluxe Black Portfolios")
- National Nonwovens 36-inch-wide wool/rayon felt in black, gray, or cream. Buy adequate yardage to cover the entire interior of the portfolio (available for purchase at a quality fabric shop or online from the Commonwealth Felt website; 100% polyester felt is not recommended)
- 1.88-inch black duct tape
- a sharp pair of scissors

A DIY portfolio flannelboard on a portable easel. (Hal Jerman)

Instructions:

1. With the interior facing up, open the portfolio on a flat surface large enough to support it. If it has interior flaps, cut them away close to the taped edge of the portfolio.
2. Lay and smooth your piece of felt on top to cover the interior of the portfolio. It should be sized to fit just to the edge, with no overhang. If the felt piece is too big, lay it flat on your work surface, put the open portfolio on top, and trace around the portfolio edge. Cut and trim to size (making adjustments as needed), then lay out smoothly on the interior.
3. Starting at the end of one long side, measure and cut a piece of tape the length of the side, with a 1-inch overhang on each end. Gently lay half the tape's width along the edge of the felt, maintaining the extra inch of tape at the ends. If the tape has not adhered in a straight line, gently pull it off and reposition where necessary. Make sure that the felt is smooth and still aligned with the portfolio.
4. Firmly press and fold the tape over to the outside of the portfolio, being careful not to catch the portfolio ties. Trim the extra double fold of tape flush with the short edges.
5. Repeat step number three on the other long edge, then with the short edges.

If this sounds like too much work, a much simpler version can be made by stretching a piece of appropriate flannel cloth inside an extra-large embroidery hoop. Or, the school supply vendor Nasco sells a 3-in-1 Portable Easel, a magnetic board, whiteboard, and flannelboard all in one on its website.

Making Flannelboard Pieces

There are several methods for making flannelboard pieces. The fabric options include piecing them from felt or coloring pieces with permanent markers to cut out on Pellon® interfacing. Pictures on paper, reproduced or hand-colored, can be laminated or covered with clear Con-Tact® paper. They are then backed with sandpaper for the flannel board, or with a piece of magnetic tape (available at hardware stores) for use on a metal cookie sheet or motor oil change pan.

If handled with just a little care, felt and Pellon® interfacing story pieces can last for decades. When making felt pieces, there should be enough simple details to make the piece's features distinct without being too elaborate. Many commercial flannelboard pieces have so much detail that they look like a complicated book illustration and are just as difficult for the audience to read. Marker-colored Pellon® pieces also should be kept on the simple side. With many figures, it is wise to leave off the facial features, which can be difficult to make look professional. Often just the addition of wiggle eyes (movable plastic eyes sold at craft stores) and a flat nose shape is enough. The best patterns for felt pieces can be found in Judy Sierra's classic flannelboard books, *The Flannel Board Storytelling Book* (2nd ed. 1997) and *Mother Goose's Playhouse*. Judy's patterns make for simple, attractive pieces. *Mother Goose's Playhouse* is full of more than a dozen nursery rhymes. Simple illustrations from books can also serve as the basis for patterns you create yourself. The Kizclub: Learning Resources for Kids website offers free reproducible patterns for nursery rhymes and preschool learning themes that could be used for laminated paper or Pellon® pieces.

Patterns for three flannelboard stories, "It's Not That Cold Outside," "Yellow Star, Yellow Star," and "The Wheels on the Bus," suitable to make using either of the following methods, are included in the appendix of this chapter.

Making Felt Story Pieces

Supplies:

- yardage or squares of felt in the right colors for your pieces (Keep scraps for details.)
- fabric or tacky glue
- tracing paper
- straight pins

- small, sharp pair of scissors with pointed tips
- pencil for tracing
- assorted sizes of wiggle eyes
- fine-tip Sharpie® for drawing features

Instructions:

1. Determine whether the size of the pattern pieces will be large enough. If not, photo-copy and enlarge the patterns.
2. Study the patterns to determine how many different parts will need to be assembled to form the figure or object. By layering clothing, hair, legs, and so on, you can easily give the felt pieces a rich dimensionality.
3. Trace each individual pattern part separately. If one part will be glued on top of an-other, the bottom part should be enlarged to allow for overlap. For example, imagine that you are assembling a baby chick piece. You would cut a basic body shape from yellow felt, cut a little wing to glue on top, and cut an orange beak and feet that will be glued underneath the chick's body. Add a wiggle eye for completion.
4. Roughly cut out your pattern pieces individually and pin them to the felt color you choose to use.
5. Cut the pieces out following the exact pattern lines. When cutting a tight corner, cut in from both directions rather than trying to turn the piece.
6. Lay a piece of tracing paper over the original drawing that was used to make the pat-terns. Assemble the felt piece to make sure everything fits, and then glue it together.
7. Add wiggle eyes and other small touches like noses and ears.
8. Most pieces don't need facial expressions.

Making Pellon® Interfacing Pieces

Supplies:

- stiff, heavyweight, non-fusible Pellon® interfacing (sold by the yard at fabric stores)
- quality artist's markers, like Prismacolor® brand
- pair of sharp scissors

Instructions:

1. Photocopy and enlarge the pictures or patterns you wish to use.
2. Cut a piece of interfacing generously larger than your picture. Lay the picture on a flat surface, and place the interfacing on top.

Assembly of a felt flannelboard piece and a back view of overlapping pattern pieces. (Hal Jerman)

Examples of drawn and colored Pellon® flannelboard pieces. (Hal Jerman)

3. Trace and color in your picture on the interfacing. *Important!* Marker ink will take some time to dry and can smudge. Always work from light to dark colors and from left to right if you are right-handed, right to left if you are left-handed.

4. When all areas have been traced and colored, outline the piece and its elements, as needed, with a black marker.

5. Cut and trim the interfacing closer to the picture. It is not necessary to exactly cut out narrow segments like legs. In fact, keeping the piece as whole as possible adds to its durability.

Using a Flannelboard to Tell a Story

When using the flannelboard, you want to put pieces up on the board as they are mentioned and take them away when they are no longer part of the story or when the board is full (whichever comes first). It is important to remember to place them on the board in a logical sequence without blocking the audience's view of them with your body. This usually means putting them up starting at the top of the opposite side of the board from where you are sitting or standing, and working your way across from top to bottom, although variations occur depending on the story or rhyme. For example, with a rhyme like Humpty-Dumpty, you would place Humpty-Dumpty and his wall in the center of the flannelboard and surround him on all sides with first the king's horses, and then all the king's men. Part of program preparation should be to practice telling your flannelboard stories and placing the pieces.

For the sake of stability, expressive storytelling, and minimizing mishaps, it is recommended to set the board up on a table or shelf, rather than holding it with one arm in your lap. A portfolio-style board can be opened and tied like a tent to stand by itself. Using a lightweight aluminum tabletop easel, available at an art supply store, requires less space to stand (only about 10 inches in depth) and positions the flannelboard at a good angle to keep the pieces on the board.

Prior to the storytime, organize your pieces in the order they will be used, from top to bottom, and place them behind or near the board. Make sure there is space to discard them as they are removed. Hiding them behind the board, if possible, will discourage the curious hands of participants.

When beginning a story, you generally will want to start by picking up all or most of the pieces in one hand. As you tell the story, you will use the other hand to put them on the board. Although you may need both hands to pick up very large pieces, in general, picking up each piece from the table as you need it slows the progress of the story and breaks your rhythm.

With some rhymes or stories, such as "I Don't Want to Wear My Coat," you will start with the figures already set up on the board. In that case, choose whether to put the pieces up before the program begins or to quickly set them up just before sharing the story. Always practice a new story at least once to understand how to coordinate placement of the pieces.

Bells, Scarves, and Shakers

By using bells, scarves, or shakers when singing a song or dancing to music, you can enhance the storytime experience. To ensure safety, wrist bells are probably best purchased from a school supplier like Lakeshore Learning. Scarves can be donated, purchased from thrift shops, or cut from inexpensive chiffon-type fabric. Scarves are fun for dancing, waving in time to the music, and tickling. Shakers can be purchased or made by parents from plastic eggs (see chapter 6), as can twinkle stars or string spiders. Using toys that the parents have made themselves will increase their sense of involvement in the activity.

With whatever supplies you bring, always have enough for both parents and children to use, and make sure that everyone is given the bells or shakers to encourage 100 percent participation. It is best to always have multiples of the same object rather than many different versions (such as musical instruments). Children under the age of three do not understand the concepts of taking turns or sharing, and it's important to minimize conflict.

Experience has shown that making noise will work with almost any rhyme or song you choose. Some favorites are "Frère Jacques," "Old MacDonald," "Ring around the Rosie," "Shake My Sillies Out," "If You're Happy and You Know It," "Twinkle, Twinkle, Little Star," and "Jingle Bells." Also use noisemakers to chant a rhyme like this:

> Shake them up, shake them down
> Shake them all around the town!
> Shake to the left, shake to the right,
> Shake them when they're out of sight *(shake behind your back)*.
> Round and round and round they go,
> Now go fast, and now go slow!

Recorded Music

Recorded music always livens up a storytime, but try to use it as only an occasional addition to your program. A downside to primarily using recorded music in lieu of singing with the group is that it limits opportunities for modeling by the presenter and practicing by your audience. It also minimizes your message about the importance of establishing the parent-child early learning connection through music and singing. When you do choose to use recorded music, care must be taken during the selection process. Consider the following guidelines:

1. Look for songs with clear single vocals accompanied by simple instrumentation. Raffi's calming, melodious voice accompanied by his guitar is an excellent example.
2. Jazz or rock versions of children's songs will appeal to teens, but make sure they have enough audio clarity to work for young children. Collections of children's songs performed by popular musicians are a fun way to blend the traditional and the contemporary.
3. Look for songs that lend themselves to the use of scarves and noisemakers. With the right music, there is an opportunity for the children to develop listening skills and learn to follow directions.
4. Expect a lack of enthusiasm for just dancing; teens may find this too embarrassing.
5. Try playing children's songs as background music while engaged in a play activity. Make an opportunity to comment on how much language children learn from listening to songs.

Some recorded favorites that many children and adults love to move to are included on the following albums.

- *One Light, One Sun*, by Raffi (1985): "Time to Sing" and "Apples and Bananas"
- *Baby-O!* by Marylee Sunseri (2005): "What'll I Do with the Baby-O?" and "Clap Your Hands"
- *Classic Nursery Rhymes*, by Susie Tallman (2002): "Skidamarink"
- *More Singable Songs for the Very Young*, by Raffi (1977): "Shake My Sillies Out" and "Six Little Ducks"
- *Rhinoceros Tap*, by Sandra Boynton (2004): "Horns to Toes" and "So Long, Doggies"
- *Singable Songs*, by Raffi (1976): "Bumping Up and Down in My Little Red Wagon" and "Spider on the Floor"
- *If You're Happy and You Know It: Sing Along with Bob*, Vol. 1 by Bob McGrath (1996): "This Little Light of Mine" and "Looby Loo"
- *Jim Gill Sings Do Re Mi on His Toe Leg Knee* (1999): "The Nothing Wrong Song," "The Tempo Marches On," and "Spin Again . . . Again"

These music collections make great background music: *Every Child Deserves a Lifetime, De Colores and Other Latin American Folk Songs, Picnic Playground, One Hundred Toddler Favorites,* and *Rock and Roll Playground*. Using an Internet music service like iTunes makes it possible to preview, download, and compile the playlist of children's songs you want. Searching by performer, title, or album makes it easy to put together a CD of tunes, or load on an MP3 player or iPod and use a stereo dock to play them.

ADAPTING AN EXISTING CURRICULUM: EVERY CHILD READY TO READ®

Every Child Ready to Read® (ECRR) is an early literacy initiative of the Public Library Association (PLA) and the Association for Library Service to Children (ALSC). It is a readily available curriculum that has been used by children's librarians with parent groups throughout the country and has been successfully implemented with teen parent groups. ECRR focuses on the development of the skills that children need to learn before and during emergent reading. ECRR recognizes that parents can be a child's first teacher and that reading is integral to helping children succeed in school and life. Librarians utilize ECRR for parents and caregivers during workshops or storytimes by highlighting activities, especially reading, that benefit their children's early literacy development and by suggesting simple ways for the adults to continue this enrichment at home. ECRR builds on the early literacy techniques that librarians have been using for years, and it formats them for teaching to parents and caregivers.

The revised version (2011) of the ECRR curriculum is updated to reflect the most current early learning research, uses less educational terminology, and emphasizes an interactive and flexible format; all of which make it quite suitable for use with teen parents (American Library Association. Association for Library Service to Children 2011). ECRR's accessible presentation of early literacy concepts and practices also is an excellent resource for the neophyte desiring a crash course on the subject. The changes to ECRR include the following components.

1. Instead of focusing equally on mastery of the early literacy skills—sound and phonemic awareness, (alphabet) letter knowledge, concepts of print, vocabulary, and comprehension—that are necessary for a strong and sustained start to the learning-to-read process, the revised curriculum incorporates new research that indicates that children acquire the first three of these skills within a finite time frame, while the latter two, vocabulary and comprehension, develop more slowly over a long period of time. The new curriculum is structured to capitalize on the fact that vocabulary and comprehension are better predictors of a child's later reading and academic success than the other three skills. It addresses children's acquisition of both types of skills, but within the context of the difference in their mode of acquisition and importance (Neuman and Celano 2010).

2. The new ECRR promotes these core values—a child's first and best teachers are parents and caregivers; young children receive many benefits and advantages from play; reading is a basic life skill; and the lifelong learning that is a fundamental role of the public library begins at birth.

3. In conjunction with literacy development, more focus is placed on reading informational texts (such as Gail Gibbons's or Steve Johnson's picture books) as the basis for the all-important attainment of "background knowledge" (i.e., knowledge of and experiences in the world), its connection to vocabulary acquisition, and its role as one of the underpinnings of reading comprehension.

4. The workshops shift from lectures to an interactive format with talking points and are intended to address learning concepts across age groups rather than being defined by specific early literacy developmental stages. Workshop components are designed for use both with groups of adults and with adults accompanied by children; and are formatted to allow individual presenters to readily adapt them to specific audiences.

5. Parents and caregivers will learn to use familiar early literacy activities—talking, reading, singing, writing, and playing—to help children develop their pre-reading skills as part of their daily life. The characteristics and benefits of stimulating learning environments—in the home, at school, or at childcare sites—is explained and encouraged.

6. The materials provided are compatible with the teen parent population's cultural, economic, educational, and linguistic diversity.

7. Booklists and handouts of simple tips and activities are available to complement the workshops in easy to access and reproduce formats.

The second edition of the Every Child Ready to Read® toolkit consists of introductions to the new research findings and early literacy, handouts, booklists, and a bibliography, promotional and marketing materials, and, most importantly, the workshop presentations. Workshop topics for parents and caregivers focus on play as a learning experience and learning about letters, words, science, and math while having "fun." There are also workshops for staff and community partners, including one on early literacy environments (Association for Library Service to Children and Public Library Association 2011). Consult the ALSC or PLA websites for additional information.

It is recommended that even trained and experienced ECRR presenters should participate in training sessions for the revised curriculum. Anyone who is planning to use ECRR who is not knowledgeable about children's literature, standard storytime presentations, or the subject of early childhood literacy should definitely consider participating in ECRR training sessions.

Early Literacy/Every Child Ready to Read® Workshop

Maryann Mori is a nationally recognized expert on presenting ECRR workshops to teen parents. Currently the director of the Waukee Public Library in Waukee, Iowa, Maryann has served as a teen specialist at the Evansville Vanderburgh Public Library in Indiana and also has wide experience in children's, adult reference, and outreach services. She has spoken at American Library Association conferences on the topic of early literacy and teen parents, and she has trained librarians throughout the Midwest in using ECRR with teen parents. The following is Maryann's ECRR Guide.

Present five key early literacy elements:

1. **The young child's development and its impact on using books with children.** Connect children's age-specific developmental skills to the types of books that they will respond to at various stages (see chapter 8, under the heading "Milestones of Early Development," and "Tips for Choosing Books for Babies and Toddlers" [Zero to Three.org 2010]).

2. **The importance of reading aloud to infants and young children.** Discuss how children acquire language through exposure to language, and discuss the importance of

reading and interactions with caregivers for brain development and future success in school and life (see above, under "Practices that Promote Early Learning").

3. **Types of children's books.** Present a diverse selection of board, toddler, and picture books, including patterned, rhyming, and concept books, and discuss what differentiates them. Also discuss how to judge whether a book is the right level for a child and confirm that all children will develop favorite books (see the appendix to this chapter: "Recommended Books, Flannelboard Stories, and Music").

4. **How to use children's books, incorporating modeling of good read-aloud techniques.** Use a doll to demonstrate how to hold and read aloud to a child; explain how to find the right time of day and mood for sharing books. Indicate that, at first, children will treat books like toys (see above, under "Modeling Read-Aloud Methods").

5. **Early childhood literacy concepts and reading.** Focus on the ECRR concepts that a child can learn from specific books, including letter names, understanding of print, sounds and phonemics, vocabulary, and comprehension. Demonstrate how to reinforce early learning when reading is done aloud (Every Child Ready to Read® [American Library Association. Association for Library Service to Children 2011]).

These topics can be covered in four workshop sessions. Each session will last about 30 to 45 minutes, and the length will depend on whether children are present. Each session will combine a storytime with a discussion of parenting skills and child development. If children are present, these concepts will be shared throughout the storytime presentation. Without children, it is possible to have a classroom-style presentation, which will still include opportunities for the teen parents to interact and discuss. In either case, you will be modeling ways to read and use books with babies and toddlers. The basic outline of the four sessions is as follows.

Session 1

1. Introduce yourself, your library, and the materials and services it offers.
2. Give an overview and introduction to ECRR.
3. Present statistics about the importance and benefits of reading to children.
4. Hand out an ECRR brochure or flyer.

Session 2

1. Offer an overview of the types of books for young children (board, toddler, and picture books).
2. Provide a summary of child development in increments: birth to 3 months, 3 to 6 months, 6 to 12 months, and 12 to 24 months.
3. Offer ideas on how to choose developmentally appropriate books for children of different ages.
4. Lead a discussion of the benefits of reading to children, emphasizing that reading is fun (see this chapter, "Practices that Promote Early Learning").
5. Hand out a list of recommended board books.

Session 3

1. Present books that promote phonemic awareness.
2. Present books that promote vocabulary.
3. Hand out a list of the rhymes, fingerplays, and songs used in your storytime sessions.

Session 4

1. Offer a review of ECRR.
2. Share how to use specific books to promote the different literacy skills.

3. Lead a discussion of childhood reading memories.
4. Give encouragement to the parents.
5. Hand out a gift board book for each parent.

ECRR Concepts to Highlight

Sounds and Phonemics

Baby babble is the predecessor of speech. Babies are naturally experimenting with sounds when they begin to babble. Phrases like "ba-ba, ma-ma, da-da" are phonemics, the sounds that make up words. Learning letter sounds, learning syllable patterns, and even playing with silly sounds are all part of language development. Reading books that include rhyming words, repeated phrases, and examples of alliteration or silly words encourages sound imitation and helps children learn to play with smaller sounds. Ask teen parents about the sounds or words their child is saying to stimulate thought and discussion about their child's language development. Parents of toddlers will likely have many examples to share. Pointing out that when young babies coo and babble they are actually learning to talk helps teen parents realize the importance of responding to their children and encouraging their children's attempts to express themselves.

Ask the questions "Why should a child learn the sound that a cow or horse makes?" and "Why should children learn animal sounds when most children do not live on a farm and may never visit a farm?" You can provide two answers: knowing the sound of a cow is perceived as general knowledge that everyone should know, and teaching babies about animal sounds helps children begin exploring the other sounds of language. Point out to teen parent audiences that not all languages use the same sound for an animal noise. The book *Hush! A Thai Lullaby*, by Minfong Ho (1996), uses the Thai-language forms of animal sounds. The book *Mung Mung: A Fold-Out Book of Animal Sounds*, by Linda Sue Park (2004), presents animal sounds in multiple languages. Stress that books with animal illustrations can be used with children as a way to identify animals and sounds, regardless of the text surrounding the story. Ignoring the text allows you to just interactively read the pictures.

Also use books like *Jazz Baby*, by Lisa Wheeler (2007), which has rhyming and an obvious rhythm to the flow of the text, to develop a child's awareness of sounds in words. Applying accelerando, or gradually increasing speed, and ritardando, or gradually slowing your pace, when reading aloud, adds even more excitement to the story. Adding actions, like clapping hands, snapping fingers, tapping toes, or dancing, when reading, increases the book's appeal.

Vocabulary

Vocabulary is learning to talk in a language and learning words and gaining the understanding that specific things have specific names. Useful to promote vocabulary development are books that:

- Focus on familiar objects that a child recognizes, like body parts, animals, vehicles, or household objects.
- Repeat the names of things.
- Give things multiple names.

In the book *Under My Hood I Have a Hat*, by Karla Kuskin (2004), the author refers to a girl's scarf as a "muffler." The text says, "My muffler muffles around my neck." If a reader does not recognize the word "muffler," the context and illustration help define it. Share an example like this with teen parents to demonstrate how books often incorporate rich vocabulary into a child's life, far more than is found in daily conversation or on television shows. Additionally, point out that studies have shown that the more words a child is exposed to, the easier it will be for the child to decipher unfamiliar words when learning how to read.

Posing the question "When is the last time you used the word 'elephant' in your conversation?" also helps teen parents realize that books present a broader range of vocabulary than daily conversation. Most teens won't recall using the word, unless they recently visited a zoo. Next ask, "Should your child be able to recognize the word 'elephant' and know what the word represents?" Most everyone will agree that every child should know how to identify an elephant. Then show some children's books that feature elephants, like the *Elmer* books, by David McKee (1989), *Horton Hears a Who*, by Dr. Seuss (1954), and *From Head to Toe*, by Eric Carle (1999). Stress again that reading introduces new vocabulary to children.

Program Tips

Keep your presentations interactive, include the parents (and children) in your activities, and encourage the teen parents to think about, and answer, your questions. Asking some of the questions mentioned earlier could get teens to think back to their own childhood. Using childhood memories to recall who read to the teen when they were young, their favorite books, and their own positive associations with reading, is a first crucial step in connecting the teens, their children, and reading. Additionally, don't forget that the books you select for your workshops should be as appealing to the teen parents as they are to children. Always allow a few minutes for chatting with the parents about their children's growth and development. Demonstrating an authentic interest in their lives and the lives of their babies is one of the best ways to develop a good rapport with the teen parents. And have fun!

CONCLUSION

Talking, reading, and singing are simple activities that promote literacy and language development. Helping teen parents give their children the gift of literacy, and making it a bonding and joyful experience for everyone, can be one of the most satisfying aspects of programming for young families. Facilitating meaningful interactions between the teen parent and the child through literacy-rich experiences will give parents confidence in their role as teachers and as mothers and fathers. It is important to remember that every early learning experience a child gets benefits their development and contributes to their long-term success.

REFERENCES

Brain Development

Brotherson, Sean. "Bright Beginnings #4: Understanding Brain Development in Young Children." North Dakota State University (2005), http://www.ag.ndsu.edu/pubs/yf/famsci/fs609w.htm.

Cobb, Jane. *What'll I Do with the Baby-O?* Vancouver, BC: Black Sheep Press, 2007.

Gopnik, Alison, Andrew Meltzoff, and Patricia Kuhl. *The Scientist in the Crib: Minds, Brains, and How Children Learn.* New York: William Morrow, 1999.

Hawley, Theresa. "Starting Smart: How Early Experiences Affect Brain Development." Zero to Three: National Center for Infants, Toddlers, and Families (2000), http://main.zerotothree.org/site/Doc Server/startingsmart.pdf?docID=2422.

The First Years Last Forever, part of the *I Am Your Child* series. Parents Action for Children. http://store. parentsactionstore.org/prostores/servlet/-strse-template/storemain/Page.

Oregon's Child: Everyone's Business. "For Parents and Caregivers: Help Your Child's Brain Develop through Love and Play" (2002), http://www.oceb.org/.
    English PDF version: http://www.oceb.org/Documents/BAWBrochureEnglish.pdf.
    Spanish PDF version: http://www.oceb.org/Documents/BAWBrochureSpanish.pdf.

Storytime Planning and Early Literacy

Cobb, Jane. *I'm a Little Teapot! Presenting Preschool Storytime.* Vancouver, BC: Black Sheep Press, 1996.

Ernst, Linda. *Baby Rhyming Time.* New York: Neal-Schuman, 2008.

Ghoting, Saroj Nadkarni, and Pamela Martin-Diaz. *Early Literacy Storytimes @Your Library.* Chicago: American Library Association, 2006.

London, Jonathan. *Froggy Gets Dressed.* New York: Viking, 1992.

MacMillan, Kathy, and Christine Kirker. *Storytime Magic: 400 Fingerplays, Flannelboards, and Other Activities.* Chicago: American Library Association, 2009.

Marino, Jane, and Dorothy Houlihan. *Mother Goose Time: Library Programs for Babies and Their Caregivers.* New York: H. W. Wilson, 1992.

Nichols, Judy. *Storytimes for Two-Year-Olds*. Chicago: American Library Association, 2007.

Numeroff, Laura Joffe. *If You Give a Mouse a Cookie*. New York: HarperCollins, 1996.

Pavon, Ana-Elba. "Infopeople Workshop—Planning, Doing, and Sustaining a Successful Bilingual Storytime" (2008), Infopeople. http://www.infopeople.org/training/past/2008/biling-storytime/.

Peck, Penny. *Crash Course in Storytime Fundamentals*. Westport, CT: Libraries Unlimited, 2009.

Rosenkoetter, Sharon, and Joanne Knapp-Philo, eds. *Learning to Read the World: Language and Literacy in the First Three Years*. Washington, DC: Zero to Three Press, 2006.

Sánchez, Marcela. "Storytimes in Languages Other Than English." (March 26, 2009) Staff Training and Development, Indianhead Federated Library System (Eau Claire, WI). http://www.hclib.org/extranet/. The presentation is listed as "Storytime Presentation."

Tarango, Laura and Valerie Wonder. "Bilingual Storytimes: Building Early Literacy and Community." WebJunction (2009), http://www.webjunction.org/early-literacy/-/articles/content/73216091.

Wattenberg, Jane. *Mrs. Mustard's Baby Faces*. San Francisco: Chronicle Children's Books, 2007.

Fingerplays, Rhymes, and Songs

King County Library System. "Tell Me a Story" wiki. http://wiki.kcls.org/tellmeastory/index.php/Fingerplays%2C_Rhymes_and_Songs.
    Has links to demonstration videos of fingerplays on YouTube.

Zero to Three: National Center for Infants, Toddlers, and Families. "Getting In Tune: The Powerful Influence of Music on Young Children's Development" (2002), www.zerotothree.org/site/DocServer/music.pdf?docID=961.

Puppets and Flannelboards

Axtell, Steve. "Developing Excellence in Puppet Manipulation." Axtell Expressions (2002), http://www.axtell.com/manip.html.

Commonwealth Felt. http://www.commonwealthfelt.com/.

Dick Blick Art Materials. http://www.dickblick.com/.

Greene, Carol. "Making Your Figure Talk," Arts in Education. http://www.carolgreene.com/education/vent/talk.html.

Kizclub: Learning Resources for Kids. http://www.kizclub.com/.
    Illustrations of nursery rhymes and everyday objects that can be used for flannelboard patterns.

Lakeshore Learning. http://www.lakeshorelearning.com/home/home.jsp.

Nasco.com. http://www.enasco.com/.

Sierra, Judy. *The Flannel Board Storytelling Book*. New York: H. W. Wilson, 1997.

Sierra, Judy. *Mother Goose's Playhouse: Toddler Tales and Nursery Rhymes, with Patterns for Puppets and Feltboard*. Ashland, OR: Bob Kaminski Media Arts, 1994.

Every Child Ready to Read®

American Library Association. Association for Library Services to Children. "Every Child Ready to Read" (2011), http://www.everychildreadytoread.org.

Association for Library Service to Children and Public Library Association. "Building on Success: Every Child Ready to Read® @your library," 2nd ed. Draft document. American Library Association, 2011.

Carle, Eric. *From Head to Toe*. New York: HarperFestival, 1999.

Dr. Seuss. *Horton Hears a Who*. New York: Random House, 1954.

Every Child Ready to Read Task Force. "Evaluation Summary and Recommended Next Steps." Association of Librarians Serving Children and the Public Library Association (2009), http://www.ala.org/ala/mgrps/divs/alsc/ecrr/ecrr_taskforce_report_july2.pdf.

Ho, Minfong. *Hush! A Thai Lullaby*. New York: Orchard Books, 1996.

Kuskin, Karla. *Under My Hood I Have a Hat*. New York: Laura Geringer Books, [2004] 1964.

McKee, David. *Elmer*. New York: Lothrop, Lee & Shepard, [1989] 1968.

Neuman, Susan, and Donna Celano. "Every Child Ready to Read: An Evaluation. Public Library Association Conference. March 25, 2010." American Library Association. Association for Library Service to Children. http://www.ala.org/ala/mgrps/divs/alsc/ecrr/index.cfm.

Park, Linda Sue. *Mung Mung: A Fold-Out Book of Animal Sounds*. Watertown, MA: Charlesbridge, 2004.

Wheeler, Lisa. *Jazz Baby*. Orlando, FL: Harcourt, 2007.

Zero to Three: National Center for Infants, Toddlers, and Families. "Tips for Choosing Books for Babies and Toddlers" (2010), http://www.zerotothree.org/early-care-education/early-language-literacy/choosing-books.html.

RESOURCES

Bibliographies

Lewis, Valerie, and Walter Mayes. *Valerie and Walter's Best Books for Children: A Lively, Opinionated Guide.* 2nd ed. New York: Quill, 2004.

Lipson, Eden Ross. *The New York Times Parent's Guide to the Best Books for Children.* New York: Three Rivers Press, 2000.

Odean, Kathleen. *Great Books for Babies and Toddlers: More Than 500 Recommended Books for Your Child's First Three Years.* New York: Ballantine Books, 2003.

Oppenheim, Joanne. Oppenheim Toy Portfolio: The Best Toys, Books & Videos for Kids. http://www.toyportfolio.com/.

Brain Development

Parents as Teachers. *Linking Neuroscience to the Care and Education of Young Children: Prenatal to Kindergarten Entry.* St. Louis, MO: Parents as Teachers National Center, 2001.

Zero to Three: National Center for Infants, Toddlers, and Families. "FAQ's On the Brain" (2010), http://main.zerotothree.org/site/PageServer?pagename=ter_key_brainFAQ.

Storytime Planning and Early Literacy

BestKidsBooksite. http://www.thebestkidsbooksite.com/.

> Offers a huge collection of fingerplays, book recommendations, storytime and craft ideas, and more, geared for librarians. Includes a "Babytime" section with a recommended infant storytime format.

¡Colorín Colorado! http://www.ColorinColorado.org/.

> A Spanish/English version of the Reading Rockets website.

Davis, Robin Works. *Toddle On Over.* Fort Atkinson, WI: Alleyside Press, 1998

Ernst, Linda. *Baby Rhyming Time.* New York: Neal-Schuman, 2008.

Maddigan, Beth. *The Big Book of Stories, Songs, and Sing-Alongs: Programs for Babies, Toddlers and Families.* Westport, CT: Libraries Unlimited, 2003.

Reading Is Fundamental. http://www.rif.org/.

> One of the most important promoters of early literacy in the United States. The RIF website offers information for educators and parents, as well as online early literacy games for children.

Reading Rockets. http://www.readingrockets.org/.

> A PBS website that provides excellent reading research and resources links, as well as age-level reading guides for parents. Baby and toddler guides are available in English and Spanish; preschool through elementary are in English and 10 other languages.

Fingerplays, Rhymes, and Songs

Ada, Alma Flor, and F. Isabel Campoy, selectors. *Pío Peep! Traditional Spanish Nursery Rhymes.* English adaptations by Alice Schertle. New York: Harper Collins, 2003.

Ada, Alma Flor, and F. Isabel Campoy, selectors. *Mamá Goose: A Latino Nursery Treasury / un Tesoro de Rimas Infantiles.* New York: Hyperion, 2004.

Brown, Marc. *Finger Rhymes.* New York: Dutton, 1980.

Brown, Marc. *Hand Rhymes.* New York: E. P. Dutton, 1985

Cole, Joanna. *Pat-A-Cake and Other Play Rhymes.* New York: Morrow Junior Books, 1992.

Cole, Joanna. *The Eensty-Weentsy Spider: Fingerplays & Action Rhymes.* New York: Morrow Junior Books, 1992.

Conners, Abigail Flesch. *101 Rhythm Instrument Activities for Young Children.* Beltsville, MD: Gryphon House, 2004.

Cousins, Lucy (illus. by). *Lucy Cousin's Book of Nursery Rhymes.* New York: Dutton Children's Books, 1999, 1989.

De Paola, Tomie. *Tomie de Paola's Mother Goose.* New York: Putnam, 1985.

Dunn, Opal. *Hippety-Hop Hippety-Hay: Growing with Rhymes from Birth to Age Three.* New York: Henry Holt, 1999.

Gayle's Preschool Rainbow. http://www.preschoolrainbow.org/preschool-rhymes.htm.

 A wide variety of fingerplays, some traditional and some adapted. Organized by broad topics such as "Animals" and "Special Occasions." Access to theme-based activities is available by subscription.

KIDiddles. http://www.kididdles.com/lyrics/index.html.

 Lyrics to children's songs, indexed by title and subject. Also can do a site search using lyric keywords. Some songs also have an instrumental of the music available to listen to. Can download music and lyric sheets.

National Network for Child Care. "Fingerplays and Action Verses for Children." National Network for Child Care. http://www.nncc.org/Curriculum/fingerplay.html.

Opie, Iona, ed. *Here Comes Mother Goose.* Cambridge, MA: Candlewick Press, 1999.

Orozco, José-Luis, selector. *Diez Deditos / Ten Little Fingers: And Other Play Rhymes and Action Songs from Latin America.* New York: Dutton, 1997.

Ra, Carol. *Trot, Trot to Boston: Play Rhymes for Baby.* New York: Lothrop, Lee & Shepard Books, 1987.

Schiller, Pam, and Thomas Moore. *And the Cow Jumped Over the Moon: Over 650 Activities to Teach Toddlers Using Familiar Rhymes and Songs.* Beltsville, MD: Gryphon House, 2006.

Trevino, Rose Zertuche. *Read Me a Rhyme in Spanish and English.* Chicago: American Library Association, 2009.

Wilner, Isabel. *The Baby's Game Book.* New York: Greenwillow Books, 2000.

Puppets and Flannelboards

Briggs, Diane. *101 Fingerplays, Stories and Songs to Use with Finger Puppets.* Chicago: American Library Association, 1999.

Champlin, Connie. *Storytelling with Puppets.* 2nd ed. Chicago: American Library Association, 1998.

Minkel, Walter. *How to Do "The Three Bears" with Two Hands.* Chicago: American Library Association, 2000.

Wilmes, Liz, and Dick Wilmes. *Felt Board Fingerplays.* Elgin, IL: Building Blocks, 1997.

Every Child Ready to Read®

American Library Association. Association for Library Services to Children. http://www.ala.org/ala/mgrps/divs/alsc/index.cfm.

American Library Association. Public Library Association. http://www.ala.org/ala/mgrps/divs/pla/index.cfm

Paris, Scott. "Reinterpreting the Development of Reading Skills." *Reading Research Quarterly* 40, no. 2 (2005): 184–202.

Sources for Flannelboard Story Sets

Artfelt Puppet System. http://www.artfelt.net/warehouse/front.htm.

 Sells felt finger puppets that can also be used as flannelboard pieces. It has sets for stories like "It Looked Like Spilt Milk," and "Brown Bear, Brown Bear, What Do You See?"

Lakeshore Learning. http://www.lakeshorelearning.com/home/home.jsp.

 Sells soft stuffed pieces for stories like *The Very Hungry Caterpillar* and *Silly Sally* and feltboard easels.

Nasco. http://www.enasco.com/.

 Nasco sells ready-made flannelboard and nursery rhyme felt sets.

Sources for Puppets and Toys

Chinaberry Books. http://www.chinaberry.com/.

 Chinaberry has expanded its wares to include low tech, traditional toys and puppets.

Folkmanis Hand Puppets. http://www.folkmanis.com.

 Folkmanis has been making attractive, durable puppets, lovable animals, for nearly three decades. They offer a range of sizes, from butterfly finger puppets to enormous fluffy dogs.

Schylling Toys. http://www.schylling.com/.

 Your choice of a variety of jack-in-the-boxes and wonderful tin reproduction toys.

APPENDIX

ADDITIONAL SAMPLE STORYTIMES

Storytime 1

Song—**"If You're Happy and You Know It"**
Fingerplays—
 "Apple Tree"
 "Tickle You Here"
 "This Little Piggy"
Book—**Here Are My Hands** by Bill Martin
Fingerplays—
 "Teddy Bear"
 "Al paso, al paso, al paso" / **"Hop, Hop, Hop"**

Song—**"Row, Row, Row Your Boat"**
Fingerplays—
 "Humpty Dumpty"
 "Eeensy, Weensy Spider"
 "Doña Araña / "Lady Spider"
 "This Little Train"
Book—**Peekaboo!** by Matthew Price and Jean Claverie
Fingerplay—**"Head and Shoulders, Baby"**

Songs—with bells
 "Frère Jacques"
 "Twinkle, Twinkle, Little Star"

Storytime 2

Song—**"If You're Happy and You Know It"**
Fingerplays—
 "Jack Be Nimble"
 "2 Little Blackbirds"
 "Knock at the Door"
Nursery Rhyme Flannelboards—
 "Hey Diddle, Diddle"
 "Baa Baa Black Sheep"
 "This Little Piggy"
Fingerplays—
 "Itsy Bitsy Spider"—use spider puppet
 "Apple Tree"
 "Row, Row Your Boat"
Book—**Old Mother Hubbard** by Jane Cabrera
Fingerplays—
 "Ring around the Rosie"
 "Rock-a-Bye Baby "—with baby puppet
 "Head & Shoulders, Baby"
Book—**Peek-a-Boo** by Roberta Intrater
Music—"Hey Ho the Rattle Oh!" Mary Lee Sanseri
Closing Song—**"Wheels on the Bus"**

RECOMMENDED BOOKS, FLANNELBOARD STORIES, AND MUSIC

Board Books

Baker, Keith. *Big Fat Hen*. New York: Harcourt Brace, 1994.
Boynton, Sandra. *Blue Hat, Green Hat*. New York: Little Simon, 1995.
Boynton, Sandra. *Moo, Baa, La La La!* New York: Little Simon, 1995.
Boynton, Sandra. *Snuggle Puppy: A Little Love Song*. New York: Workman Pub., 2003.
Brown, Margaret Wise. *Goodnight Moon*. New York: HarperFestival, 1991.
Campbell, Rod. *Dear Zoo*. New York: Little Simon, 2007.
Carle, Eric. *From Head to Toe*. New York: HarperFestival, 1999.
Carle, Eric. *The Very Hungry Caterpillar*. New York: Philomel, 1994.
Carle, Eric. *The Very Busy Spider*. New York: Penguin, 1984.
Cousins, Lucy. *Doctor Maisy*. Cambridge, MA: Candlewick Press, 2001.
DePaola, Tomie. *Tomie's Baa Baa Black Sheep and Other Rhymes*. New York: Putnam Publishing, 2004.
DePaola, Tomie. *Tomie's Little Mother Goose*. New York: Putnam Publishing, 1997.
DePaola, Tomie. *Tomie's Mother Goose Flies Again*. New York: Putnam Publishing, 2005.
Fleming, Denise. *The Everything Book*. New York: Henry Holt, 2000.
Hill, Eric. *Where's Spot?* New York: G. P. Putnam's Sons, 2000.
Katz, Karen. *Counting Kisses*. New York: Little Simon, 2001.
Katz, Karen. *Mommy Hugs*. New York: Little Simon, 2007, 2006.
Katz, Karen. *Where Is Baby's Bellybutton?* New York: Little Simon, 2000.
Laden, Nina. *Peek-a-Who?* San Francisco: Chronicle, 2000.
London, Jonathan. *Wiggle, Waggle*. San Diego: Red Wagon Books, 2002.
Martin, Bill. *Brown Bear, Brown Bear, What Do You See?* New York: H. Holt, 1996.
Martin, Bill. *Here Are My Hands*. New York: H. Holt, 1998.
Murphy, Mary. *I Like It When*. San Diego: Red Wagon Books, 2002.
Murphy, Mary. *I Like It When . . . /Me Gusta Cuando . . .* Orlando, FL: Libros Viajeros/Harcourt, 2008.
Manning, Jane. *My First Baby Games*. New York: Harper Collins, 2001.
Oxenbury, Helen. *All Fall Down*. New York: Little Simon, 2009, 1987.
Oxenbury, Helen. *Clap Hands*. New York: Little Simon, 2009, 1987.
Oxenbury, Helen. *Say Goodnight*. New York: Little Simon, 2009, 1987.
Patricelli, Leslie. *Big Little*. Cambridge, MA: Candlewick Press, 2003.
Patricelli, Leslie. *Quiet Loud*. Cambridge, MA: Candlewick Press, 2003.
Shaw, Charles. *It Looked Like Spilt Milk*. New York: HarperFestival, 1993.
Smith, Jerry. *The Wheels on the Bus*. New York: Grosset & Dunlap, 1991.
Taback, Simms. *Peek-a-Boo Who?* Maplewood, NJ: Blue Apple, 2006.
Williams, Sue. *I Went Walking*. San Diego: Harcourt Brace, 1996.
Williams, Sue. *I Went Walking / Sali de Paseo*. Orlando, FL: Harcourt, 2006.
Williams, Sue. *Let's Go Visiting*. San Diego: Red Wagon, 2003.
Wood, Audrey, and Don Wood. *Piggies*. Orlando, FL: Red Wagon, 1991.
Wood, Audrey, and Don Wood. *Piggies / Cerditos*. Orlando, FL: Libros Viajeros, Harcourt, 2008.
Wood, Audrey, and Don Wood. *Quick as a Cricket*. Swindon, UK: Child's Play (International), 1998.
Wood, Audrey, and Don Wood. *Silly Sally*. San Diego: Red Wagon Books, 1999.

Books to Read Aloud

Aliki. *One Little Spoonful*. New York: HarperFestival, 2001.
Aliki. *Welcome, Little Baby*. New York: Greenwillow Books, 1987.
Baicker, Karen. *I Can Do It Too!* Brooklyn, NY: Handprint Books, 2003.
Cimarusti, Marie. *Peek-a-Moo*. New York: Dutton's Children's Books, 1998.
Cousins, Lucy. *Maisy Big, Maisy Small*. Cambridge, MA: Candlewick Press, 2007.
Cousins, Lucy. *What Can Rabbit Hear?* New York: Tambourine Books, 1991.
Cousins, Lucy. *What Can Rabbit See?* New York: Tambourine Books, 1991.
Cousins, Lucy. *Where Is Maisy?* Cambridge, MA: Candlewick Press, 1999.
Davis, Katie. *Who Hops? ¿Quién Salta?* Orlando, FL: Libros Viajeros, Harcourt, 2005.
Dr. Seuss. *Mr. Brown Can Moo! Can You?* New York: Random House, 1970.
Gentieu, Penny. *Baby! Talk!* New York: Crown Publishers, 1999.
Hines, Anna Grossnickle. *1, 2, Buckle My Shoe*. Orlando, FL: Harcourt, 2008.
Intrater, Roberta. *Peek-A-Boo, You!* New York: Scholastic, Inc., 2002.
Johnson, Kelly. *Look at the Baby*. New York: Henry Holt, 2002.
Kubler, Annie. *Itsy Bitsy Spider (Sign and Singalong)* Auburn, ME: Child's Play, 2004.

Kubler, Annie. *Twinkle, Twinkle, Little Star (Sign and Singalong)* Auburn, ME: Child's Play, 2004.
Lobel, Anita. *Hello, Day!* New York: Greenwillow, 2008.
Murphy, Mary. *I Kissed the Baby.* Cambridge, MA: Candlewick Press, 2003.
O'Connell, Rebecca. *The Baby Goes Beep.* Brookfield, CT: Roaring Brook Press, 2003.
Price, Matthew, and Jean Claverie. *Peekaboo!* New York: Alfred A. Knopf, 1985.
Raffi. *Wheels on the Bus.* New York: Crown, 1990, 1988.
Rowe, Jeannette. *Whose Nose?* Boston: Little, Brown, 1998.

Stories and Rhymes for Flannelboards

Carle, Eric. *The Very Hungry Caterpillar.*
Langstaff, John. *Oh, A-Hunting We Will Go.* New York: Atheneum, 1974.
Mack, Stan. *Ten Bears in the Bed.* (recommend shortening to five–seven bears)
Shaw, Charles. *It Looked Like Spilt Milk.*
"Yellow Star, Yellow Star." (A holiday variant of *Brown Bear, Brown Bear, What Do You See?* Text and patterns are at the end of this chapter.)
Traditional. "The Farmer in the Dell."
Traditional. "I Don't Want to Wear My Coat." (Lyrics and patterns are at the end of this chapter.)
Traditional. "Old MacDonald."
Traditional. "The Wheels on the Bus." (Lyrics and patterns are at the end of this chapter.)
Nursery Rhymes: "Baa Baa Black Sheep," "Hey Diddle Diddle," "This Little Piggy," "Two Little Blackbirds."

Recorded Music

Give these albums a listen. Use the songs you like and that will work for your activity.
Boynton, Sandra. *Rhinoceros Tap.* Cambridge, MA: Boynton! Recordings: Rounder, 2004.
Every Child Deserves a Lifetime. Los Angeles: Shout Factory, 2007.
Gill, Jim. *Jim Gill Sings Do Re Mi on His Toe Leg Knee.* Oak Park, IL: Jim Gill Music, 1999.
McGrath, Bob. *If You're Happy and You Know It: Sing Along with Bob.* Vol. 1. Teaneck, NJ: Bob's Kids Music, 1996.
One Hundred Toddler Favorites. 3-CD set. Redway, CA: Music for Little People, 2005.
Orozco, Jose-Luis. *De Colores and Other Latin American Folk Songs.* Berkeley, CA: Arcoiris Records, 1994.
Orozco, Jose-Luis. *Diez Deditos / Ten Little Fingers.* Berkeley, CA: Arcoiris Records, 1997.
Peterson, Carole. *Dancing Feet.* [S.l.]: Macaroni Soup, 2008.
Picnic Playground. [S.l.]: Putumayo World Music, 2009.
Raffi. *Baby Beluga.* Vancouver, BC: Shoreline Records, 1980.
Raffi. *More Singable Songs for the Very Young.* Vancouver, BC: Shoreline, 1977.
Raffi. *One Light, One Sun.* Vancouver, BC: Shoreline, 1985.
Raffi. *Rise and Shine.* Willowdale, ON: Shoreline, 1982.
Raffi. *Singable Songs for the Very Young.* Vancouver, BC: Shoreline, 1976.
Rock & Roll Playground. [S.l.]: Putumayo World Music, 2010.
Schnitzer, Sue. *Wiggle and Whirl, Clap and Nap.* Boulder, CO: Wee Bee Music, 2000.
Sunseri, Marylee. *1, 2, 3, Sing With Me.* Pacific Grove, CA: Piper Grove Music, 1999.
Sunseri, Marylee. *Baby-O! Activity Songs for Baby Playtime and Lapsit.* Pacific Grove, CA: Piper Grove Music, 2005.
Sunseri, Marylee. *Mother Goose Melodies.* Pacific Grove, CA: Piper Grove Music, 2003.
Tallman, Susie. *Children's Songs, A Collection of Childhood Favorites.* United States: Rock Me Baby Records, 2004.
Tallman, Susie. *Classic Nursery Rhymes.* San Francisco: Rock Me Baby Records, 2002.
The Wiggles. *You Make Me Feel Like Dancing.* Port Washington, NY: Koch Records, 2008.

Storytime Observation Checklist

Circle one answer.

1. Parents sit with their children.

   Yes / No

2. Parents sing songs with their children.

   Yes / No

3. Parents follow the librarian and do the fingerplays.

   Yes / No

4. Children are paying attention and participating.

   Yes / No

5. Parents are not involved in what's going on.

   Instead they are . . .

   - Text messaging

   - Talking

   - Reading

   - Taking a nap

   - Doing something else

   _____

6. What did you like most about the program?

Storytime Observation Checklist

Circle one answer.

1. Parents sit with their children.

   Yes / No

2. Parents sing songs with their children.

   Yes / No

3. Parents follow the librarian and do the fingerplays.

   Yes / No

4. Children are paying attention and participating.

   Yes / No

5. Parents are not involved in what's going on.

   Instead they are . . .

   - Text messaging

   - Talking

   - Reading

   - Taking a nap

   - Doing something else

   _____

6. What did you like most about the program?

Reproducible Storytime Observation Checklist. (Ellin Klor)

From *Serving Teen Parents: From Literacy to Life Skills* by Ellin Klor and Sarah Lapin.
Santa Barbara, CA: Libraries Unlimited. Copyright © 2011

Favorite Fingerplays 1

Jack Be Nimble
Jack be nimble,
(bounce child)
Jack be quick,
(bounce child)
Jack jump OVER the candlestick!
(lift child over head)

This Little Piggy
This little pig went to market,
This little pig stayed home,
This little pig had roast beef for dinner,
This little pig had none.
This little pig cried "Wee, wee, wee,"
All the way home.
(Touch a toe or finger for each "pig.")

Head and Shoulders, Baby
Head and shoulders, baby, clap 1, 2, 3.
(touch child's head and shoulders)
Head and shoulders, baby, 1, 2, 3.
(speed up) Head and shoulders, head
and shoulders, head and shoulders, head
and shoulders, baby, 1, 2, 3!
(repeat pattern)
Knees and ankles, baby, 1, 2, 3, ...
Touch the floor, baby, 1, 2, 3, ...

Knock at the Door
Knock at the door,
(knock forehead)
Peep in, *(touch eyes)*
Lift up the latch *(touch nose)*
And walk in. *(put finger in mouth)*

The Eeentsy-Weentsy Spider
The eentsy-weentsy spider went up the water spout,
(fingers "climb" while raising arms)
Down came the rain & washed the spider out,
(lower arms while fingers make "rain")
Out came the sun, *(arms form a circle)*
and dried up all the rain, *(fingers drift up)*
And the eentsy-weentsy spider went up the spout again!
(fingers "climb" while raising arms)
(open out fingers one at a time)

Scary Eyes
See my big and scary eyes,
(circle eyes with fingers)
Look out now, a big surprise,
BOO!
(shout & take fingers away from eyes)

Catch a Fish
One, two, three, four, five,
(start with closed fist & count out fingers)
I caught a fish alive!
(make a "catching" gesture by snapping hand)
Why did I let it go?
(release & open fingers)
Because it bit my finger so! *(shake thumb)*

Row, Row, Row Your Boat
Row, row, row your boat,
Gently down the stream,
Merrily, merrily, merrily,
Life is but a dream!
(make rowing motions with arms or cycle child's legs)
(repeat rhyme speaking slowly, then switch to double speed for last two lines)

Ring around the Rosie
Ring around the rosie, *(bounce)*
Pocket full of posies. *(bounce)*
Ashes, ashes, *(lift)*
We all fall down! *(lower)*
The cows are in the meadow, eating buttercups,
Thunder,lightning *(gently shake baby)*
We all stand up! *(lift baby)*

Beehive
Here is the beehive, *(make a fist)*
But where are the bees?
They're hiding inside, where nobody sees.
(point to fist)
Look out now, they're coming alive! *(shake fist)*
Let's count them – 1, 2, 3, 4, 5!!

Favorite Fingerplays 2

Old MacDonald
Old MacDonald had a farm, E-I-E-I-O!
And on this farm he had a duck, E-I-E-I-O!
With a quack, quack here, and a quack, quack
there, Here a quack, there a quack, everywhere a
quack, quack. . . .
Old MacDonald had a farm, E-I-E-I-O!!
Sing with other animals: dog—woof, cat—meow,
cow—moo, pig—oink

Apple Tree
Way up high in the apple tree, *(raise arms)*
Two little apples smiled at me. *(cup hands)*
I shook that tree as hard as I could, *(shake arms)*
Down came the apples, *(drop hands to lap)*
Mmm, were they good!! *(rub tummy)*

Teddy Bear
Round and round the garden goes the teddy bear.
("walk" fingers in a circle on child's tummy)
One step, two step,
(take two "steps" toward head with fingers)
Tickle him under there!
(tickle child under chin)

Humpty Dumpty
Humpty Dumpty sat on a wall,
(bounce)
Humpty Dumpty had a great fall.
(open legs and let baby "fall")
All the king's horses and all the king's men
Couldn't put Humpty together again.

Where Is Thumbkin?
Where is Thumbkin? Where is Thumbkin?
(hands behind back)
Here I am, here I am. *(bring thumbs out)*
How are you today, sir. *(one thumb bows to other)*
Very well, I thank you. *(other thumb bows)*
Run away, run away. *(put hands behind back)*
Where is Pointer? . . .Tall Man? . . . Ring
Man? . . . Pinkie? . . . Whole Family *(all fingers)*

Here's the Train
Here's the train going down the track, "Choo, choo,
choo," *(make "chugging" motions with arms)*
Now it's going forward, *(chug again)*
Now it's going back. *(chug slowly)*
Ring the bell, "Ding, ding, ding!" *(ring bell)*
Hear the whistle blow, *(hold hand at mouth & say
"whoo, whooo!")*
What a lot of noise it makes,
as down the track it goes!

Rock-a-Bye Baby
Rock-a-bye baby, *(rock child)*
On the tree top *(lift child)*
When the winds blow,
The cradle will rock. *(rock child)*
When the bough breaks *(lift)*
The cradle will fall.
And down will come baby,
Cradle and all. *(lower)*

Two Little Blackbirds
Two little blackbirds sitting on a hill,
(hold up bent index fingers & close other fingers)
One named Jack, and one named Jill.
(wiggle index fingers at each other)
Fly away, Jack; fly away, Jill.
("fly" each hand behind your back)
Come back, Jack; come back, Jill.
("fly" each hand to front)

The Bubble Song
1 little, 2 little, 3 little bubbles *(count with fingers)*
4 little, 5 little, 6 little bubbles,
7 little, 8 little, 9 little bubbles,
10 little bubbles go POP! POP! POP! *(clap hands)*
Pop, pop, pop those bubbles,
Pop, pop, pop those bubbles,
10 little bubbles go POP! POP! POP!
(clap hands)

Pancake
Mix a pancake, stir a pancake,
(pretend to stir batter in a bowl)
Put it in a pan. *(pour "batter" into pan)*
Cook a pancake, flip a pancake,
(flip the pancake)
Catch it if you can!
(pretend to grab pancake in the air)

Open, Shut Them

Open, shut them, open, shut them,
(open & close hands)
Give a little clap.
Open, shut them, open, shut them,
Lay them in your lap.
Creep them, creep them, *(walk fingers up)*
Way up to your chin,
Open up your little mouth, but do not let them in!

The Wheels on the Bus

The wheels on the bus go round & round, round &
round, round & round, *(roll arms)*
The wheels on the bus go round & round,
all through the town!
The horn on the bus goes beep, beep, beep . . .
(beat open hand on fist)
The wipers on the bus go swish, swish, swish . . .
(move arms back & forth)
The doors on the bus go open & shut, open & shut
(open & close arms)
The people on the bus go up & down, up &
down . . .
(stand up & sit down)
The baby on the bus goes whaa, whaa, whaa . . .
(cradle arms and rock)
The parents on the bus say "I love you," "I love
you" . . .
(hug child)
All through the town!

If You're Happy and You Know It

If you're happy and you know it, clap your hands.
If you're happy and you know it, clap your hands,
If you're happy and you know it,
Then your face will surely show it,
If you're happy and you know it, clap your hands.
... Wiggle your toes! Pat your head! Shout hooray!
etc.

Motorboat

Motorboat, motorboat, go so slow,
(stand and spin slowly holding child)
Motorboat, motorboat, go so fast,
(spin a little faster)
Motorboat, motorboat, STEP ON THE GAS!
(spin faster)

Twinkle, Twinkle, Little Star

Twinkle, twinkle, little star,
(hold hands high and open/close them)
How I wonder what you are!
Up above the world so high,
like a diamond in the sky!
(make diamond shape with fingers)
Twinkle, twinkle, little star,
how I wonder what you are.

Hickory Dickory Dock

Hickory dickory dock, *(swing arms)*
The mouse ran up the clock.
(run fingers up arm to head)
The clock struck one,
(clap hands over head)
The mouse ran down,
(run fingers down arm)
Hickory dickory dock. (swing arms)

It's Not That Cold Outside
(Sung to the tune of "Mary had a Little Lamb")

I don't want to wear my gloves,
wear my gloves, wear my gloves,
I don't want to wear my gloves,
It's not that cold outside!
(Repeat, substituting other clothing.)
I don't want to wear my scarf . . .
I don't want to wear my hat . . .
I don't want to wear my coat . . .
I don't want to wear my boots . . .
I don't want to wear my shirt . . .
I don't want to wear my pants . . .
ACHOOO!
Guess I better wear my pants,
wear my pants, wear my pants
It's really cold outside!
(Repeat, substituting other clothing.)
Guess I better wear my shirt,
Guess I better wear my boots,
Guess I better wear my coat,
Guess I better wear my hat,
Guess I better wear my scarf,
Guess I better wear gloves,
IT'S REALLY COLD OUTSIDE!

Favorite Fingerplays 4

Frère Jacques
Frère Jacques, Frère Jacques,
Dormez vous? dormez vous?
Sonnez les matines, sonnez les matines,
Din, din, don! Din, din, don!
Are you sleeping, are you sleeping?
Brother John? Brother John?
Morning bells are ringing, morning bells are ringing,
Ding ding dong, ding ding dong.

Doña Araña
(se imitan con las manos las acciones de la araña)
Doña Araña se fue a pasear
Hizo un hilo y se puso a trepar,
Vino el viento y la hizo bailar.

Al paso, al paso, al paso
*(El adulto sienta al niño en una rodilla.
El movimiento de la pierna aumenta con las
palabras de la rima.)*
Al paso, al paso, al paso,
Al trote, al trote, al trote,
Al galope, al galope, al galope.

The Noble Duke of York
The noble Duke of York, he had ten thousand men,
He marched them up to the top of the hill,
And he marched them down again.
And when you're up, you're up, *(lift child)*
And when you're down, you're down, *(lower child)*
And when you're only half way up,
You're neither up nor down!
(lift child to center, lift child high, lower child)

Pop! Goes the Weasel
All around the cobbler's bench,
The monkey chased the weasel;
The monkey thought 'twas all in fun,
Pop! Goes the weasel!
A penny for a spool of thread,
A penny for a needle.
That's the way the money goes,
Pop! Goes the weasel!

Great Big Ball
Make a little tiny ball, like this.
(Use finger & thumb)
Make a middle size ball, like this.
(Use fingers and thumb of both hands)
Now make a GREAT BIG BALL like this!
(Use arms)
Now let's count them—one, two, three!
(Repeat shapes from large to small shapes again)

(English translation)
Lady Spider
*(imitate the spider's actions with hand
movements)*
Lady Spider spun a thread
To climb as high as the elephant's head.
Along came the wind and made her dance.
Along came a storm, and she lost her chance.

(English translation)
Hop, Hop, Hop
*(The adult has the child sitting on one knee. The
movement increases with the words of the rhyme.)*
Walk, walk, walk.
Trot, trot, trot.
Gallop, gallop, gallop!

Pat-a-Cake, Pat-a-Cake
Pat-a-cake, pat-a-cake, baker's man.
(clap slowly with rhythm)
Bake me a cake as fast as you can;
Pat it and roll it and mark it with B,
(pat and roll the dough, and write a letter "B")
And put it in the oven for baby and me.
*(push "cake" into oven,
and point to child and self)*

Tickle You
Hug you here, hug you there,
Hug you, hug you, everywhere!
Tickle you . . .
Bounce you . . .
(match actions to words)

From *Serving Teen Parents: From Literacy to Life Skills* by Ellin Klor and Sarah Lapin.
Santa Barbara, CA: Libraries Unlimited. Copyright © 2011

It's Not That Cold Outside
(Sung to the tune of "Mary had a Little Lamb")

I don't want to wear my gloves,
wear my gloves, wear my gloves
I don't want to wear my gloves,
It's not that cold outside!

(Repeat, substituting other clothing.)
I don't want to wear my scarf ...
I don't want to wear my hat ...
I don't want to wear my coat ...
I don't want to wear my boots ...
I don't want to wear my shirt ...
I don't want to wear my pants ...

ACHOOO!!
Guess I better wear my pants,
wear my pants, wear my pants
It's really cold outside!

(Repeat substituting other clothing.)
Guess I better wear my shirt,
Guess I better wear my boots,
Guess I better wear my coat,
Guess I better wear my hat,
Guess I better wear my scarf,
Guess I better wear gloves,
IT'S REALLY COLD OUTSIDE!!

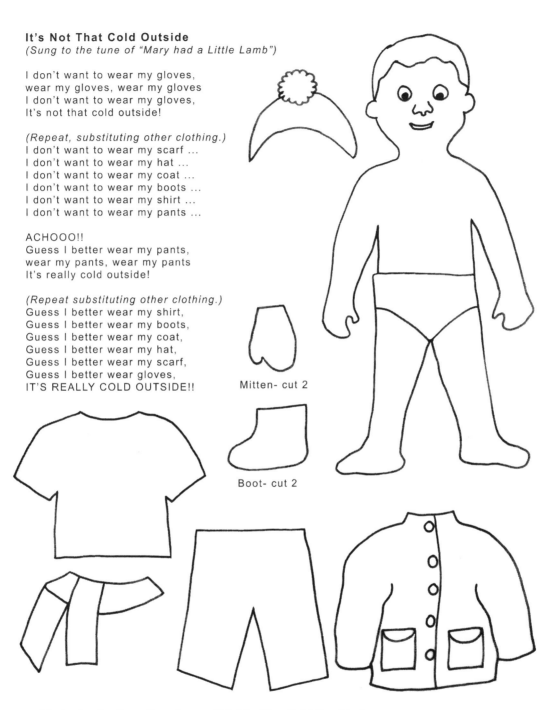

Mitten- cut 2

Boot- cut 2

Patterns and lyrics for the flannelboard story "It's Not That Cold Outside."
(Jan Irving and Robin Currie (lyrics) Ellin Klor (patterns))

Yellow Star, Yellow Star ...
(Patterned after Brown Bear, Brown Bear, What Do You See?)

Yellow star, yellow star, what do you see?
I see a pair of blue mittens looking at me.
Blue mittens, blue mittens, what do you see?
I see a green hat looking at me.
Green hat ...   purple stocking ...
Purple stocking ..brown boots....
Brown boots ...   golden bell ...
Golden bell ...   red and white candy cane ...
Candy cane ....   gingerbread man ...
Gingerbread man ...   red flower (pointsettia) ....
Red flower ...   white snowman ...
Snowman .....   Pine tree ,,,,
Pine tree ...   Santa Claus ...
Santa, Santa, what do you see?
I see presents for children everywhere, that's what I see!

Mittens (cut 2)

Patterns and text for the flannelboard story "Yellow Star, Yellow Star . . ." (Ellin Klor)

Yellow Star, Yellow Star ...

Boots (cut 2)

Patterns for the flannelboard story "Yellow Star, Yellow Star . . ." (Ellin Klor)

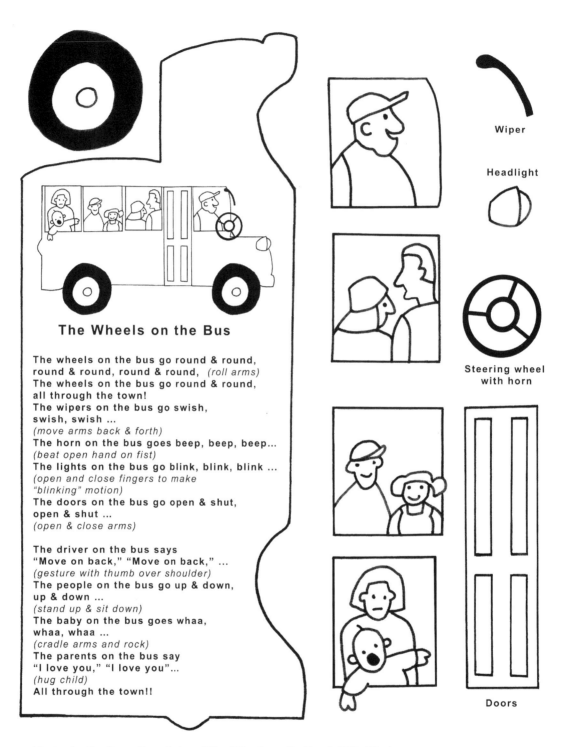

The Wheels on the Bus

The wheels on the bus go round & round,
round & round, round & round, (roll arms)
The wheels on the bus go round & round,
all through the town!
The wipers on the bus go swish,
swish, swish ...
(move arms back & forth)
The horn on the bus goes beep, beep, beep...
(beat open hand on fist)
The lights on the bus go blink, blink, blink ...
(open and close fingers to make
"blinking" motion)
The doors on the bus go open & shut,
open & shut ...
(open & close arms)

The driver on the bus says
"Move on back," "Move on back," ...
(gesture with thumb over shoulder)
The people on the bus go up & down,
up & down ...
(stand up & sit down)
The baby on the bus goes whaa,
whaa, whaa ...
(cradle arms and rock)
The parents on the bus say
"I love you," "I love you"...
(hug child)
All through the town!!

Wiper

Headlight

**Steering wheel
with horn**

Doors

Patterns and lyrics for the flannelboard story "The Wheels on the Bus." (Ellin Klor)

8

TEEN PARENT FAMILIES: PLAYING AND LEARNING TOGETHER

Every day can be a learning experience for a young child, if parents and caregivers are aware of opportunities when they occur, and if they have the knowledge and energy to act on them. A key aspect of everyday learning is verbalizing and affirming experiences with children. Through this process, they recognize how language is used to explain and identify their environment, a significant concept in language development. Seeing the world through the child's eyes, and supporting the child's exploration, are intuitive skills for some parents, but other mothers and fathers could benefit from the modeling and teaching of these techniques. Many libraries have recognized the value of introducing parent-child play activities as an adjunct to the storytimes they offer to the general public. Whether the activities are called "early learning" or "school readiness," motivated parents are eager to give their children enrichment activities. Librarians working with teen parents can create the same connections for them using early literacy, everyday learning, and play. As discussed in chapter 6, the library can be a powerful resource for recreation. Within this context, teen parents can also learn how the library's resources, like materials on play and parenting, can help them become better parents.

MILESTONES OF EARLY DEVELOPMENT

It is important to have a basic understanding of the milestones of infant and toddler development in order to plan effective, age-appropriate programs and activities for young children. This background knowledge is also beneficial to have on hand to pass on to parents whenever necessary. Children's development can be categorized into five areas: physical, language, cognitive, social, and emotional. From birth to 18 months, a child's development progresses so rapidly that scientists divide it into three-month increments. From 18 months to three years, changes are charted on a six-month basis. In brief, the age-based developmental stages, adapted from Zero to Three's "Your Baby's Development" (Parlakian and Lerner 2008) and *The Complete Resource Book for Infants*, by Pam Schiller, are outlined below.

- **Birth to 3 months:** The baby becomes familiar with parents and caregivers and responds to them; she uses body language, facial expressions, and sounds to communicate her condition (sleepy, hungry, happy, etc.). She starts to grasp objects and follow moving objects with her eyes (tracking); she learns to trust that her needs will be met.

173

- **3 to 6 months:** The child learns to control her body (she can sit up with help, roll over, and hold her head steady). She uses her mouth, hands, and fingers to explore and pick things up; she communicates with sounds, actions, and facial expressions (smiles and laughter). She enjoys interactive games like patty-cake, swipes at objects, and will bounce when standing in a grown-up's lap.

- **6 to 9 months:** The child is learning to think and solve problems (she copies what adults do to see how things work). She can pick up small objects and put them in her mouth, including finger foods. She sits independently, and she may be able to scoot or crawl. She babbles and uses her voice to express feelings like happiness and anger; she copies actions like waving "bye-bye" and shaking her head for "no." She responds to baby games like peekaboo. Her personality and temperament begin to show (she may be active or an observer; she may like calm or busy environments).

- **9 to 12 months:** She understands what is being said to her and can follow simple directions. She mimics speech when babbling and may be able to say a word or two. She can creep and crawl and can roll a ball and tear paper. She understands that things exist even when they are out of sight (object permanence). She looks at books; she likes to repeat actions again and again to understand how things work (and is also building memory). She communicates with gestures, pointing, crawling, and pulling up, and she explores objects by shaking or banging them. She can drop objects into an open box and fit nesting boxes together.

- **12 to 15 months:** She is starting to walk, alone or with help, and can crawl up stairs. She can turn the pages of a book and throw a ball. She uses actions to communicate needs and can use some words. She will say "No" and demonstrate a desire for more independence. She likes to copy the actions of others, such as using the telephone or stirring a pot.

- **15 to 18 months:** The child can walk, scribble with a crayon, build a block tower, and feed herself. She can understand simple questions and directions and communicates with a combination of sounds and actions. She is becoming aware of her emotions and those of others (and may repeat actions that make someone laugh). She may struggle with her own emotions and have tantrums. She is good at problem solving (she repeats actions to figure them out, and she imitates what others do).

- **18 to 24 months:** The child is learning many new words and may make two-word sentences. She needs help with self-control and frustration. She uses imagination for pretend play and likes figuring things out by filling, dumping, opening, closing, and sorting objects. She tries to do things independently, such as getting dressed. She enjoys nursery rhymes and can match sounds to animals. She may be able to listen to a short story. She can use playdough, finger paint, work a simple puzzle, and string large wooden beads.

- **24 to 30 months:** The child can walk up stairs steadily, walk backward, and balance on one foot. She communicates feelings and wants with language. She engages in pretend play using objects for unintended purposes, such as a box for a toy bed. She laughs at silly things. She is interested in being with other children and will copy what they do, but she is challenged by sharing.

- **30 to 36 months:** The child has mastered many physical skills; she can pedal a tricycle, dress herself, draw a line, turn a knob, or unscrew a cap. She uses language to express her thoughts and feelings. She uses as many as 900 words, asks questions, knows her first and last names, and can understand sentences with more than one idea. She can remember yesterday's events, act out stories, and use some logic in everyday situations. Friends are important to her.

The significant developmental changes that occur in the first three years of life, particularly in the first year, are nothing short of amazing. The critical factors enabling young children to reach these developmental milestones are ongoing, repeated, and positive interactions and experiences with adults. What is also clear is that activities need to be developmentally appropriate for the child's age and maturity level. Children cannot be expected to do things that are beyond their physical and intellectual abilities. This can often be a challenging concept for teen parents; from their own developmental perspective, they assume that young children can think in the same way that they themselves do. It is important to be aware, and make teen parents aware, that in many instances, if a child rejects a book, toy, or activity, the cause may be that it is developmentally too old or too young for them.

WHAT ABOUT PLAY?

Maria Montessori's adage "Play is the young child's work" conveys the critical notion of how babies and children grow and learn. Understanding and promoting this concept is vital to children's development. It is essential to help teen parents see the importance of play as much more than simply having fun. Many teen parents had minimal exposure to interactive play with their own parents when they were children, and they will often need guidance on how and why to show their children how to play a game or do an activity. Even with newborns, the teens can practice the one-person conversation technique discussed below and will often enjoy the activities themselves. Through these types of activities, the parents get a glimpse of what early learning is about. Teaching young parents about the importance of play for their children is best done by doing and showing, with casual discussion (rather than lecture) integrated into the program. An immediate experience gives teens a frame of reference for understanding. These experiences and your guidance and direction should convey to the teen parents that through play, children learn and develop:

- Gross motor skills, from crawling, to standing, walking, jumping, and climbing
- Hand-eye coordination and small muscle dexterity in their fingers and hands
- Socialization, through the interaction of playful games (peekaboo, etc.)
- Communication and language development through sounds, gestures, facial expressions, talking, and listening
- Early thinking, including memory use, problem solving, and imagination
- Early learning concepts, including cause and effect, object permanence (the understanding that things still exist even when you can't see them), spatial relationships of objects, and use of symbols (toy versions of real things, pictures that represent real things, words that name objects and actions) (Miller 1999)

And how do babies and toddlers learn?

- They learn through their senses—touch, taste, smell, sight, and hearing.
- They learn from imitating what others do.
- They learn from a variety of types of play—quiet, active, solitary, with others.
- They learn through repetition and trying things themselves.
- They learn by moving at their own speed (Warner 1999).

Basic Baby Play

Simple, interactive parent-child play, like peekaboo games, tickling, and bouncing, can be harder to introduce to teen audiences than activities that utilize objects and have a concrete format. Teen parents can feel ill-at-ease acting goofy in front of their peers and others. Often the most successful way to demonstrate this sort of play is to have the parents share in small groups what they enjoy doing with their children. In the process of sharing, library staff have an opportunity to build on what the teens are already doing, recognize their strengths, present the importance of play, and suggest effective techniques.

To find quality learning activities, rather than reinventing the wheel, take a look at *The Early Learning Initiative for Wisconsin Libraries* (Huntington 2005). It has many suggestions online for age-appropriate learning activities, which accompany its "Sample Library Programs for Infants." Also consult the books *Oppenheim Toy Portfolio: Baby and Toddler Play Book* (Oppenheim and Oppenheim 2001) and *Baby Play and Learn* (Warner 1999). Perfect for library staff, *Read It! Play It! With Babies and Toddlers* (Oppenheim and Oppenheim 2006) matches stories geared for infants and toddlers with play activities and has excellent suggestions on read-aloud enrichment techniques. Ideas to try include classic peekaboo games, including those using scarves; and tickle games like "Tickle You Here, Tickle You There; Tickle You, Tickle You Everywhere!"

PLANNING SUCCESSFUL PROGRAMS

Parent-child programs using planned activities and supplies take some logistical development. Be sure to consider these basic factors.

1. The age range of the children in the group
2. The number of children and parents
3. The best time during your visit to schedule the activity, identifying when children are alert and calm (avoid nap and meal times)
4. The early learning experience that you hope to share
5. The features and limitations of the physical facility where you will be working
6. The total time available for setup, the activity, and cleanup
7. The cost and availability of supplies

Working out these details is easier than it might seem. Many books on developmental activities and play specifically list the skills that each activity promotes and indicate the appropriate age range of the activity. These include *Baby Play: 100 Fun-filled Activities to Maximize Your Baby's Potential*, edited by Wendy Masi and Roni Cohen Leiderman; *Toddler Play: 100 Fun-filled Activities to Maximize Your Toddler's Potential*, edited by Wendy Masi; *Read It! Play It! With Babies and Toddlers*, by Joanne and Stephanie Oppenheim; *Simple Steps*, by Karen Miller; and *365 Activities You and Your Toddler Will Love*, by Nancy Wilson Hall.

Involving the teen parents in helping you plan your program has multiple benefits. The most significant advantage with this planning technique is buy-in and commitment from the teen parents to the program. It is also another way to introduce them to early learning concepts, and to the wealth of helpful ideas to be gleaned from library resources. Pre-select from books and websites a number of activities that seem feasible and ask the teen parents to look at them and suggest which they would like to try. You can mention the early learning concepts involved as you discuss their choices. Plan with them the logistics of the activity setup, necessary supplies, and preparation work. Whenever possible, have them help you set up the activities.

Selecting Activities

An important goal behind introducing parent-child activities to teen parents is to encourage them to try the activities at home, or to be inspired to try something similar that they can enjoy as a family. If everyone has a great time doing the activity with you, they may decide to incorporate it into their routines at home. Here are guidelines for selecting activities.

1. Always check to make sure that none of the supplies could be a potential choking hazard for the child.
2. Make sure that the activity is age appropriate and will work for the age range of the children in your group. Look for activities that can be used in different ways by different ages of young children.
3. Use inexpensive household materials as much as possible so that the activity is easy to replicate at home.
4. Try to avoid activities that are really messy, will need to dry for more than a few minutes, require a lot of cleanup, or use materials that children might like to, but shouldn't, put in their mouths.
5. Always ask about possible food allergies. As a general rule, avoid foods containing peanuts (a common allergen) because many babies and toddlers have not been exposed to them yet.

6. Do not use activities that could be dangerous if a parent's attention strays.

7. Plan your activities so that there is a minimal chance for discord. Under the best of circumstances, young children are not able to share until at least age three. Make sure that there are always enough materials so that all participants can have their own brush, ball, or whatever the activity requires.

Programs that include parent-child activities can be in a variety of different formats, depending on the needs, age, and interest levels of the teen parents in your program and their children. Consider using the following program designs.

1. **One or more interactive activities during or after a storytime.** This approach works well with activities that have short setup time and are easy to coordinate with the storytime, such as making music with homemade instruments and playing with puppets or toys. Necessary supplies can be readily available for distribution in baskets or bins. These baskets should be kept hidden until you are ready to use them. Otherwise, toddlers will want to get the items out right away, when the presenter may not be ready to have the items used. With its pairings of books and play activities, *Read It! Play It! With Babies and Toddlers*, by Joanne and Stephanie Oppenheim, makes it easy to plan a smooth transition from storytime to playtime.

2. **Several activities highlighting early learning concepts, with or without discussion afterward.** You may choose to have all the activities involve the same concept, or they can involve multiple concepts. Focusing on one concept creates a stronger message, but if program time is limited and your visits are infrequent, it may make sense to try to cover several. When putting together this type of activity session, the "station" approach—often used in preschools, where different activities are set up around the room and children and parents move from one to another as they choose—works well. Generally, plan on the entire session lasting 25 to 30 minutes, with three activities, each at separate tables, or in separate areas. Make sure that the stations and chairs are set up so that parents sit with their children and share the activity with them. Parents and children can rotate from one station to the next as they like. Keep everything unstructured enough so that a child can linger as long as he or she wants at any activity.

3. **A "learning lab" for parents.** If you are working with parents only, it is possible to put together a learning lab where the parents do the activities themselves, and then you discuss what children would learn from the activities. Set the experience up by discussing what children can learn from play, give the parents a list of early learning skills, and ask them to identify what each activity would teach their children. You will be surprised at how much pleasure the teens will derive from trying the activities.

With all of these formats, it is important to have staff (library or on-site at the partner agency) involved to demonstrate and initiate activities and model the role of the parent in play activities. Even just one person floating around from activity to activity, engaging and involving participants as they move around, is extremely beneficial. Keep in mind that the linchpin to playing and participating in the activity is language development. Encourage parent-child dialogue throughout the program, most importantly by engaging in it yourself.

Introducing Activities

Similar to the storytime model, use these interactive play activities as starting points to highlight specific early learning concepts. The following basic concepts about early learning experiences and play should be consistently mentioned at every program.

- Children learn through repetition.
- Children learn best in a loving environment where parents and caregivers support their exploration. This means conversing with the child about what you are doing as you do it and helping them to make discoveries on their own.
- There is no right or wrong way to do these activities. Children learn through experimentation.

In addition, mention the specific early learning skills and developmental benefits that the program's activities demonstrate. Examples include hand-eye coordination, language development, visual discrimination, fine motor skills, classifying skills, and problem solving. Before starting, always give parents and staff a tour of each activity, demonstrating what to do. This is your opportunity to introduce the concepts you want to emphasize as you model each step.

Behaviors to Model

When you participate with the parents and children in these activities, you are able to model critical parenting behaviors for teen parents. Most likely, you will find yourself spontaneously responding to interactive behavior in the following ways.

- **Exploration and discovery:** Allow the child to explore the toy or object with limited adult intervention. Describe to the child what he or she is doing and what is discovered. Show children how to do an activity, such as filling a cup with sand, but then let them do it themselves. Help only enough to avoid frustrating the child (Zero to Three, "Make the Most of Playtime").

- **The one-person conversation:** This important concept demonstrates for young children how conversations work and reinforces the connection between language and experiences. Very simply, the adult makes comments and asks questions about the play activity, and then answers them as well.

- **Praise:** Acknowledge and praise children as they accomplish things, whatever it may be. Look for ways to make positive comments (Masi 2001).

- **Sharing:** Children are not really capable of sharing until at least age three. It is important to make sure that teen parents do not expect their toddlers to be able to share. It is wise to mention this when orienting parents to the program's activities. However, adults can introduce the concept by playing turn-taking games such as rolling a ball back and forth (Parlakian and Lerner 2009).

- **Post-activity discussion:** Taking time for a discussion after the activities is especially effective because parents can respond to what they saw and experienced. A question to generate discussion might be "What did your child like doing best?" Also consider asking "How did you help your child?" or "Did your child do anything she had never done before?"

EVERYDAY LEARNING

With the intention of providing activities that are fun, are educational, and encourage bonding, programs can be planned to focus on a specific aspect of everyday early learning, such as sensory experiences, problem solving, or music. When working with a group of children that has a wide range of ages and are developmentally at different stages, try to choose open-ended activities that can be done at a range of levels, from simple to complex. Although the stated age and interest level may be as young as one year, most children under four years will continue to enjoy the activities, although they may complete them quickly. Encourage parents whose children are not yet able to participate to join in themselves and show their children how to do the activity. Ask them to explain the activity to their children as well, allowing the parents to practice the one-person conversation technique to foster language development.

The web resource from Washington Learning Systems *Supporting Early Literacy in Natural Environments: Activities for Caregivers and Young Children*, by Angela Notari-Syverson and Kristin Rytter, recommends simple everyday learning topics, such as "playing with sounds," "talking about food," and "learning my name." It can serve as a springboard for planning activities. The specific suggestions for parents on how to do and talk about the activities with their children are extremely helpful. For example, "talking about food" gives simple questions to ask about food when eating and suggests extended activities, such as counting and comparing sizes of edibles like raisins.

Sensory Experiences

All humans experience the world through their senses, but for the young child, with limited understanding of why and how things happen, sensory experiences can be quite powerful. Some children are sensitive to sensory stimulation, and care must be taken to recognize a child's individual limits, especially in regard to loud or sudden noises (such as popping balloons). The following are activities to try that enhance learning through the senses. Look for more suggestions for sensory play on the Preschool Express by Jean Warren website on the "Toddler Station: Sensory Exploration" webpages.

Sound and Music

Homemade Band

The Homemade Band is a fun way to learn through sound and music. Begin with children who are 9 to 12 months. Different "instruments" will work for different ages; measuring spoons, for example, may be used like a rattle by a six-month-old baby. Parents of young infants can participate themselves while sitting with their children.

Supplies:

Have enough sets of instruments for both parents and children.

- wooden spoons (for thumping)
- metal and plastic bowls (for thumping on)
- measuring spoons (for shaking)
- plastic cups (for knocking together and drumming on)
- metal soup spoons
- wrist bells
- plastic shaker eggs or bottle shakers (can be homemade; see chapter 6)
- child-friendly music with a strong beat (optional)

Instructions:

1. Lay the homemade band instruments out on tables or the floor, pairing spoons with bowls, etc.
2. Demonstrate how to use the instruments.
3. Encourage parents to play with the instruments too, showing their children what to do, and taking turns using different items with their children.
4. Add recorded music with a strong beat, or even singing, and bang along with the tune.

Other ideas include the "Freeze Dance" from *Toddler Play: 100 Fun-filled Activities to Maximize Your Toddler's Potential*, edited by Wendy Masi, "shakers" from the Preschool Express by Jean Warren website, or try this melodious mix of books and music:

Musical Storytime

Songs and rhythm enhance any storytime. The following is an example of a song-based storytime to round out your music play. Remember to include the following talking points at some point throughout the musical storytime: (1) music builds memory skills; (2) the musical beat emphasizes the cadence and phrasing of words; (3) music can calm both parent and child; (4) music encourages creativity when you make up new verses or words; and (5) music is a way to introduce young children to their ethnic and family heritage by singing or playing favorite songs.

1. For the opening song and book, sing with the book *If You're Happy and You Know It*, by Jane Cabrera.
2. Include the fingerplays/songs "Row, Row, Your Boat" and "Head and Shoulders, Baby, One, Two, Three."

3. Sing a song with puppets: "Grandpa's Farm" from *One Light, One Sun* (Raffi 1985).

4. Play a singing game: "Ring-around-the-Rosie" (sing twice, just humming the second time).

5. Include a book to sing: *Wheels on the Bus* (Raffi 1988).

6. Play a recorded song: "Morningtown Ride" from *Baby Beluga* (Raffi 1980) and use shakers, bells, or scarves.

Touch

Finger Painting with Pudding

Some children may be hesitant to touch something new. Encourage the parents to show the young children that it is safe to touch the pudding, especially when it comes to licking your fingers. This activity works with children who are 12 months or older.

Supplies:

-   dinner-size plastic plates, metal pie pans, or trays (one for each child)
-   vanilla instant pudding (one box makes enough for four children)
-   2 to 3 mixing bowls
-   mixing spoons for stirring
-   damp washcloths or paper towels

Instructions:

1. Have the parents mix the pudding, and let it sit until it thickens.

2. Set plates, trays, or pans around low tables, with two chairs at each place. If cleanup is a problem, the tables and floor may be covered with plastic or newspaper, or you can work outside.

3. Before beginning, children and adults should wash their hands.

4. Seat one child with a parent at each place.

5. Put a big dollop (or two or three) of pudding on each plate or pan.

6. Encourage parents to stick their fingers in the pudding and show their children how to swirl it around or make a picture.

7. Let everyone play with the pudding as long as they like.

8. Have damp paper towels or washcloths ready to wipe hands and faces once the activity is completed.

Cornmeal Tray (nine months or older)

Supplies:

-   5-pound bag of cornmeal
-   clean dishpan or tray with 2- to 3-inch sides
-   small paper cups or measuring cups

Instructions:

1. Pour cornmeal into the dishpan or tray.

2. Add cups for filling and emptying.

3. Plunge your hands into the cornmeal, and feel its silky softness. Play with cups, filling and emptying them. Talk about how the cornmeal feels on your hands and how it looks when you pour it.

Textures (nine months or older)

Supplies:

- scraps (at least 4-inch by 4-inch) of papers and fabrics with different textures—sandpaper, cellophane, velvet or corduroy, lace, flannel, corrugated paper, fake fur or sheepskin, foil, silk
- table, child's height
- cookie sheet or tray

Instructions:

1. Lay two or three scraps on the tabletop or tray at a time.
2. Touch the scraps, or gently brush the child's arm with them, and talk about the differences in how they feel.
3. Use vivid words to describe the scraps, such as scratchy, bumpy, sleek, velvety.

Try a "Tactile Walk" from *The Complete Resource Book for Toddlers and Twos*, by Pam Schiller, to see how much you can feel with your feet as you step from textured surface to surface. This activity is ideal for children age six months or older. Infants who are just starting to stand can be supported on their "walk." It is recommended that you advise the group (prior to the group's meeting) that shoes and socks will be removed for a special activity. Some teens may feel better about participating if they've had advanced warning and an opportunity to make sure that they aren't wearing socks with holes.

No-Cook Playdough

Playdough is an excellent, inexpensive learning toy to enhance a tactile experience. Have each parent make a batch of playdough, so that there is plenty to play with and also to take home. Just be sure that everyone understands that it's not for eating. For younger children who might be inclined to taste the playdough, put a big blob of the dough in a sealed sandwich bag for squishing. Encourage expectant teens and/or parents with infants to play with it themselves. This is ideal for children age 15 months or older.

Supplies:

(Makes one 2- to 3-cup batch)

- 2 cups flour
- 1 cup salt
- 1 tablespoon vegetable oil
- 1 cup water (or slightly more, if needed)
- food coloring
- quart-size resealable plastic bags
- wooden spoons for mixing
- measuring cups
- mixing bowls
- cookie cutters, small rolling pins, wooden Popsicle sticks

Instructions:

Each parent can make their own batch of playdough, either with their child's participation or solo. If possible, allow time for parents and children to experiment manipulating the finished playdough together.

1. Mix the flour, salt, and oil together in mixing bowls.
2. Add several drops of food coloring to the water.

Playdough—fun to make, fun for play. (Vickie Shelton)

3. Add the water in small increments while stirring the flour mixture until it forms a ball of dough.
4. Knead the dough until it is soft and pliable.
5. The parent and the child can sit together and play with the dough. They can use hands and tools to roll it, fold it, make balls of it, and cut out shapes. Parents of very young children can do most of the work, and narrate what they are doing for their children.
6. Parents can take their playdough home and store it in a sealed plastic bag in the refrigerator.

Smell

Smellers, small plastic containers holding scented herbs, spices, citrus peel, or scented oils (adapted from *Pint-Size Science*, by Linda Allison and Martha Weston, and the Preschool Express by Jean Warren website), are ideal to have the teen parents help you prepare. They can quiz each other on the smells before introducing them to their children. Encourage the parents to gradually move the smeller close their child's nose to avoid upsetting the child. This activity is right for children age 15 months or older.

Early Thinking and Problem Solving

Young children naturally pose and solve problems almost every waking moment. What happens if I push on the door? What's under the blanket? It cannot be emphasized enough to teen parents that children are learning from their exploration. These activities create opportunities for the teen parents to appreciate the infant/toddler brain hard at work trying to understand the world. Here are examples of simple, inexpensive interactive learning experiences.

Learn to "play with cereal and crackers" from *365 Activities You and Your Toddler Will Love*, by Nancy Hall (2006). Children learn to sort, fill, and identify colors using oyster crackers and colored cereal pieces. This is an opportunity to show parents how to model doing the activities for their children. Recommended for children 12 months or older.

Everyone, from 1 to 100, loves to open packages and tear off the wrapping. For children from 18 months, watching a parent wrap a toy (without tape) and then getting to "unwrap" it involves problem solving as well as fun. Follow the instructions for "unwrapping toys" found in *Toddler Play: 100 Fun-filled Activities to Maximize Your Toddler's Potential*, by Wendy Masi (2001).

Debrief with the parents after the activities are completed. What did their children do? What did they like? What did they learn? Could they see themselves trying this at home again with their children? Emphasize the interconnectedness between play and learning, and point out specific moments when their children were having fun.

Nature Walk

Transforming a walk around the block into a nature walk requires only a little mindfulness on the part of parents. Taking a group walk in a local community garden, park, or nature preserve, guided by a few suggestions, strongly illustrates for teen parents their children's natural curiosity and interest in the world around them. Even if an idyllic sylvan glade is not within walking distance, give this a try. It is important for parents to recognize the learning value of their own neighborhood. The "At the Park" section of the Born Learning website offers suggestions to turn a walk into a learning experience for infants, toddlers, and preschoolers. As the group facilitator, when suggesting a nature walk, it is also important to be mindful of any safety concerns in the neighborhoods where the teen parents live (see chapter 2).

In conjunction with this program, provide your group with a list of local low- or no-cost outdoor recreation sites. Compiling a local list based from a larger resource gives you the opportunity to vet it for cost and age appropriateness. Also, ask your teen parent group to share places they enjoy taking their children to add to the list. An example of a comprehensive resource to use as a starting point from the San Francisco Bay Area is the Bay Area Kid Fun website, which lists outdoor fun spots such as beaches, parks, farms, and gardens.

Need some ideas when planning your nature walk? The Nature Rocks website, founded by the Children and Nature Network and supported by The Nature Conservancy, provides suggestions for nature awareness activities for children of all ages, grouped by available time, in environments ranging from the backyard to regional parks. Growing concern over the disconnect between children and nature has resulted in a grassroots movement to bring the natural world back into children's lives. Through the Children and Nature Network you may be able to locate an organization in your area that would be interested in working with teen parent groups.

Simple Nature Activities for Early Learning

This program incorporates a nature walk, group craft activity, and related storytime program. Integrating experiences, literature, and creativity makes for the ultimate learning experience. Remember to always check out your destination in advance, and think through the specific avenues of discovery to be highlighted during the walk. Two simple handouts, "Talking about Things Outside," from *Supporting Early Literacy in Natural Environments* (Notari-Syverson and Rytter 2006), and the "Nature Guide" from the Children, Nature, and You website, offer great ideas to enhance the learning experience for the teen parents and their children.

When introducing the Nature Walk program to your teen parent group, describe what the planned activities during the walk will include, so parents know what to expect. Try telling the parents, "We will take a walk and introduce your baby/toddler to the world of nature. Enjoy the sunshine, and talk about what you see and find. Point out interesting plants, flowers, bugs, rocks, and so on as you walk and stop to look at them. If your child is walking and talking, let him or her take the lead and you follow. Get down to his or her level to see the world from your child's viewpoint." To encourage parents' participation, give them a copy of the "Nature Walk Checklist," found in the appendix of this chapter, which reiterates these suggested activities. This activity is most effective if you take the teen parents for a trial walk though the park or garden first and show them specific features that they can share with their child. Then they can bring the children out and repeat the walk.

Wendolyn Bird, director of Tender Tracks Trails and Tales, recommends that you listen and feel during your nature walk.

1. Find a comfortable place to sit. Close your eyes and listen to all the sounds you can hear. What are they like? Which direction did they come from? Who might have made them?
2. Close your eyes again, and this time, feel the sunlight and air touching your face or arms. Where is the sun? What direction is the breeze blowing? How does the air feel? Warm and gentle? Cool and brisk?

Also try looking for critters, bugs, and other interesting small things:

1. Turn over a rock on the ground and see what you find. Look for pillbugs, ants, etc.
2. Then ask (and answer) some questions:
   a. What do you see?
   b. Does it look like anything else?
   c. How does it move? Does it crawl? Slither?
   d. Can you count its legs?
   e. What color is it?
   f. How does it feel? Smooth or bumpy?
   g. Does it make any sounds?
   h. Does it smell? Can you smell it?
3. Try to identify the creature or guess its name.

"Leaf looking," from *I Love Dirt!* by Jennifer Ward, is another great activity for toddlers and preschoolers. Parents and children collect a few leaves that appeal to them, and then talk about their characteristics (size, shape, color, texture, etc.). Be sure to avoid walking through areas with poisonous plants. As a precautionary measure, remind parents that some plants are poisonous and children should not put them in their mouths.

Trees also warrant attention on your nature walk. In *Toddler Play: 100 Fun-filled Activities to Maximize Your Toddler's Potential*, editor Wendy Masi explains how to use all your senses to really get to know a tree. *Trails, Tails and Tidepools in Pails* (Docents of Nursery Nature Walks 1995) recommends collecting "outdoor smells" like dirt, pine needles, grass, and flower petals, and taking time to get a great big "sniff" of each. Both of these activities are best for children who are 18 months or older.

Another approach to take is to consider this walk as a sensory experience. Discuss with parents how children learn through their senses and give examples from nature such as the smell of herbs or flowers, the colors of plants and flowers, the textures of leaves and dirt, the taste of edible herbs, and the sound of birds or insects in the garden. Leading parents and children on a sensory walk works best if there is time to orient the parents with an advance walk-through. Staff can also accompany small groups of parents and children as they explore the park or garden and keep the activity interactive.

Create a temporary memory of your nature walk by making a nature collage from nature oddments gathered on your walk.

Group Nature Art Collage

Supplies:

- plastic bag for each parent
- roll of clear Con-Tact® paper
- small slips of paper
- ink pens
- 6-inch wide strips of paper, as long as possible, folded in half lengthwise
- stapler and staples
- (optional for individual collages) yarn and paper punch

Instructions for Parents:

1. Bring a plastic bag on your walk. Collect leaves, small rocks or sticks, pods, or flowers that you find on the ground, and put them in your bag.
2. Tell your child the name of each item as you pick it up.
3. Describe each item.
   a. What color is it?
   b. Is it hard or soft? Wet or dry?
   c. What shape and size is it? Round? Long? Big? Small?
   d. Compare the sizes of things: "This leaf is bigger than this one."
4. Bring your bag of treasures back to the meeting room.

Instructions for Staff:

1. Give each parent a small slip of paper and a pen. Ask parents to write their names and their children's names on the slip, along with a comment about what they enjoyed on the nature walk.
2. Unroll and cut a six-foot length of Con-Tact® paper, laying it either on a table or on the floor. Peel away the backing paper with the sticky side facing up.
3. Ask the parents and children to lay their notes and some of their nature walk treasures down on the Con-Tact® paper.
4. Unroll another sheet of Con-Tact® paper, unpeel it, and lay it over the first, encasing the collected treasures and trying to avoid wrinkles as best you can.
5. Frame the collage with the long strips of colored paper, encasing the edges in the fold and stapling it down every few inches.
6. Hang your nature collage at a low enough height so that the children can look at it.
7. Ask parents to point out their contributions to the collage, and read to their child what they wrote.

Individual Nature Art Collage

1. Cut a 12-inch by 12-inch rectangle of Con-Tact® paper for each child.
2. Pull away one half of the backing paper and fold it back, so that half of the sticky side of the paper is exposed.
3. Have parents write a memory of the walk and arrange notes and nature treasures on the Con-Tact® paper.
4. Unpeel the rest of the paper, and fold it over to encase the collage.
5. Punch two holes at the top, and thread a piece of yarn through them to make a hanger.

When you are back from your walk, cement the relationship between experiences and books with a garden storytime.

A Garden Storytime:

1. Sing an opening song: "If You're Happy and You Know It."
2. Present several fingerplays: "Jack Be Nimble," "Two Little Blackbirds," and "Round and Round the Garden."
3. Read a book: *Brown Bear, Brown Bear What Do You See?* by Bill Martin.
4. Present several fingerplays: "Eentsy Weentsy Spider" (with spider puppet), "Apple Tree," and "Row Row Your Boat."
5. Tell a garden-themed flannelboard story: "The Giant Carrot," from *Mother Goose's Playhouse* by Judy Sierra.
6. Present several fingerplays: "This Is the Way We Water the Plants," "Ring around the Rosie," and "Rock-a-Bye Baby."

Small nature art collage. (Hal Jerman)

7. Read a book: *I Love Bugs*, by Philemon Sturges.
8. Present several fingerplays: "Here Is the Beehive" (with bee puppet), and "Twinkle, Twinkle Little Star."
9. Include music: "In My Garden," from *One Light, One Sun* by Raffi.
10. Include a closing song, such as "Wheels on the Bus."

"This Is the Way We Water the Plants" Song

(Sung to the melody of "Here We Go Round the Mulberry Bush.")

This is the way we water the plants.

(Infants—Parent sits with the baby in his or her lap and raises the baby's arms to form a spout and tips the baby to one side.)
(Toddlers—Parent helps child pretend to be a watering can, forming a handle and spout, and tip from the waist to water the flowers.)

Water the plants.
Water the plants.
This is the way we water the plants
Whenever they get dry.
We water the plants so they can grow,

(Infants—Parent slowly lifts baby overhead.)
(Toddlers—Parent shows child how to imitate a seed growing by first crouching on the ground and then slowly standing.)

So they can grow.
So they can grow.
We water the plants so they can grow,
Right up to the sky.

INTERACTIVE PLAY ACTIVITIES FROM BOOKS AND WEBSITES

There are many excellent compilations of activity ideas for infants and toddlers. The resources geared toward parents seem to work best. While you will find some useful ideas in them, the books written for day-care providers tend to be a little too "educational" and less oriented toward parent-child bonding. Here is a selection of activities.

From *365 Games Smart Babies Play*, by Sheila Ellison and Susan Fernandi, try the "Put In—Take Out" game (for ages 6 to 12 months) or the "Big or Little Sorting Game" (for 18 months or older), or play "Scarf Magic," using a paper towel tube and a string of scarves (for 6 months or older). Find directions for activities like water painting with big brushes, foil squeezing, playing with office supply–type stickers, and "Press and Stick Collages" in *First Art: Art Experiences for Toddlers and Twos*, by MaryAnn Kohl.

Making a puppet from a plain white sock and engaging it in a three-way conversation, exploring the feel and textures of an assortment of different papers, and collecting squishy items to squeeze are all great ideas to use with babies and young toddlers found in *Baby Play and Learn*, by Penny Warner. *365 Activities You and Your Toddler Will Love*, by Nancy Hall, suggests activities such as edible finger-painting on crackers and playing "sandbox" in a dishpan filled with oatmeal.

Improve children's coordination and problem solving by stacking paper cups, tearing newspaper (messy, but fun), or hiding small toys in boxes with hinged lids. These ideas are from *Simple Steps*, by Karen Miller.

The website Preschool Express by Jean Warren is a treasure trove of simple, inexpensive, and age-appropriate crafts and play activities. Find out how to play with tissue paper and learn concepts from pots and pans in the "Toddler Activities" section.

CONCLUSION

Young children need everyday learning and play for successful development. Teen parents may not be aware of the importance of these activities or know how to make the most of the opportunities they present. Experiencing the fun of engaging in age-appropriate play with their children encourages teen parents to incorporate these activities into their daily routines, thereby benefiting the child both in terms of development and by strengthening the parent-child bond.

REFERENCES

Allison, Linda, and Martha Weston. *Pint-Size Science: Finding-Out Fun for You and Your Young Child.* Boston: Little, Brown, 1994.

Bay Area Kid Fun. http://www.bayareakidfun.com/.

Bird, Wendolyn. Listen and Feel. (information sheet, Children, Nature, and YOU, n.d.)

Born Learning.org. "Learning On the Go: At the Park." http://www.bornlearning.org/default.aspx?id=14.

Cabrera, Jane. *If You're Happy and You Know It.* New York: Holiday House, 2005.

Children and Nature Network. "Grassroot Leadership Campaigns." http://www.childrenandnature.org/movement/campaigns/.

    Identifies organizations throughout the United States and Canada dedicated to reconnecting children and nature.

Children, Nature and You. "Nature Guide." http://www.childrennatureandyou.org/Online%20Nature%20Guide.pdf.

    A delightful information sheet filled with simple outdoor activities and experiences for children.

Docents of Nursery Nature Walks. *Trails, Tails and Tidepools in Pails: Over 100 Fun and Easy Nature Activities for Families and Teachers to Share with Babies and Young Children.* Santa Monica, CA: Nursery Nature Walks, 1995.

Ellison, Sheila, and Susan Fernandi. *365 Games Smart Babies Play.* Naperville, IL: Sourcebooks, 2005.

Hall, Nancy Wilson. *365 Activities You and Your Toddler Will Love.* San Francisco: Weldon-Owen, 2006.

Huntington, Barbara. "Early Learning Initiative for Wisconsin Public Libraries." Wisconsin Department of Public Instruction (2005), http://dpi.wi.gov/pld/pdf/earlylearning.pdf.

Kohl, MaryAnn, with Renee Ramsey and Dana Bowman. *First Art: Art Experiences for Toddlers and Twos.* Beltsville, MD: Gryphon House, 2002.

Martin, Bill. *Brown Bear, Brown Bear, What Do You See?* New York: Henry Holt, 1996.

Masi, Wendy, and Roni Cohen Leiderman, eds. *Baby Play: 100 Fun-filled Activities to Maximize Your Baby's Potential.* San Francisco: Creative Publishing International, 2001.

Masi, Wendy, ed. *Toddler Play: 100 Fun-filled Activities to Maximize Your Toddler's Potential.* San Francisco, CA: Creative Publishing International, 2001.

Miller, Karen. *Simple Steps: Developmental Activities for Infants, Toddlers, and Two-Year-Olds.* Beltsville, MD: Gryphon House, 1999.

Nature Rocks. http://www.naturerocks.org/.
    Find nature anywhere in the United States by your address or zip code; discover ideas for experiencing nature based on child's age, time available, and type of environment.

Notari-Syverson, Angela, and Kristin Rytter. "Supporting Early Literacy in Natural Environments: Activities for Caregivers and Young Children." Washington Learning Systems. http://www.walearning.com/media/downloads/english-infant-activities.pdf. Highly recommended as a source of early learning topics to develop into activity programs.

Oppenheim, Joanne, and Stephanie Oppenheim. *Oppenheim Toy Portfolio: Baby and Toddler Play Book.* New York: Oppenheim Toy Portfolio, 2001.

Oppenheim, Joanne, and Stephanie Oppenheim. *Read It! Play It! With Babies and Toddlers.* New York: Oppenheim Toy Portfolio, 2006.

Parlakian, Rebecca, and Claire Lerner. "The Truth about Play." Zero to Three: National Center for Infants, Toddlers, and Families (September 2009), www.zerotothree.org/site/DocServer/The_Truth_About_Play.pdf?docID=9381.

Parlakian, Rebecca, and Claire Lerner. "Your Baby's Development." Zero to Three: National Center for Infants, Toddlers, and Families (2008), http://www.zerotothree.org/site/PageServer?pagename=ter_par_agebasedhandouts.

Raffi. *Baby Beluga.* Vancouver, BC: Troubador/Shoreline, 1980.

Raffi. *One Light, One Sun.* Vancouver, BC: Shoreline Records, 1985.

Raffi. *Wheels on the Bus.* New York: Crown, 1988.

Schiller, Pam. *The Complete Resource Book for Infants: Over 700 Experiences for Children from Birth to 18 Months.* Beltsville, MD: Gryphon House, 2005.

Schiller, Pam. *The Complete Resource Book for Toddlers and Twos: Over 2000 Experiences and Ideas!* Beltsville, MD: Gryphon House, 2003.

Sierra, Judy. *Mother Goose's Playhouse: Toddler Tales and Nursery Rhymes, With Patterns for Puppets and Feltboard.* Ashland, OR: Bob Kaminski Media Arts, 1994.

Sturges, Philemon. *I Love Bugs.* New York: HarperCollins, 2005.

Ward, Jennifer. *I Love Dirt! 52 Activities to Help You and Your Kids Discover the Wonders of Nature.* Boston: Trumpeter Books, 2008.

Warner, Peggy. *Baby Play and Learn.* New York: Meadowbrook Press, 1999.

Warren, Jean. "Toddler Activities." Preschool Express by Jean Warren. http://www.preschoolexpress.com/toddler_station.shtml.
    One of the best resources on the web for age-appropriate toddler activities.

Zero to Three. "Make the Most of Playtime." Zero to Three: National Center for Infants, Toddlers, and Families. http://www.zerotothree.org/child-development/play/make-the-most-of-playtime.html

RESOURCES

Alliance for Childhood. "Time for Play, Every Day: It's Fun—It's Fundamental." http://www.allianceforchildhood.org/sites/allianceforchildhood.org/files/file/pdf/projects/play/pdf_files/play_fact_sheet.pdf.

Center on the Emotional and Social Foundations of Learning, Vanderbilt University. "Making the Most of Playtime." http://www.vanderbilt.edu/csefel/familytools/make_the_most_of_playtime2.pdf.
    Explains play skills and suggests how to play with infants to three-year-olds.

Ginsburg, Kenneth R. "The Importance of Play in Promoting Healthy Child Development and Maintaining Strong Parent-Child Bonds." *Pediatrics* 119, no. 1 (January 2007), http://www.aap.org/pressroom/playFINAL.pdf.

Kuffner, Trish. *The Toddler's Busy Book.* Minnetonka, MN: Meadowbrook Press, 1999.

Louv, Richard. *Last Child in the Woods: Saving Our Children from Nature-Deficit Disorder.* Chapel Hill, NC: Algonquin Books, 2006.

Nurik, Cindy Bunin, with Jane Schonberger. *Fun with Mommy and Me: More than 300 Together-Time Activities for You and Your Child.* New York: Dutton, 2001.

Press, Judy. *The Little Hands Art Book: Exploring Arts and Crafts with 2-to-6-year-olds.* Charlotte, VT: Williamson, 1994.

Schiller, Pam, and Jackie Silberg. *The Complete Book of Activities, Games, Stories, Props, Recipes, and Dances for Young Children.* Beltsville, MD: Gryphon House, 2003.

Appendix

Nature Walk Checklist

Mark off each activity -

- ♣ Smell something—a flower, herb, leaf, dirt- and talk about it.
- ♣ Look at a bug, and talk about it.
- ♣ Turn over a rock & see what's underneath, and talk about it.
- ♣ Close your eyes and feel the sun, and talk about it.

Look up at the sky. Do you see -

- ♣ Clouds?
- ♣ Clear blue sky?
- ♣ Birds?

Pick up a leaf. Is it -

- ♣ Big?
- ♣ Small?
- ♣ Smooth?
- ♣ Fuzzy?

What shape is it?

- ♣ Pointed?
- ♣ Round?
- ♣ ***Use your plastic bag to collect small leaves, grass or flowers for the nature collage.***

Nature Walk Checklist

Mark off each activity -

- ♣ Smell something—a flower, herb, leaf, dirt- and talk about it.
- ♣ Look at a bug, and talk about it.
- ♣ Turn over a rock & see what's underneath, and talk about it.
- ♣ Close your eyes and feel the sun, and talk about it.

Look up at the sky. Do you see -

- ♣ Clouds?
- ♣ Clear blue sky?
- ♣ Birds?

Pick up a leaf. Is it -

- ♣ Big?
- ♣ Small?
- ♣ Smooth?
- ♣ Fuzzy?

What shape is it?

- ♣ Pointed?
- ♣ Round?
- ♣ ***Use your plastic bag to collect small leaves, grass or flowers for the nature collage.***

Reproducible Nature Walk Checklist. (Ellin Klor)

Index

ABOUT THE AUTHORS

ELLIN KLOR is a children's librarian at the Santa Clara City Library in Santa Clara, California. Her work focuses on family literacy, including outreach to teen parent groups and families living in transitional housing. Ellin has been a presenter on children's services and literature topics for the California Library Association, the Santa Clara Reading Council, and the Jewish Coalition for Literacy. Ellin holds an MLS from the Simmons College Graduate School of Library and Information Science. She serves as a trustee of The Girls' Middle School in Mountain View, California, and lives with her husband and daughter in Palo Alto.

SARAH LAPIN is a senior community program specialist at the San Mateo County Library in San Mateo, California. Her work focuses on adult and family literacy program development, outreach, and direct service. Sarah has had the opportunity to pursue her commitment to family literacy through her work with the library, as well as with a number of nonprofit community organizations serving diverse populations, including teen parents and immigrant families. She holds a master's degree in social work from the University of Southern California. Sarah has been a presenter on family literacy topics at the California Library Association and California Family Literacy Conferences. She lives in San Francisco.

MARYANN MORI has presented the topic of library services for pregnant/parenting teens at ALA, PLA, and several state and regional conferences. She has written for *Library Worklife*, *The Informed Librarian Online*, and *Public Libraries*. Her work has been included in books published by the American Library Association, and her chapter about teens' use of social networking sites was published in *Social Networking Communities and E-Dating Services* (IGI, 2008). Formerly a teen specialist librarian for the Evansville Vanderburgh Public Library (Indiana), Mori is currently director of the Waukee Public Library in Waukee, Iowa. She graduated from the University of Illinois with an MSLIS.

13876924R00128

Made in the USA
Lexington, KY
16 March 2012